The Incompetent Manager
The causes, consequences and cures of managerial derailment

For Alison, who knows what I am on about
and
for Bob and Joyce Hogan who have made their special area of interest
the topic of management incompetence.

The Incompetent Manager

The causes, consequences and cures of managerial derailment

ADRIAN FURNHAM
Professor of Psychology, University College London

W
WHURR PUBLISHERS
LONDON AND PHILADELPHIA

British Library Cataloguing in Publication Data

A catalogue record for this book
is available from the British Library.

ISBN 1 86156 370 1

Contents

Preface

This is not a typical, heroic, magic-bullet, how-to-do-it book for managers. It is, in fact, almost the opposite: it explores how, when and why managers fail and derail, why incompetent managers are hired in the first place, how to understand the causes of management failure – particularly in terms of personality traits and disorders – and how to pick up the pieces.

Many books describe how to be a competent or successful manager. But relatively few describe how to spot or avoid incompetence. This book aims to fill this gap in the market.

The sheer number of management books available today may be an index of the amount of incompetence in the business world. These books are often simple-minded and patronizing, and they tend to follow a formula – one that sells books, but one that paradoxically may encourage incompetence. Consider some of the rules associated with writing a best-selling business book:

- The book must be simple. It must argue that one single idea, technique or approach is the 'secret' of good management. Best-sellers are peppered with anecdotes, parables, vignettes, stories – case studies that supposedly act as testimonies to the central theme that business is easy. But business is not simple and managing people is not easy – it is like herding cats. No one technique can overcome or even control the myriad issues in people or product management.
- The book must argue that human behaviour is (easily) changeable. If this is true, why are people in therapy for years? Ask any smoker or dieter about behaviour change. Talk to psychotherapists. Changing behaviour is expensive and time-consuming, and requires personal commitment. It is virtually impossible to change behaviour legally and ethically if the person does not want to change.
- The book must emphasize that the individual (worker or manager) is the unit of change. This psychological level of analysis is comprehensible and

attractive but it neglects social and economic factors. Even if you could change individuals, the appropriate company infrastructure (accounting, ergonomics, IT systems) must be in place for the change to succeed.

- The book must stress the individual manager's control. Indeed, the message for poor bewildered managers floating on an ocean of problems is that, quite simply, they can become masters of their fate, captains of their own ship. Books even argue that empowering others somehow increases control. But managers and their staff are interdependent; by encouraging maverick, crypto-autocratic techniques, traditional how-to-do-it books more often lead to tears than to desired targets.

- The book must provide a manual of steps and principles. The how-to approach must be set out in a style somewhere between a computer manual and a child's book. It must give the impression that people, markets and customers are logical, rational automatons and that, if you simply follow a set number of steps, all will be well. As we all know, this approach does not work, even with computers.

- The book must suggest that the technique is universally effective. The idea is that whether you manage Alaskans or Zambians, people are basically people. Furthermore, it does not matter whether you are in manufacturing or the service industry, the technique will work for you. This is obvious nonsense but it is needed for worldwide sales.

- The book 'proves' that you will see an immediate short-term payoff. Despite what you have heard about magic bullets and wonder pills, the book suggests that you can achieve change and success (or basically whatever you want) easily, quickly and without effort. Note that there is little talk about cost – monetary, temporal or personal – but a lot of talk about outcome. In fact, the precise nature of the process is rarely explained.

- The book provides lists of happy customers. These may be quotes on the back of the book – so-called extracts from reviews. They may be case studies where clients have graciously consented to 'having their story told'. There are never criticisms, moments of doubt or a score card that mentions the downside of the process.

- The book must not be counterintuitive. It must be common-sensical but dressed up in modish jargon. Better to have an old wives' tale, a modern myth repackaged in the idioms and PR of today, than uncomfortable empirical truths that defy common sense.

- The book must say that there is no conflict in the workplace and that management and labour never disagree. The notion that what is good for management may not be good for workers never comes up. The message is all about how all the different stakeholders in the company will benefit from the new technique. You should never, ever mention that the advocated process might even lead to conflict.

- The book invites ownership through adaptation. The idea is that the reader needs to interpret the 'general principles' set out in the book for his or her own purposes. The fact that this contradicts the claim of universalism does not matter. It is the basic trick of all fortune tellers – I speak vaguely, you interpret specifically. Indeed, the book may be internally inconsistent on a number of points, but this is glossed over.
- The book should stress that management is a romantic, heroic activity. Saving companies has replaced saving virgin princesses as the favoured activity of today's folk heroes. Restoring the health of the company is more important than the work of Dr Kildare. Managers 'boldly go' to the new frontier, like conquerors on a heroic voyage. They are the crusaders of tomorrow.
- If these observations characterize popular business books, then they may well be the cause rather than the cure of many managerial problems. This book doesn't follow the standard recipe.

Bookstores and libraries will find this book difficult to classify. It is not a self-help book in the tradition of *The One-Minute Manager*, *The 10 Day MBA* or the many (bland and well-known) 'Secrets of the Successful Manager'. It may be used for self-understanding, or to enlighten managers who have crashed and burned, but it is not like most management books. It does not offer simple solutions but it does offer some insight into an unspoken plague – the incompetent boss.

It might be classified under humour. This would be a compliment ... but the book aims to do more than just amuse. The Dilbert books and cartoons are actually profound statements of organizational behaviour, and many serious insights are presented in jest.

If the book ends up under 'General Management', then it will rub shoulders with some unlikely companions because its message is profoundly different from many, and in fact it is a gloomy one – namely, that the average manager is more likely to be incompetent than competent, and incompetence is hard to cure. Some organizations seem almost consciously to select for, train and encourage incompetence; not surprisingly, then, they also seem unwilling or unable to deal with the problem of the incompetent manager.

Many management books simplify rather than clarify: they assume people are rational, rather than rationalizing, and that management is a technique to be learned. The average middle manager, caught up in a capricious economic climate, is offered formulas, slogans, homilies and techniques that supposedly ensure good management in the complex and paradoxical world of work. Thus the poor manager, caught between the consultant and the employee, is offered new, different and often contradictory messages every few years. First they had to concentrate on morale, then on communication, then on strategy, then on corporate culture. After that they had excellence, then empowerment, then they moved back to leadership. And leadership involved MBO (management buy-outs), then TQM (total quality management), then culture audits, 360° feedback, focus groups and transformational leadership.

The problem with many popular management books is not that they describe, prescribe and proscribe processes that are fundamentally wrong, but rather that they propose overly simple solutions. Thus advocates of the now-popular emotional intelligence (EQ) argue that attention to people issues will provide a competitive edge and that success at work depends on something more than rational, analytical decision-making. They argue that EQ is twice as important as IQ, that EQ becomes more important as one moves up an organization, and that it can be learned. Goleman's (1998) theme is that too many managers are 'smart but emotionally dumb' and that people at work should not be judged by their IQ, training, expertise and experience, but by how well they 'handle themselves and others'. People skills are increasingly important in the new economic world order, but the evidence suggests that, as IQ rises, EQ drops.

But a closer reading of Goleman's EQ book reveals typical shortcomings. There is always evidence by anecdote: folksy case studies that are supposed to be typical. The evidence never passes any scientific tests and the results can be given alternative explanations. There is also a tendency to 'neologize the banal', with talk of emotional labour and leveraging diversity, when simpler terminology is available. When the academic literature is cited, it is usually a selective reading of theories and evidence aimed primarily to support the theory. And, finally, good evidence is often misquoted and misinterpreted.

Sceptics regard this as repackaging old ideas to create work for training consultants. Cynics see managers casting around for quick fixes and silver bullets to solve intractable human problems.

Organizations have been around since the beginning of human society. We are now born in, and usually die in, organizations. All our major rites of passage occur in organizational contexts and some are well run by quietly competent people. How they got to be that way is the subject of this book. The book is divided into three parts. It begins with an introductory chapter reviewing the literature on managerial military incompetence. The first part of the book then deals with the concepts of competence and incompetence. Chapters 2 and 3 primarily spell out certain issues that are common in organizational life. Chapter 4 closely examines the concept of competence; it focuses in particular on the competency concept so popular today in the human resources literature and what that concept tells us about incompetence.

Part II of the book gets to the heart of the matter. Chapter 5 looks at the concept of personality and why it is so important for understanding management failure. Chapter 6 looks at management derailment through the personality disorders: what it looks like and what causes it. Chapter 7 shifts the focus to management teams and why some of them end up as incompetent.

The final part (Part III) has just one chapter (8) but for many readers it may be the most important. It looks not at cause but cure: what to do with the incompetent manager. No magic bullets here but some understanding of the options.

Adrian Furnham
London, 2003

PART I
INCOMPETENCE AT WORK

CHAPTER ONE

Management Incompetence

1.1. Introduction

Nearly everyone has worked for an incompetent manager. Some have never worked for anyone else! Bad managers can and do make everyone's life miserable. They can also threaten the future of the organization that hired them. This book is about incompetence: what it looks like, what causes it and what can be done about it. Although there are many causes of management failure and incompetence, one of the most important and poorly understood is the personality of those who select, appoint, promote and themselves become senior managers. The book will therefore take an unapologetic psychological approach to this problem.

Management is a popular topic of conversation at work and at the dinner table. Bewildered and bullied employees need to make sense out of their experiences with an incompetent boss. The spouses and friends of these people must listen to the frustrated and increasingly desperate reports of life at work. The long-suffering staff of the managerially incompetent seek sympathy for their plight, and help for themselves and sometimes for their boss. Managerial incompetence is probably a more frequent topic of conversation than managerial competence. Although this situation is understandable, it is surprising that so little has been written about the topic.

Three areas of research are germane to this issue. The first is research on military incompetence; this concerns the problem in one particular and very consequential sector. The second is the very limited writing on the psychology of management incompetence per se. The third is on fads and fashions at work.

This first chapter looks at each of these areas of literature in turn because each informs the central thesis of this book.

1.2. Life and Death and Incompetence

It has been fashionable, at least among the baby-boomer generation, to mock the military. Hence the view that military intelligence is an oxymoron. It is, however, clear to many professional and amateur historians that military officers throughout history have demonstrated courageous and far-sighted leadership of an outstanding nature and that the future of nations has turned on their capabilities. To lead great armies in a foreign theatre of war with all the concomitant dangers and difficulties makes running a medium-sized business (or country) look like child's play.

However, every major nation has experienced military defeat, often with significant consequences. Careful analysis of the causes of defeat points to many factors, one of which is the pathologies of certain military officers, who are in fact no more competent than managers in any other sector of organizational life.

There are few good psychological analyses of incompetent military leadership. A clear exception is the book by Norman Dixon (*The Psychology of Military Incompetence*), which inspired the title of this book. Dixon's book and his theme are important because, although military organizations are specialized, they are not unique. Indeed an analysis of management in the military naturally applies to all uniformed services (fire, ambulance, police) and others besides. In fact, a 'command and control' management style and culture can be found in many organizations that have a uniform code, not of dress, but of behaviour.

Dixon (1981), an ex-military man and experimental psychologist, claims that military incompetence is tragically expensive, predictable and preventable. Incompetence in the military is fundamentally no different from that in business, politics or state service, except that:

- military organizations may attract a minority of people who are particularly prone to failure at high levels of command;
- the nature of militarism serves to accentuate the less adaptive personality traits in leaders;
- military officers are not democratically elected and few are sacked, dismissed or demoted for their incompetence;
- the consequences of bad military decisions are often incredibly high.

Incompetence involves, first, *a serious waste of human resources and failure to observe one of the first principles of war – economy of force*. This failure derives in part from an inability to make war swiftly. It also derives from certain attitudes of mind. Next, it involves *a fundamental conservatism and clinging to outworn tradition*, an inability to profit from past experience (owing in part to a refusal to admit past mistakes). It also involves a failure to use or a tendency to misuse available technology. Third, incompetence results from *a tendency to reject or ignore information* that is unpalatable or that conflicts with preconceptions. Another problem is *the tendency to underestimate the enemy and overestimate the capabilities of one's own side.* Penultimately, *indecisiveness* and a tendency to abdicate from the role of decision-maker lead to incompetence. Finally, *an obstinate persistence in a given task* despite strong contrary evidence is the hallmark of incompetence.

There are several explanations for military disasters. The first is that military (and indeed managerial) incompetence might be attributed to lack of intellectual ability. Is low intelligence among officers a necessary and sufficient explanation for military disaster? Although there is evidence that some military commanders were not especially bright, and that IQ was never a major criterion for selection or promotion, this does not seem an important, sufficient or parsimonious explanation for military failure.

What is true, however, is that the military harbours a culture of anti-intellectualism. The tendency to denigrate the intellectual values of inquiry, criticism and innovation, and to promote the values of tradition and conformity is, of course, not unique to the military. This may sound like an argument by academics designed to promote their style of management, but it seems that academic organizations are often better models of management competence than the military. However, the point is important – if an organization ignores or despises intellect, it will have long-term consequences, most importantly during times of change and the attendant stress. Organizations with incompetent managers are often either deeply anti-intellectual or uncritically in awe of quasi-intellectual (for example, consultant-based) solutions. Both attitudes towards intellectual inquiry are unhealthy.

The essence of a military organization is 'an ever-increasing web of rules, restrictions and constraints presided over by an elite, one of whose motives was to preserve the status quo' (Dixon, 1981: 172). It is, of course, possible to characterize the civil service or many large multinationals in much the same way. Is the obsessive–compulsiveness of military behaviour, particularly manifest in the constant need for cleanliness, personal pride and orderliness, the root cause of incompetence? The ritualization of behaviour can be deeply constraining. Furthermore, the ritual is deceptive because it is always almost exclusively concerned with outward show, and soon becomes a substitute for thought. Dixon clearly sees the parallels between obsessive–compulsive neuroses and military life:

> One underlying feature of such symptoms is that they are repetitive, stereotyped and occur without insight into their origins. Another is that they centre around cleanliness and orderliness. Finally, they are often defences against anxiety or suppressed anger. This is clear from the great distress which may be occasioned by their forcible prevention. (Dixon, 1981: 148)

This theme will be explored in the second part of the book.

Organizations have rules or codes of honour. The code of honour is designed to ensure that threatening situations are met by fight rather than flight. The snobbishness found among many officers may reflect an under-lying sense of inferiority because only the socially insecure need to feel snobbish:

> Whatever else it may be, sensitivity to criticism is a measure of insecurity. It implies a weak ego that, in turn, and by way of compensation, manifests itself in particular character-traits, one of which is snobbishness. Whether this ego-weakness is due to some early shock to self-esteem, or fear of the breakthrough of unacceptable impulses, or some combination of these two influences, the individual so afflicted develops certain defences that help to minimise his painful feelings. This finds support in yet another feature of military organisations – their cult of anti-effeminacy. (Dixon, 1981: 207)

Arrogance, pomposity and hubris certainly characterize many captains of industry who later fall from grace. It is the excessive self-esteem that is the clue. Military incompetence, like managerial incompetence, is really a fail-ure of leadership. Military leaders (that is, officers) are, however, rather different from managers in most other organizations because:

1. They are appointed rather than emerge – the average soldier has no say in the sort of officer (leader) he or she gets.
2. Military leaders have considerable power over their subordinates and can literally order them to do their bidding – the force of law rather than per-suasion.
3. They can be autocratic and information flows strictly through the chain of command.

The concept of authoritarianism may explain military incompetence. The model military leader is a paterfamilias – the all-powerful, all-knowing father figure in the authoritarian Victorian family. In Dixon's discussion of authoritarianism, he relies heavily on the classic psychoanalytical study of prejudice entitled *The Authoritarian Personality* (Adorno et al., 1948), pub-lished more than 50 years ago. The authors of that book were trying to understand the origins of anti-Semitism in Nazi Germany; they traced it to the concept of authoritarianism, and they identified a number of factors that seemed to cause it.

Authoritarianism contributes to military incompetence in various ways. Research shows that authoritarians are more dishonest, irresponsible, untrustworthy, suspicious and socially conforming than non-authoritarians (authoritarian tendencies can be easily measured). Authoritarians are less insightful and empathic and are less likely to understand the opposition's intentions. They seem unable to relinquish cherished traditions and to adopt technical innovations. They underestimate the ability of the opposition. They demand obedience and loyalty in juniors at the expense of initiative and innovation. Authoritarians are deeply concerned about their reputations and the criticism of seniors. They are also particularly quick to blame others for their shortcomings. Many authoritarians tend to be obsessive–compulsive types. Authoritarians are more likely to believe in supernatural forces, and therefore fate. They also have generalized hostility and a lack of humanity.

In short, authoritarians are hostile, dogmatic people with closed minds. Hence, they are attracted to the cult of muscular Christianity and the stoicism and the dominance–submission relationships in military life. Obviously, they may be attracted to other organizations that resemble the uniformed services – for example, the church and, in many countries, government service. There are, of course, degrees of authoritarianism: it is not an all-or-nothing issue. In addition, many people and organizations try to hide their authoritarianism in an effort to appear 'politically correct'.

Authoritarians are attracted to organizations that fulfil their needs and vice versa. Hence, over time more and more people of the same persuasion populate organizations. The peacetime army, like a large national utility, can soon be a homogeneous mass of crypto- and even proto-authoritarians.

Dixon (1981) develops his own quite specific theory of military incompetencies (Figure 1.1).

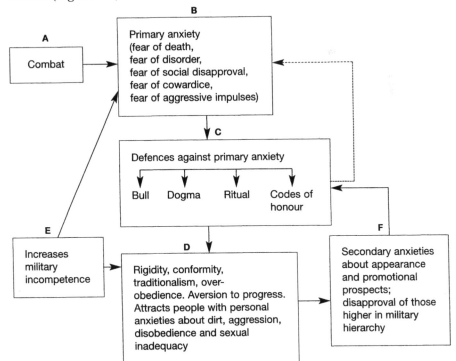

Figure 1.1 Dixon's (1981) theory of military incompetencies.

Combat (A) produces several sorts of anxiety (B). To reduce these anxieties (and increase efficiency), aspects of militarism (C) are developed. These reduce primary anxiety (the 'dashed' arrow). But defences against primary anxiety (C) necessarily make for rigidity of thinking, and so on (D). They will also tend to attract individuals with personal anxieties about dirt and aggressions.

Both aspects of D often have two adverse effects. First, they directly reduce military competence (E), thereby increasing primary anxiety in the combat situation. Second, they evoke a number of secondary (social) anxieties (F). Both these effects will tend to increase D, thereby constituting a vicious circle of cause and effect.

Dixon notes:

> In developing this thesis, emphasis was laid upon those devices whereby fear is stilled, aggression evoked and disorder prevented. Military organisations were depicted as sometimes cumbrous and inflexible machines for the harnessing and direction of intra-species hostility beneath whose often brightly decorated exterior the psychological process of 'bull' authoritarianism, codes of honour, anti-intellectualism, anti-effeminacy, sensitivity to criticism and fear of failure have contributed to incompetence, both directly and indirectly.
>
> These processes make for incompetence because, since their primary object is control and constraint, they themselves tend to become inflexible and unmodifiable. They resist change, block progress and hamper thought. Just as once useful but now irrelevant drills rob overt behaviour of any verve or spontaneity, so ancient rules and regulations, precious formulae and prescribed attitudes become an easy substitute for serious cerebration. (Dixon, 1981: 306)

Dixon argues that the military personality is drawn to, and seems to have an emotional investment in, using force to solve problems and manage others. They are, of course, not unique in this. Incompetent military leaders are emotionally dependent, socially conforming and religiously orthodox, and they distrust the new and strange. They also lack creativity, imagination, aesthetic appreciation, cognitive complexity, independence and altruism. They are anxious and self-doubting, and the lethal combination of high anxiety and low self-esteem in part makes their behaviour bizarre and unpredictable, with literally awful consequences. The urge simply to give orders, control others and follow rigid codes of conduct epitomizes the failed military manager. They are the classic 'control freak' managers. The opposite traits of tact, flexibility and imagination seem associated with managerial success in the military or elsewhere.

There is a consistent pattern underlying military fiascos. The pattern includes: a tendency to underestimate the capabilities of the enemy relative to one's own capabilities; an inability to admit mistakes, and a tendency to blame them on others, which makes it difficult to learn from experience; a fundamental conservatism that inhibits change and ignores technical advances; a failure to use reconnaissance adequately; a tendency to discount warning signals that indicate things are going wrong; passivity and procrastination; failure to take the initiative and exploit advantages gained; and, finally, a predisposition to use frontal assaults, often against the enemy's main line of defence.

Authoritarian people are attracted to military organizations and are more likely to succeed in them. This is consistent with the finding that we are all attracted to organizations because of their values and the way they 'go about things'; people seek out jobs that fit their personalities. It is difficult to 'prove' retrospectively that all failed military leaders were authoritarians, and it would be unwise to attempt to explain everything in these terms. Authoritarianism is, however, one factor in the complex pathology of the incompetent manager.

Dixon's analysis was obviously inspired by Freudian ideas and the psychiatric literature. This is not a common approach in the management literature but it is an important one and is a theme explored further in Chapters 5 and 6. Certainly, the similarity between military and management incompetence is striking.

1.3. The Incompetent Manager

Incompetence is not a curious and rare phenomenon in the world of management: it is more often the rule than the exception. Ask the average person to rate the people for whom he or she has had to work all his or her life and typically what we find is that more than half of managers are rated as 'mildly', 'amazingly' or even 'dangerously' incompetent. The same is true if you ask managers to rate their peers. But this is more than just blaming others.

Many lazy, incompetent or unskilled staff blame their performance on their managers, as a worker might blame their tools for their poor performance. But competence, unlike beauty, is not just in the eyes of the beholder. It is possible to describe, observe and see the consequences of good management.

Incompetence is not simply the absence of competence, just as health is not the absence of illness. Incompetence is usually associated with interpersonal flaws and lack of ability. Clever, charming psychopaths are usually incompetent managers. So too are the people whose careers are predicated on getting along with senior management, and who ultimately are 'Peter Principled' (promoted beyond their level of competence) based on lack of performance – when it is finally discovered.

Incompetent managers are found in all sectors, in all countries. Some environments are more conducive to incompetent managers than others. Large public utilities, government departments and other 'non-profits' are a sort of club of the incompetent. Incompetent managers select, train, promote and model incompetence. If a potentially competent manager gets hired into a company run by incompetent managers, the only model he or she will ever see is incompetence. Thus incompetence gets perpetuated.

This process also, in part, accounts for incompetent corporate culture. The entire organization acquires an incompetent style (see below) which influences how the organization does things. Incompetent corporate cultures are not easy to change.

In tropical climates, when a house is infested with ants, bees or fungus, drastic steps are taken to eradicate them. The pest controller uses heavyweight toxic materials to deal with the problem, knowing any remaining vestige of the insect or plant life will allow it quickly to reappear and lead to a reoccurrence of the problem. Few organizations ever go in for pest controller consultants. However, when companies collapse – literally like buildings with termites – they may be rebuilt only if the incompetence is eradicated.

Courtis (1986), in a book entitled *Managing by Mistake*, noted that:

> ... basic and essential management principles are being flouted everywhere. Mistakes made by incompetent managers fall crudely into five categories:
>
> 1. Errors of omission (failure to act or communicate).
> 2. Errors of commission (doing things you ought not to have done).
> 3. Qualitative errors (doing the right thing inadequately or by the wrong method).
> 4. Errors of timing (doing the right thing too early or too late).
> 5. Credibility errors (doing the right thing, at the right time, but in such a way as to irritate everyone or discredit the action). (Courtis, 1986: ix)

Managerial incompetence causes employee stress, which leads to illness and absenteeism, which in turn leads to greater costs to the company. Vicious circles like this are frequently a function of managerial competence levels.

As for how to detect the potential bad manager, Courtis suggests that one clue will be a tendency towards *scapegoating culprits for personal errors*: 'The school system of identifying culprits in order to punish them (to prevent repetition of the offence) very seldom works in business and shouldn't be considered' (Courtis, 1986: 2). The incompetent manager finds others to blame for problems; the competent manager finds a way to prevent the problems from reoccurring. Hence the use of the phrase 'blame-storming groups' to find culprits after management blunders: 'Management by blame is particularly nasty in the management of people. Looking for bad points becomes infectious. Managers whose logic and business decision-making is otherwise impeccable can descend to childish and petty attitudes in their dealing with people' (Courtis, 1986: 4). Incompetent managers are often *pessimistic fatalists* who exaggerate failure and spend their energy on finding scapegoats rather than on diagnosing the cause of the failure. Scapegoating often ruins long-term relationships. Good managers understand that exceptions to rules and processes will occur. Few systems can be constructed to take account of all possible situations and, even if they can, they will be extremely cumbersome and complex. When exceptional circumstances occur, they command immediate attention and can be easily dealt with.

Incompetent managers are *poor delegators*, even though they do not know it. They delegate tasks not objectives; and they blur accountability so as to make it impossible for their staff to use their initiative. Hence the delegatee is demotivated and fails – which proves to incompetent managers that delegation doesn't work.

Incompetent managers *forget that their job is to take a longer view*. This does not mean ignoring daily events and recording and analysing them appropriately. Trivia need to be identified, delegated or ignored. 'The short-sighted and narrow minded walk through their work laying a minefield for their staff, colleagues and successors' (Courtis, 1986: 11).

Incompetent managers believe in luck, competent ones do not. As Courtis says,

> Luck is bunk. However, what is popularly dismissed as luck, when it is not just coincidence, often hides a degree of forward planning or problem analysis, which the owner may be unwilling to share or be doing without fully appreciating the skill involved. (Courtis, 1986: 12)

There is a large psychological literature that shows that instrumentalists – people who take charge of their own careers – are likely to succeed whereas fatalists are likely to fail. Many incompetent managers believe that luck, chance or powerful people, and not themselves, is the key to their success.

Incompetent managers don't think through the potential costs and benefits associated with the (adequate) performance of a particular job. Such an evaluation depends on a good job analysis for the position in question. Recruitment and selection are expensive – but so is losing good people. The cost of turnover created by poor management can be much greater than the costs of either selection or recruitment. Incompetent managers treat selected candidates as cannon fodder rather than as potential customers. And badly treated employees then become 'ill-will ambassadors' for the company.

Good managers take seriously the process of inducting new employees into their organization. They explain the written and unwritten rules, and the taboos and unusual quirks of the company. They introduce new people to all those who will be important to their doing their job well, regardless of their rank. It is also important to manage corporate reputation.

Incompetent managers often underestimate the role, importance and intelligence of their support staff: 'it is entirely possible that the IQ of the average secretary exceeds the IQ of the boss. The thoughtful manager will take advantage of this rather than be frightened' (Courtis, 1986: 34).

Ultimately, people are in business to make money. The primary aim of all jobs should be to maximize profit and efficiency through good products, services and so on. All competent senior managers should regularly evaluate which of their major activities they can best afford to downsize, why they have not chosen to downsize an activity and, if not downsized, how they can make it more profitable in the future.

Serious adversity often helps to weed out managerial incompetence. The possibility of failure helps the competent manager concentrate, assess priorities, make sacrifices, identify key objectives and make tough decisions, while simultaneously ignoring office politics and other distractions. Potential failure may also help management groups pull together into real teams. Crisis is a sort of Darwinian process for revealing incompetence, some of which may be cured and some not. But it is equally important not to over-compensate when confronted by a problem. Management by crisis rather than reason is the hallmark of an incompetent manager. Failing to plan, monitor and ask difficult questions is yet another sign of incompetence.

Incompetent management encourages crime (theft, bogus worker compensation claims, sabotage); bad managers don't understand the difference between security and insurance, and the costs of crime can be exorbitant. Insurance is a backstop when security fails. Incompetent managers lead their staff to become whistleblowers and absentees.

The importance of regular, clear, honest communication cannot be overestimated. Gossip abhors a vacuum: idle speculation and damaging rumours are often the result of employees trying to make sense of what is happening around them. Incompetent managers choose inappropriate media to communicate to the wrong people badly. Often their writing, like annual reports, is boring, costly, incomprehensible, insulting and wrongly aimed. It is a sort of in-house junk mail – volume mailings only expecting a minority response. Bad writers fail to consider how readers will react to their memos; will they be offended, pleased, informed, provoked to respond, or apathetic?

Many features of management incompetence will be considered in this book. What is suggested so far, however, is that incompetent managers, like traffic wardens, are ubiquitous. They are found in all industries, in all sectors and at all levels. They may be accountants or advertising executives, in consumer behaviour or computers, engineers or executives. They have a lot in common because they have similar characteristics and similar management behaviours.

1.4. The Psychology of Managerial Incompetence

Furnham (1998, 2000a) has reviewed the topic of management incompetence: although he acknowledges that many incompetent managers may be 'psychologically disturbed', he also notes other reasons for incompetence.

One is that managers fall victim to fads perpetrated by consultants. Another reason is that managers often have bizarre beliefs and myths about how to manage. Furnham maintains that many incompetent managers hold and follow management myths for five reasons:

1. They don't get clear, specific feedback on their style so they cannot learn from experience.
2. They are superstitious and it takes careful and honest analysis and experimentation to dispose of superstition.
3. Most have had a pretty erratic (often poor) formal management education.
4. Many are simply desperate for answers and will follow anyone or any theory that has sufficient self-proclaimed confidence.
5. Many managers hate, and are frightened by, ambiguity and uncertainty and conform to myths simply to avoid these.

Furnham (2000a) presented a 'theory' of management incompetence that takes the form of a vicious cycle (Figure 1.2). It does not explain how managers become incompetent but rather tries to explain why they stay that way.

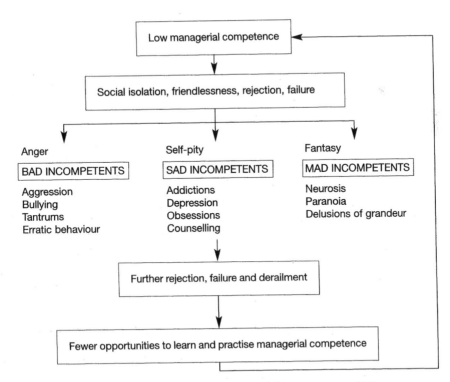

Figure 1.2 The causes and consequences of managerial incompetence (MI).

So the cycle spirals down. The helpless, hapless and hopeless manager simply becomes more so.

Furnham defines the three types as follows:

1. The sad, inadequate manager is often one who is prone to depression and self-pity. Many have a fine future behind them and probably will never reach their potential. Colleagues and schoolmates poring over photographs often remark of the sad, incompetent managers that, although they clearly had some promise, was never reached. They may turn to pharmacological solutions (drink and drugs) to try to improve their sorry state, but with little success.

2. Bad: Some inadequate and incompetent managers are bad in the moral sense. The bully, the selfish, egotistical bastard and the psychopath are all well known in the managerial dungeons of notoriety. These managers often succeed in the short run. Indeed, it is a sad fact that some also succeed in the long run, threatening the happy myth that good wins out in the end. They can succeed in some companies in particular sectors during specific phases of the economic cycle, but they rarely last.

3. Mad: Some incompetent managers simply become deranged over time. They live in a fantasy world where they think they are successful, adaptive, healthy individuals. They start by believing their own press statements and strictly censoring negative feedback. They may develop a whole range of neurotic and psychotic symptoms before anyone seriously thinks of men in white coats. (Furnham, 2000a: xvii)

We need to be able to explain both the origins of incompetence and why it continues ... why we have vicious and virtuous cycles and why some managers get caught in a web of failure. The answers will be discussed in technical detail in Chapters 5, 6 and 7.

1.5. Fads, Fashions and Folderol in Management

Folderol is defined as 'a showy useless ornament, a trifle, a nonsense, a meaningless refrain in some old songs'. Incompetent managers are dedicated to management folderol; this leads them to jump on every new management bandwagon and then zealously apply the dictates of the new idea. A devotee of folderol rarely notices what inevitably happens – the same idea/technique is repackaged the second time around. Management fads, like fashion fads, move in cycles.

It has been observed that the length of women's skirts is correlated with the economy – short skirts in bullish times, long skirts in bearish times (although if one takes into account the cost of material, it should be the other way around). Just as skirts go up and down, so management ideas come in and out of fashion. People have not changed fundamentally for two hundred thousand years and, to some extent, nor has the work that they do.

People monitor computers as their grandparents monitored weaving machines. Rewards, expectations and lifestyles have changed, but how you manage people has not necessarily changed.

An applicant for a top management job was asked what he later confessed to be an extremely difficult question by an inquisitive but sceptical member of the selection board: 'What has been the major development in management science since the war?' Floundering and flummoxed, the applicant attempted slow babbling while speaking, only to be interrupted by another member of the selection board, who tried to help by saying: 'OK – this century, not just the past 50 years'. The candidate gave no satisfactory answer. The implication was obvious. Either he was ignorant or management science had not come up with anything. The candidate's CV suggested the first was not true so the answer must be the latter. The central question is, why are there fads and fashions in management? There are fashions in all sorts of behaviour. The key issues are:

- Why do managers embrace them so enthusiastically?
- What determines a change in fashion from the end of one fashion to the adoption of another?
- What are the consequences of slavish fashion following?

The answer to the first question is probably quite simple – *desperation*. Incompetent managers like the idea of a simple fix, a magic bullet that provides, once and for all, a solution to people problems and product management. They rarely understand that they are the problem. Furthermore, because incompetent managers are frequently uncritical, they genuinely believe that the new treatment works. Like the obese diet addict who tries every new remedy but ends up getting fatter, so incompetent managers embrace and discard faddish tricks and enthusiasms as children discard toys.

The second question is usually dictated by two things: *consultant and management incompetence*. Clearly a new fad is needed when it is discovered, at great cost, that the previous fad is not working or, worse, is even causing harm. A second reason could be when management consultants see that a product market is saturated and that the S curve is beginning to affect their growth. The brighter consultants then seek their own fad, although being first does not necessarily mean making more money. It is the old game of supply and demand – as the demand for a new solution occurs, so it is supplied. Big fads, like measuring corporate culture or re-engineering, may last a year. Small fads have a shelf life of about three years.

The third question is easiest to answer. The consequences of faddish management, with all the swings and turnabouts that it implies, are profoundly disrupting. It is bad enough to endure the 'slings and arrows' of the market without dealing with the idiosyncrasies of fad-obsessed managers.

In her excellent book *Fad Surfing in the Boardroom: Reclaiming the courage to manage in the age of instant managers*, Shapiro (1996) systematically examines and exposes modern management myths.

1. *Mission statement*: The continuing fad of writing and rewriting valuable and hopefully self-fulfilling mission statements, is patently a waste of time. Shapiro sensibly argues:

   A. 'Forget the quest for a start-to-finish blueprint: It's the stepwise approach that increases the odds for success' (Shapiro, 1996: 5).
   B. 'Forget the broad-based, democratic visioning process: It's those who control the resources who are the gate-keepers to the dream' (1996: 12).

   Shapiro believes that many mission statements are talismans, hung in public places to ward off evil spirits. They should be short, powerful, removable, chargeable and credible. They have no power beyond the ability to serve as a public statement of an organization's desired values and aims.

2. *Strategic planning*: Once strategic plans are completed, they are out of date. In this sense planning is important but the plan is not. Wooing serendipity and exploiting opportunities are more relevant than following plans. What incompetent managers do is write the plan and feel it is done. A competent manager keeps looking at the figures, looking for patterns in the data and remaining sensitive to discontinuance and unpredicted changes.

3. *Delayering, right-sizing and re-engineering*: For more than 15 years the faddists have sought to destroy one major bogeyman, the idea that decision-making in hierarchical organizations is slow, inefficient and too political. Hierarchy stands for everything that is bad, yet it is inconceivable to think of a non-hierarchical organization. It is accountability and authority that matter, not hierarchy per se. Renaming jobs, redesigning organizational charts and believing you are making a contribution are hallmarks of the incompetent manager.

4. *Obsession with corporate culture*: It is true that every organization has an 'internal game that sets the rules for how to survive and excel within the organization', sometimes called 'corporate culture'. Although it is true that unofficial rather than explicit rules determine success in an organization, it is also true that there is no clear relationship between knowing the real rules and how this actually contributes to success. If one believes that corporate culture is worthy of investigation *and* change, then it is crucially important to uncover the 'real rules of the internal game', so that 'one can then move to alter those rules that stand in the way of the needed changes' (Shapiro, 1996: 62). Clearly, incompetent managers have no idea how to access the rules that govern the real culture, let alone knowing how to change them.

5. *Communication in open environments*: Incompetent managers talk about openness and the real flow of honest and accurate information in organizations. Every realistic manager knows 'there is nothing to gain and maybe much to lose by contributing ideas and observations' (Shapiro,

1996: 67). The grapevine is perhaps the most reliable source of information, *not* emails, in-house publications and CEO videos.

6. *Empowerment, delegation and real responsibility*: 'Empowerment' is a new
   word for 'delegation'. Real delegation involves devolving power to those
   lower in the organization. But power sharing or power distribution can be
   very destabilizing. Ultimately the success of empowerment depends on an
   employee's good judgement, which itself may be a correlate of intelligence,
   experience and so on. Incompetent managers believe that empowerment,
   whether people want it or not, is the secret of good management.

7. *Obsession with customers:* Customer satisfaction is crucial – unsatisfied customers go to one's competitors. But incompetent managers in weak
   companies often erroneously believe that their internal systems and structures are customer friendly. They believe that satisfied customers are loyal
   and that they already know all they need to about their customer's needs.
   They often deliberately filter out news that they do not like and tend to
   remember only self-fulfilling data. Incompetent managers talk a good deal
   about 'customer focus' but get obsessed with what they like about products – such as certain technical features.

8. *Belief in brand loyalty:* Incompetent managers forget that customers have
   choices, and are more and more sophisticated. They forget that customers
   desert them when they think they are being taken for granted. All products and services have subtle intangibles that customers notice – and
   incompetent managers do not. Every product has a cost–benefit ratio in
   the eyes of the customer.

9. *Obsession with fads:* Shapiro calls total quality management 'total quality
   mayhem: When cookbook compliance creates quality quagmires' (1996:
   173). Re-engineering is no more than a licence to print money for consultants. Incompetent managers may well be alert to cost-cutting strategies
   but rarely do they see the consequences of them.

Thus, management gurus and consultants 'help' and encourage managers
to become incompetent by making them reliant on simple and simplistic formulas that in themselves are harmless and often ineffectual. However, they
often give the impression that management involves little more than the
application of new 'magic-bullet' techniques.

There are often debates in psychology as to whether therapy is liberating
or imprisoning. Does it free people (from anxiety, guilt, destructive behaviours) or make them addicted to, and dependent on, therapists? Some
(grown, adult) patients seem unable to make any decisons, even mundane
ones, without first consulting their therapists. It's good for the therapeutic
income if not the process. The same happens in business: replace therapist
with management consultant and you have the roots of consultancy dependency. A desperate search for simple solutions to difficult problems of which
oneself is a major factor can lead the incompetent manager to become

addicted to consultants who may or may not be helpful and who encourage or discourage unhealthy dependency and addiction. In this sense, the incompetent manager may exacerbate the problem by calling in consultants.

1.6. Anti-preneurs and Absurd Behaviour

It has been fashionable to create neologisms around the word entrepreneur. Hence we have intrapreneur, which captures the idea that some people may work within organizations to bring about success. Many studies have attempted to list (even to understand) the particular mix of needs, traits and abilities required to be a successful entrepreneur. It is unlikely, but possible, that successful entrepreneurs may once have been incompetent managers – the two seem antithetical. It could be that early in their careers they had a managerial job that was deeply unsuited to their talent and temperament. They may have been incompetent as a result of this poor fit but have quickly moved on.

To a large extent, incompetent managers are unlikely to be entrepreneurially oriented and probably rather anti-entrepreneurial. They possess none of the drive, courage, zeal and ability of the entrepreneur, and may be jealous of them. In this sense they are anti-preneurs. Indeed, it may be useful to benchmark the signs of incompetence by contrasting them with the attributes of entrepreneurs. The list provided by Born and Altink (1996) provides an excellent starting point:

Table 1.1 The essential differences between entrepreneurs and anti-preneurs

Entrepreneurs	Anti-preneurs
• Clear market orientedness	• Ignorance of market issues
• Perseverance	• Quick to give up/despair
• Decisiveness	• Ditheringness and dependence
• Flexibility	• Rigidity
• Realistic attitude	• Dogmatic attitude
• Good problem analysis	• Weak problem analysis
• Takes initiative	• Follows, never leads
• Uses financial control information	• Ignores financial control information
• Impressive planning/organizational capacity	• No systematic, comprehensive planning
• Creativity	capacity
• Good tolerance for stress	• Conventionality
• Skill in negotiation	• Stress prone, poor coping
• Person-oriented leadership skills	• Limited negotiation skills
• Verbal communication skill	• Little person insight (self or other)
• Reflection/learning capacity	• Neither articulate nor clear in verbal
• Task-oriented leadership	communication
• Excellent social relations	• Inability to be self-critical or learn from actions
• Outside socio-political awareness	• Poor at task analysis, work assignment
• Good written communication skill	• Socially insensitive and unskilled
	• Mainly internal in interests, scanning
	• Poor at formulating interpretable and
	succinct documents

Another psychologist who objects to the simplistic answers and gimmicks offered by 'self-help' books is Farson (1996) in his splendid book *Management of the Absurd*. His thesis is this:

> The confused manager careering from trend to trend cannot become an effective leader as long as he or she continues to believe in simplistic techniques. But a manager who can appreciate the absurdities and paradoxes of business relationships and organisations is surely going to be far less vulnerable to fashions, and therefore stronger as a leader. (Farson, 1996: 13)

He distinguishes stupidity – foolish mistakes – from absurdity, which is a result of unreasonable, ridiculous, irrational behaviour. But, the author notes: 'Paradox and absurdity keep us off balance. In so doing, they produce the humility, vitality, and creative surprise that make life so worth living' (Farson, 1996: 15).

Farson sets out a long list of paradoxes that at first glance may seem to be inconsistent jumbles, but that on further reflection seem to be quite reasonable: the opposite of a profound truth is also true. Thus we need full, open, honest communication in organizations, but we also need diplomacy and tact, which are euphemisms for information distortion. Next, nothing is as invisible as the obvious. The best management decisions come through simply taking a fresh look at the state of affairs everyone has taken for granted. Third, the more important a relationship, the less management skills matter. Spontaneity, genuineness and caring are not skills to be learned, they are natural products of important relationships. Once you find a management technique that works, give it up. Most prevent closer human relationships. One needs to transcend techniques in order to be really competent. Again, paradoxically, effective managers are not in control. Qualities such as persuasion, tenacity, patience, courage, firmness, enthusiasm and wonder are more useful than the ability to manipulate and control. Most problems that people have are not problems, they are predicaments. Problems can be solved, but predicaments must be coped with, and most managerial problems are the latter – complicated, inescapable dilemmas. There is no simple solution.

Technology creates the opposite of its intended purpose. Like side effects from drugs and surgery, there are many unanticipated costs of technology. For instance, while pursuing the vision of the paperless office, the use of paper has increased. Furthermore, we think that we invent technology, but it invents us. Just as travel created the possibility of having suburbs, computer networks have created virtual companies and teams. The more we communicate, the less we communicate. There is an optimal amount of communication (both information and channels), beyond which it becomes dysfunctional. Most communication problems are actually balance-of-power problems.

All corporate climate surveys point out communication problems, but it is unclear what the solution is. In communication, form is more important than content. The music is as important as the lyrics; the style is as important as the meaning of the words. The hidden agenda or meta-message is in the form. Equally, listening is more important than talking. Listening may be inappropriate and confining, and can be disturbing. It is more than patiently hearing what others have to say, and few people (other than therapists) are trained to do so. Praising people does not motivate them. Praise can be threatening (can they repeat the act?); it may be a way to gain status over them (the praiser is the judge); it may constrict creativity because it routinizes behaviour; it may be associated with criticism (positive comments until the last word); it may help distance oneself from others. Another paradox. Every act is a political act. All management acts and decisions are about the redistribution or enforcement of power.

Never forget that the best resource for solving any problem is the person who presented it. Students learn more from each other than from their teachers. Participatory management has the expertise and power of self-help groups. And, most importantly, organizations that need the most help will benefit from it least. Psychotherapy works best for the least mentally ill; punishment works for 'goodies' not 'baddies'. Seriously ill organizations are deeply resistant to change. The people who can change call for help, not those who don't or can't. Individuals are pretty indestructible – organizations are very fragile. Individuals can and do withstand incredible situations, but organizations are little more than bonds between people, and they are fragile. They need nurturing. Furthermore, big changes are easier to make than smaller ones. Gradualism often meets with more resistance than bold moves.

We learn more from our successes and others' failures. Personal failure often leads to demoralization but the failure of others teaches us about vulnerability. Personal failure is a good teacher only if we can analyse, without fear or favour, its causes and consequences, and few want to do this or are capable of it. Planning is an ineffective way to bring change. Inside planners are often blind to what needs changing most; they are often too low in the organization and don't understand top-level concerns. The fact that planning is confined to one department is self-limiting; it does not consider political issues when instituting changes; it neglects the fact that changes will have to be made as one goes along and that self-interest can be a serious barrier to effective planning. Organizations change best by surviving calamities. Yet most managers try to avoid crises, some of which lead to essential changes that ultimately save an organization. People we think need changing are pretty good the way they are. Because bad news has more impact than good and because it is easier to blame individuals than situations, managers spend too much effort trying to change people. Select well and trust the staff rather than try to change them. Every great strength is a great weakness. Strengths become weaknesses when we rely too heavily on them: the tenacious need to know when to give up; the careful need to know when to relax; the self-critical need to know when to be more self-accepting. Furthermore, weaknesses can be strengths – feelings of inadequacy can create a strong need to achieve. Morale is unrelated to productivity. Hard work determines productivity, whereas morale may in fact reduce it. But a manager's morale may lead him or her to manage better, which, in turn, leads to greater success.

There are no leaders, only leadership. The real strength of leaders is their ability to get the best out of the group. Being dependent on one heroic person is a recipe for failure. The more experienced the managers, the more they trust simple intuition. Experienced and wise managers can scrutinize problems more quickly and accurately, and that is often called intuition. Leaders cannot be trained, but they can be educated. Good leaders do not know how they came to be good at the task or, indeed, what makes them so good. Training attempts to develop skills and techniques; education is about information and knowledge. Education is, or should be, liberating; it should develop new perspectives. In management, to be a professional, one must be an amateur. Amateurs do things out of passion. Professionals need skill, knowledge and competence, but they also need the joy and commitment of the amateur.

The moral of the above is that a lot of what one has been told is wrong. It is as if all the magic-bullet books are propagating not just simplicities but wrong advice. One does not have to agree with all of the above, but the message is clear: incompetence may be the result of following conventional wisdom.

1.7. Obsolescence

Are incompetent managers simply dinosaurs that should have been made obsolete (redundant)? Although there are lots of distinctions to be made regarding obsolescence, most observers agree that professional obsolescence occurs when an individual uses theories, techniques or concepts that have been surpassed because they have been proven to be less effective or powerful. Managerial obsolescence usually refers to a person being unwilling or unable to keep up to date with salient developments in the field. A crude index of obsolescence can be calculated by dividing the current knowledge/skills of an individual manager (numerator) by current knowledge in the field (denominator), which is usually fast growing.

Jones and Cooper (1980) define managerial obsolescence as 'the extent to which a manager's knowledge and skills have failed to keep pace with the current and likely future requirements of his job' (1980: 11). They highlight six significant factors often associated with obsolescence:

- *Age*: This depends on the sector, although people in highly technical areas (engineers, scientists) seem to peak before the age of 40. Paradoxically, older managers often rate themselves as the least obsolete and younger managers as the most obsolete.
- *Professional and technical qualifications*: Qualifications can be a good predictor of obsolescence because having many qualifications is often a sign of motivation and ability to learn in the first place. There is a cycle whereby better qualified people get more demanding jobs from which they learn more all the time and are thus less likely to become (or even feel) obsolete.
- *Work experience and mobility*: Mobility, in terms of both career changes and geography, is one way to ensure that skills and knowledge are developed.
- *Self-confidence about ability to learn*: Those who seek out and enjoy learning and feel that they can master new skills do so and are less likely to be seen as obsolete.
- *Attitudes to the importance of updating*: Obviously realizing the need for, and benefits of, technical and informational updating is itself a powerful predictor of not becoming obsolete. The way people choose, albeit hypothetically, to use business sabbaticals is a good index of their potential for (not) becoming obsolete.
- *Membership of professional associations*: Professional associations may be a good means to prevent the onset of obsolescence, unless of course their primary function is social rather than educational.

So, the obsolete manager is likely to be middle-aged, to have stuck to one job in one company, to doubt his or her learning ability but not see the necessity of updating, and not to be a member of a professional organization.

If an incompetent manager is middle-aged, middlebrow and middle ability, it is often cheaper to replace him or her with a younger and more 'gung-ho' person. The bad manager could be given a lesser job – for example, 'Manager of Special Projects' – but that may be pointless because he or she may simply poison others or act as a poor role model. The third option involves more than plastic surgery and it's highly unlikely, which leaves the final option.

1.8. Conclusion

Incompetence in the military serves as a good model for particular types of management incompetence. Both can be explained in large part by the personality and pathology of managers, which determine the endless errors that managers make. Furthermore, incompetence breeds incompetence: the vicious and virtuous cycles occur such that both competent and incompetent managers tend to become more so over time. The whole situation is made worse by consultants selling simple silver-bullet solutions to problems.

As noted above, the remainder of this book is divided into three parts. In the first, there is general exploration of the subject matter, looking at some of the more amusing features of management failure and how business writers have talked about them (Chapters 2 and 3). Next, the concept of competence and, more specifically, competency is explored: a word used so often by human resource people today.

The second part of the book picks up the theme of this first chapter. It examines the role of personality in the workplace. Another long chapter explores pathological incompetence and the dark side of the personality – and how it affects management performance. This part will also look at how people work in teams and how we have both competent and incompetent teams.

In the final part of the book possible cures are described. A theme is that we need to understand the cause of the problem before we can cure it: diagnosis precedes treatment. And one has to admit that in some cases the prognosis is poor.

CHAPTER TWO

The Nature of Incompetence

2.1. Introduction

To be a good manager is not easy. Employees are fickle, capricious, irascible and even mean – although it could be argued that managers often get the staff that they deserve. Competition in the workplace is never ceasing and quickly shows up weaknesses. Managers have to be simultaneously strategic planners and counsellors; they are supposed to create a sense of continuity while chaperoning change, and they are supposed to be experts with people, systems and technology all at once. They are expected to be both leaders and followers, to set clear goals in an unclear environment, and to talk, to listen and to be eternally sensitive to ever-demanding customers.

Managers are supposed to know about, and be good at, budgeting, which is a matter of worrying before, during and after spending money. Nowadays they are expected to have business degrees, which for many is little more than a certificate permitting them to manage without using their intelligence. All around us we see one-ulcer managers holding down two-ulcer jobs.

Rarely are managers carefully selected or well trained. Most organizations assume an apprenticeship–Darwinian system in which one is supposed to learn management skills and techniques *on the job*. Then, after being promoted into management as much for one's tenure and politics as for one's performance, one is expected to be able to manage. It is assumed that there is a natural selection process whereby the strong and talented succeed and the rest either fail or never get promoted further. Both of these assumptions are fundamentally flawed. Apprenticeship (on-the-job training) is never enough to ensure the acquisition of skills because few (trainer) managers see training as their job. Indeed, most of them are poor models and educators. Although the ideas of shadowing and mentoring are now common, for the most part the shadowers learn little, the shadowed get annoyed and both remain in the dark! Mentoring can help with politics, but not with the acquisition of skills. Managers need to be developed and helped, and not just given pass-or-fail challenges. The Darwinian method of choosing managers is as likely to result in the top management being egocentric and narcissists and being mistakenly seen as talented leaders.

Sometimes having a strong characteristic or quality means that you are particularly good at business functions requiring that skill but that you are poor at others. Thus, as McCall (1998) notes, managers who are:

Market driven are admirably resourceful, entrepreneurial, risk takers and doers *but* are often inconsistent, undisciplined individualists who ignore or bypass corporate systems.

Operations driven are almost the opposite of the above – they build and use business systems well and have a reputation for efficient team work *but* they are not very sensitive to customers, often averse to change and are not good at corporate strategy and the big picture.

Finance trained are famous for their analytical skills, their detailed strategic thinking and their attention to the bottom line *but* are often weak at persuading those who have to turn their ideas into action and get results.

Human resources driven are persuasive, obliging team players; they are often systems oriented and technically sophisticated *but* (paradoxically) their cautious conformity to the system makes them poor leaders.

This implies that one often has to trade off certain natural skills and talents in particular areas of the business. Hence the idea of matrix management, business units and the like, which attempt to bring heterogeneous teams together in order to compensate for the potential shortcomings of individual players.

Some writers have even suggested that managerial incompetence can precipitate organizational accidents and disasters. Turner (1994) argues that organizational disasters are the result not only of problems with technology, but also of problems with administrative and managerial controls. He believes that, in the incubation period of any disaster, sloppy management is a necessary precondition for a subsequent breakdown. Sloppy management is associated with communication problems, so that crucial information is not sent to the appropriate people but rather to people who do not appreciate its significance. Rigid hierarchies are also a problem, because they slow down the transmission of information:

> Danger signals include multiple groupings attempting to deal with complex, ill-defined and prolonged tasks; shifting goals, roles and administrative arrangements; out-of-date regulations; and professionals who are pre-occupied because of pressure of work or for other reasons. Virtually all of these preconditions reflect poor management of one kind or another. (Turner, 1994: 217)

Organizations known for their high reliability (for example, air traffic control) trade off and balance requirements for such things as quick but accurate information and decisions and appropriate levels of hierarchy. They understand optimal levels of section or group dependence and interdependence, and most crucially who takes responsibility for what.

Incompetence in the middle ranks of management is often the result of senior managerial incompetence, which in turn is often characterized by particular axioms. A common MBA mistake is to assume that technical competence is more important than human competence. Another is to espouse certain values (teamwork, empowerment, emotional intelligence) while acting so as to undermine, rather than model, them. A third is hubris – managers believing in their own super-competence (they are visionary leaders) so that resistance to their ideas is seen as disloyalty. Incompetent managers seek favourite solutions when in trouble – merging, downsizing, re-engineering – irrespective of the nature of the problem. They believe that they are motivated by rewards (bonus) but others are motivated by punishment (fear or redundancy). They believe that if they put in place best-practice systems (performance appraisal, financial controls, quality assurance), this will ensure that their staff can be controlled and better managed. They talk about empowerment but really believe that power is a zero-sum game – the more they give away, the less they have.

All of this leads to books such as *101 Biggest Mistakes Managers Make and How to Avoid Them* (Albright and Carr, 1997). This particular book documents managerial mistakes in dealing with worker performance, making assignments, dealing with customers, providing information, relationships with other work groups, using technology, managing teams, dealing with your boss, your reactions as part of the organization and essential management skills. A great deal of the book goes over old territory which looks common-sensical and self-evident – for example, 'not keeping your workers fully trained'; 'not dealing with substandard work'; 'ignoring your customers'. But the authors analyse such important but less discussed issues as poor worker retention, not using the appraisal process to improve work performance, letting workers delegate back to management, not letting the workers deal with customers, trying to solve performance problems with technology, ignoring the boss's important issues and ignoring office politics.

Some incompetent managers engage in an exhausting process of looking for opportunities and problems, incorrectly diagnosing them and then ruthlessly applying the wrong remedy. Other managers are just lazy, and spend their time chatting with shareholders and lunching with clients while others do the work. Still others are idealists and utopian speculators whose beliefs increase in strength in direct proportion to how far they are from the problem.

Nearly 40 years ago the academic psychologist Laurence Peter described the now famous Peter Principle: 'In any hierarchy, individuals tend to rise to their levels of incompetence.' Although his book was rejected by 13 publishers, when it was finally published it became an immediate best seller. Indeed, Peter made the concept of incompetence popular long before competence or incompetency was on the lips of every manager.

In a later book entitled *Why Things Go Wrong* he spelled out a number of corollaries to the Peter Principle:

- The cream rises until it is sour.
- For every job in the world there is someone, somewhere, who can't do it. Given enough promotions, that someone will get the job.
- All useful work is done by those who have not yet reached their level of incompetence.
- Competence always contains the seeds of incompetence.
- Incompetence plus incompetence equals incompetence.
- Whenever something is worth doing, it is worth finding someone competent to do it.
- The Peter Principle, like evolution, shows no mercy.
- Once an employee achieves a level of incompetence, inertia sets in and the employer settles for incompetence rather than distress the employee and look for a replacement.
- Lust gets us into trouble more than sloth.
- There is a tendency for the person in the most powerful hierarchical position to spend all of his or her time performing trivial tasks.
- It's harder to get a job than to keep it.
- Equal opportunity means everyone will have a few chances at becoming incompetent.
- The higher up you go, the deeper you get.
- Incompetence knows no barrier of time or place.
- The higher one climbs the hierarchical ladder, the shakier it gets.
- Climb the ladder of success, reach the top, and you'll find you're over the hill.
- In a hierarchy, the potential for a competent subordinate to manage an incompetent supervisor is greater than for an incompetent superior to manage a competent subordinate.
- Colleges can't produce competence but they can produce graduates.
- Being frustrated in your work can be disagreeable, but the real disaster may be when you're promoted out of it.
- More competent individuals resign than incompetents get fired.
- The ability of the potentially competent erodes with time, while the potentially incompetent rises to the level where his or her full potential is actualized.

Peter (1985) also set out a number of wickedly funny and often political-ly incorrect principles related to his general theme. Thus he noted:

The Competence Principle: The way to avoid mistakes is to gain experience. The way to gain experience is to make mistakes.

The Sexist Principle: Most hierarchies were established by men who mono-polized the upper levels, thus depriving women of their rightful share of opportunities to achieve their own levels of incompetence.

The Levitation Principle: When the foundation of a pyramid erodes, the top can still be supported on nothing but money.

The Evaluation Principle: Either super-incompetence or super-competence may be offensive to the establishment.

The Investment Principle: Fools rush in where wise men fear to trade.

The Expectative Principle: What happens is not only stranger than we imagine, it is stranger than we can imagine.

> Individuals may be selected on a basis of competence, for their entry-level jobs, but as they move up they tend to become arranged just as distribution theory would predict: the majority in the moderately competent group, with the competent and incompetent comprising the minorities. (Peter, 1985: 72–3)

Peter became well known for his wry and funny observations. But he did not fully discuss the aetiology from a psychological perspective. He seemed to imply that organizations get the managers they deserve and that incompetence is more about managerial systems than personal pathology. But organizations do not create incompetence: they may foster it, even reward it. Its origins lie in the individuals: those high- and low-flyers that end up being managers.

2.2. High- and Low-flyers

Organizational gurus talk a lot about high-flyers: how to recruit, select, man-age and nurture the 'Wunderkind' of tomorrow. For those of us with a fine future behind us, these multilingual, multinational, multi-talented young people are a considerable threat. The Oxbridge First, topped off with the Harvard MBA; five years at McKinsey and six months working for a devel-oping country charity; tanned and chiselled good looks with excellent taste in clothes; energy and health – all of this is enough to make you sick.

There are many theories about where high-flyers come from: stories of childhood loss or deprivation, trading in the playground, brushes with the law and so on. These stories have led people to speculate on the factors that pre-dict business success. In any case, everyone, it seems, wants their organization to be full of high-flyers. Even the support staff are supposed to be super-human. Job ads encode this by talking about wanting people who are 'good in a crisis', 'eager to adapt' and 'multi-skilled'. The fact that high-flyers are often spoilt mavericks who are difficult to manage is conveniently overlooked.

Although newly recruited high-flyers may be the key to future development, the processes of selection and succession management are both a gamble. In each case, you are trying to find people who will succeed in the turbulent, uncertain future that is organizational life. Captains of industry, consultants and charlatans have all speculated on factors that are important, generating lists of factors for both selecting in and selecting out. Thus, Sir James Blyth, former MD of Plessey, noted desirable characteristics such as raw intellect, forthright honesty, determination and physical durability. He also memorably asked: 'Is he a shit? If yes, reject him: more prejudice, but in the end, why work with too many people you don't like? Usually, you inherit more than enough – why hire more?'

The lists of ideal characteristics of managers that gurus and researchers have come up with are remarkably similar. Characteristics that are frequently mentioned include determination, learning from adversity, seizing chances and opportunities, being achievement oriented, having a well-integrated value system, intrinsic motivation, effective management of risk, a well-organized life, clear objectives, a pragmatic approach, dedication to the job, sound analytical and problem-solving skills, and people skills and so on.

The trouble with these lists is that they are purely speculative. Hence, although there is some marginal overlap and agreement among them, it becomes impossible to distinguish between two equally plausible lists. So one has to do some expensive, but important, research. Somewhat belatedly, the gurus are turning their attention to those at the other end of the spectrum. Researchers tend to categorize managers rather differently when considering their long- or medium-term future. One useful taxonomy of different management types is:

- High-flyers: Great potential for future development.
- Senior managers: Will probably make, though not to board level – that is, they will have one or two more promotions. They are clearly rated good, but not the very best.
- Ceiling reached: Competent in current role, but that is their limit. Little more to offer; working at the limits of their capabilities.
- Unpredictably fragile: Able, but unstable; technically competent, but psychologically not well adjusted. Personal problems and/or skills deficits render them fragile.
- Derailed: Those who have lost the script or who have not adapted to new ways and are living on borrowed time. Dinosaurs struggling to fit in with the new corporate culture.

Letting go, outplacing or redeploying managers ('sacking', for those who are not yet suitably PC) is neither pleasant nor easy. It can be very expensive and may lead to strikes. On the other hand, it is usually unwise to retain the clearly incompetent. So how does one recognize the low-flyers? There are different signs for the three less successful groups.

Ceiling reached

These people are not victims of the glass ceiling. In many ways, they are fortunate. They have reached their potential, maximized their skills and exploited their talents. They are not Peter Principled, they really are at their appropriate level. The trouble is, they are not particularly talented. On the low side of average, they are particularly difficult to spot, especially in big organizations. The following are their key characteristics:

- Change averse, ready to oppose any form of innovation.
- Slow to learn: not too hot on computers, new systems or new ways of dealing with customers.
- Retirement obsessed: counting the days until retirement, even planning a second career.
- Uncomfortable around the young: rather hesitant in being associated with young Turks who show them up.
- Organocentric: little interest shown in competitors and general business affairs.

Displaying three out of five of these tendencies may be a warning sign. Such people are often the 'solid citizens' of organizations. Loyal and long serving, they have a wealth of useful knowledge and experience that can be exploited. The danger is in promoting them one level more than they can handle. It is better to offer a generous and early retirement package.

The unpredictably fragile

These are the neurotics of an organization, who are prone to hysteria, mood swings, hypochondria and depression. They may have real talent – they may be creative, linguistically gifted and interpersonally sensitive, but they are fragile and must be handled with kid gloves. Indeed, sometimes so much effort has to be put into appeasing and mollycoddling them that it is hardly worth the trouble. The telltale signs of this group are:

- Frequent emotional outbursts: these can be with staff, superiors, customers or even shareholders.
- High rate of absenteeism: well known in the organization for a bewildering range of rare but persistent ailments.
- Special rules: demanding unique conditions around issues such as smoking, silence, room colours and so on.
- Counselling obsessed: paradoxically, as eager to give counselling to others as they are to receive it.
- Temporally odd: they may come in to work very early or leave very late.

The derailed

These poor souls have a tenuous grasp of reality. They may be paranoid or unrealistic optimists. They are often followers of crackpot gurus and have problematic personal lives. In the old days, various nationalized utilities used to shelter these casualties of the corporate battlefield. What might their identifying characteristics be?

- Peculiar interests and obsessions: most of which have little or nothing to do with work.
- Occult leanings: may use graphology or crystals in selection or management meetings.
- Bewildered: by the speed of change and the required adaptation. Can often be seen gazing into space.
- Narcissistic: demanding, opinionated, yet clearly wrong and, worse, having a reputation for it.
- Paranoid: a perpetual concern with the meaning of internal memos, the behaviour of the CEO, what the consultants are really up to!

How did the derailed come to be in the job in the first place? Did the job break them (we pause for a speech about job stress these days) or was it poor selection? Were they the friends of someone, or coyly attractive in the interview? Was a retiring and alienated human resources director trying to place a time bomb in the organization as a parting 'present'?

Although it is important to learn from one's mistakes, the most urgent task for an organization is to deal with a derailed manager. The evidence from counselling evaluation studies is that clients don't get better, and that counsellors get worse. So don't bother with counselling as a solution to fixing these people, although it might be used as a carrot to tempt the derailed to leave. Offer outplacement counselling, job search, aromatherapy, crystal gazing – anything! Your priority must be to get rid of the derailed before the whole train flies off the tracks. Chapter 8 deals with the cures for incompetence.

2.3. The Difficult People Approach

A number of popular books and courses concern how to deal with difficult people. Sometimes these people are given the more politically correct label of 'negative people' (Kravitz, 1995). Self-help books give us the usual interpersonal skills advice: avoid taking their anger personally, defuse conflict by focusing on issues and be willing to compromise (Kravitz, 1995). But is this sufficient or even effective? Some books tell us how to deal with difficult customers (Morgan, 1996). There are books for bosses that help them to deal with difficult employees and co-workers. Broustein (1993) believes that difficult employees can be classified as new, inconsistent, unbalanced, mediocre, marginal and intolerable. No doubt the same could be said of bosses. However, it is unclear whether unbalanced should be in the middle of the list rather than at the end of the list.

Cava (1993) classifies difficult co-workers into six categories: shirkers, buck-passers, putter-offers, over-achievers, critics and interruptors. He also has seven categories of problematic employees: buck-passers, bottle-neckers, the error-prone, daydreamers, time-wasters, poor housekeepers and the downright dishonest. Bramson (1992) classifies difficult bosses into six types:

1. *Degrading bosses* or bullies. These are subdivided into ogres and fire-eaters but what they have in common is their need for power, self-validation and previous hot temper.
2. *Artful dodgers* who are not there for you (the employee). They may be stallers, wafflers or super-delegators and can be immobilized by self-doubt or conflict.
3. *Tight-reins* or those who hold the reins too lightly. They may be power-clutchers, paranoids or perfectionists, but what they have in common is a need for certainty and a lack of trust.
4. *Know-it-alls* are the bulldozing experts who require no assistance what-soever.
5. *Unscrupulous or offensive* bosses are those with essentially aberrant values. They can be further classified into scallywags, schemers or skunks.
6. *The sweet boss turned sour* is the final and totally self-explicable category.

However, if one is after a great list of problem people it would be hard to beat Honey (1992), who lists 50 types (or at least characteristics) of poor employees (see Table 1.2).

Table 1.2 Fifty types of problem people

Abdicator	Defensive	Manipulator	Scatterbrained
Absentee	Ditherer	Martyr	Secretive
Apathetic	Dogmatic	Meddler	Self-conscious
Arrogant	Eccentric	Nagger	Slapdash
Authoritarian	Flippant	Overpowering	Tactless
Boaster	Gamesman	Perfectionist	Temperamental
Bolshie	Gossip	Pessimist	Two-faced
Bore	Humourless	Plagiarist	Vague
Buck-passer	Impulsive	Prejudiced	Whinger
Bureaucrat	Intimidator	Procrastinator	Workaholic
Circuitous	Judgemental	Quarrelsome	Worrier
Coaster	Kow-tower	Reserved	
Conservative	Lazy	Sarcastic	

Honey believes that problem people waste time and money, create unnecessary stress and distort decisions. Consider the following three examples of this descriptive approach:

Bolshie people tend to be disobedient, rebellious, bloody-minded and obstructive – a depressing list! Often in conversation the bolshie person appears surly but reasonably compliant. The extent of their defiance only becomes apparent subsequently when it is revealed that they have not done what you wanted them to do. When questioned, they will often be bolshie about the very fact that they are being questioned, and fail to articulate their grievances. It is the equivalent of customers voting with their feet rather than troubling to explain why they are rebelling. Bolshie people don't necessarily *choose* actions rather than words; they often feel unable to express themselves adequately in any other way. Articulate people are more likely to verbalise their grievances and come across as grumblers (see Whinger).

Bolshie people are a problem because you cannot trust them to do what you need. They require a disproportionate amount of close supervision. It is also likely that their bolshieness will spread to other colleagues on the 'one rotten apple in a barrel' principle. Who knows, you could even have a full-scale mutiny on your hands! (Honey, 1992: 44; emphasis added)

Impulsive people can be a joy or a menace. They are a joy when spontaneity is appropriate but a menace when it is necessary to play it by the book. Impulsive people are often carried away by their own enthusiasm and, of course, they see their behaviour as an asset rather than a problem.

Impulsive people create problems when you want consistency. They are inclined to be unpredictable and arbitrary, depending on the mood they are in. They have scant regard for anything bureaucratic (see Bureaucratic), for rules, regulations and procedures. Their philosophy is very much that 'rules are there to be broken'. There are plenty of occasions when this is admirable but unfortunately impulsive people are not very good at judging when to switch their impulsiveness on and off. They are therefore inclined to behave impulsively when it is singularly inappropriate and this often has far-reaching and damaging consequences. For example, many employment practices to do with hiring, firing and safety at work are regulated by legislation. Left to their own devices impulsive managers would ride roughshod through such restrictive red tape and hire and fire at whim.

Such discretionary behaviour is frowned upon because it is the enemy of order, standardisation and quality. All legislation, whether in society at large or within an organisation or community, is an attempt to curtail impulsive behaviour. Not to do so would result in anarchy and chaos. (Honey, 1992: 96)

People who *whinge* have got grumbling down to a fine art. They are given to whining and moaning about things that happen to them. Their basic philosophy is that life should always be fair and when it isn't (which is most of the time) they whinge. They moan because other people are paid more than they are, have a better working environment and resources, have a fairer boss, have more cooperative colleagues, have a better bus service and so on and so on. Despite the fact that life is patently not fair, and that nobody ever said it would be, whingers hang on to their basic belief that it *should* be. This means that whenever there is a disparity between what they believe should happen and what actually happens, they are upset and whinge.

Whinging is a problem because it is infectious; it rapidly takes a hold and reduces people's morale. Whole conversations between people can amount to one long moan. It is invariably unproductive, however, for it is rare for whingers to take any initiative to improve the situation. If they did, they might run out of things to grumble about and that would never do! It's always up to other people, 'them' as opposed to 'us', to do something to correct the supposed injustice. (Honey, 1992: 86; emphasis added)

These descriptions are rich, amusing and true to life. But they tell us little of *why* people are like that. Why is one person impulsive and another a whinger? What is the cause of the pathology ... if that is what it is.

At the beginning of his book Honey (1992) states his assumptions about the source of these problems. This is not frequently done in texts of this kind. Note the optimistic nature of these assumptions:

1. There is no such thing as a problem person, only problem behaviours.
2. All problem behaviours are 'made, not born'.
3. All problem behaviours fall into one of two categories: you are suffering from either too much or too little behaviour.
4. Problem behaviours have to be viewed situationally.
5. Different approaches are needed depending on whether the problem behaviour is a 'one-off' or is habitual.

These assumptions are partly correct (and politically incorrect) and partly wrong. And by looking for quick cures they often fail to explore the real, fundamental, intrapersonal nature of the problem before tying to fix it. Number 2 is patently wrong. We know that there is a genetic basis to various complaints and the prognosis for change is poor. We are prepared to admit that various physical problems have inherited, physical causes that can be managed, not changed. But many people in management seem quite unwilling to accept that the same is true of psychological problems. Indeed, we know that impulsivity has a physical basis (Furnham, 1999).

Equally, while problem behaviours may have 'to be viewed situationally', this does not mean that situations are the exclusive cause of these problematic, maladaptive behaviours. Managers choose and change as well as respond to the situations that they are in. The difficult people approach has rich descriptions but naïve answers.

Brinkman (1994) identified 10 unwanted management types:

The Tank: Pushy, ruthless, loud, forceful with intensity and precision. They give no mercy and believe that the end justifies the means.

The Sniper: They have an enthusiasm for finding weaknesses in others and sabotaging them with public putdowns and knives in the back.

The Know-it-alls: People who believe they are omniscient and tell you so all the time – but who will not listen to you.

The Think-they-know-it-alls: Legends in their own minds: exaggerating, bragging, misleading and distracting.

The Grenade: They frequently and uncontrollably blow their tops and everyone in range gets caught.

The Yes Person: They over-commit to please but do not deliver, leaving a chain of unkept commitments.

The Maybe Person: The great procrastinators who put things off until too late.

The Nothing Person: They believe knowledge is power and tell nothing: they give no feedback whatsoever.

The No Reason: Doleful and discouraging, they are known as the abominable no-men.

The Whiner: Wallowing in their woe, these people carry the weight of the world on their shoulders.

This is yet another amusing but semi-arbitrary list that does not explain how these managers came to be as they are. We might recognize some of them, but these typologies do little other than to categorize types of incompetence. We need a theory of *why* people behave like that.

Lloyd (1999) does not mince words on this topic; his book is titled *Jerks at Work*. The book is written in a question-and-answer format, and deals with everyday issues around management incompetence: the manager with wild and unpredictable mood swings; the 'open door' manager who does not listen; the imperfect perfectionist; those who run frequent blame-storming sessions stealing credit for the work of their staff; those who turn everything into a crisis to suit their hyper-management style. More unusually perhaps, Lloyd lists both fellow employees (peers) and subordinates who are 'jerks at work' and how to deal with them. Here he does resort to typologies: the spreader of ill-will; the noisemaker; the ancient historian; the amateur psychologist; the teaser; the blame deflector; the media freak; the bragger; the slug; the slacker; the meanie; the reporter; the cautionist; the linguist and so on.

All these books attempt some diagnosis and then list a number of tactics to deal with the problem: how to stop those who intimidate; those who won't communicate; and so on. The major problem with the 'difficult person' approach listed above is that the categories are often terribly confused. They mix up people with personal pathology who lack skill and knowledge with people who learned their incompetence by having been rewarded for it in a previous corporate culture. Nor is it ever clear how common each type is in each business sector, or the prognosis for cure.

Some writers assume that only extreme types are bad: too impulsive is the apparent seeming opposite of too obsessional, too fast versus too slow. But little is said about the aetiology of these tendencies. Are they only difficult at work or equally hard to live with at home? Have they always been difficult? How did the organization come to hire these difficult people? Indeed, has the organization actually modelled and rewarded these difficult behaviours? What evidence is there that these difficulties can be overcome, essentially by relying on the skills and enthusiasm of individuals or groups of employees?

Most problematic of all is the idea that one needs to cope with, rather than change or remove, the difficult person. Some behaviour problems are relatively easy to cure through education, carrot-and-stick or other relevant training methods. However, the idea that real pathologies are easy to cure is quite misleading. Various forms of managerial neurosis are pretty immune to therapy of all sorts, particularly the 'talking cures'. Therapists are quick to point out that treatment works only if the patient *wants to change*. Difficult bosses rarely want to change.

The word 'difficult' is too bland and too neutral. Many difficult bosses are incompetent and inadequate to the demands of their jobs. Labelled thus, it is clear why learning coping strategies are of limited value – because they require others to adapt to, help or try to influence the boss. Some difficult bosses are 'stress-carriers' almost in a genetic sense just as Queen Victoria was a carrier of haemophilia: they spread their incompetence, unhappiness and pathology around organizations to the detriment of all concerned. Others are too dim to master new technologies and ways of behaving. They have been Peter Principled and reached their ceiling.

It would be nice to believe that all people are changeable. Indeed, this assumption underlies a lot of management training. Therapists will tell you that all change is slow, painful and gradual, and that not everyone succeeds at the task. Many cannot, and will not, be changed. And certainly it is unlikely that a manager's employees will be powerful change agents. Learning coping skills and instituting training courses is not enough for 'difficult' people at work. The cure is often, alas, much more drastic.

2.4. Management Styles of the Incompetent

In his witty *Cynic's Guide to Management*, McKibbin (1998) lists 25 management styles, all incompetent and all familiar. He focuses on a person's particular style of management rather than his or her abilities, personality and pathology. The book is more humorous than analytical, but the styles are well-known manifestations of incompetence. The styles are arranged alphabetically:

Abdication Management: Abdicating responsibility by calling in others (nearly always management consultants). This is most often done when decisions are difficult or involve personal pain. The strategy is extremely expensive but has the advantage that, if the whole thing fails, the consultant can be blamed.

Alibi Management: Obtaining, refining and rehearsing a long list of alibis as to why service fails. They may be human (staff shortages, sickness), mechanical (an incident at Swindon), electrical (signalling problems), vague (the incoming flight arrived late) or 'acts of God' (the weather).

Ballcock Management: A lavatorial analogy where managers contribute precious little to organizational success, being kept afloat by the hard work of others until a cut-off point is reached beyond which they cease to rise. This occurs either when subordinates/peers get 'fed up' carrying the ballcock manager or seeing them take credit for what they quite clearly have not done.

Beehive Management: Here managers emulate the drones in beehives. Occasionally beehive organizations have more than one corpulent 'queen' and extensive elaborate dances occur (meetings, lunches) to decide on winners. Sometimes drones can outnumber workers, but that is a recipe for disaster.

Convoy Management: This is where management proceeds at the pace of the 'slowest-witted' manager. Convoy management rejoices in the rule of 'precedent' – doing things in the way in which they have always been done. Fear of innovation and procrastination are the marks of convoy management.

Crisis Management: This is not the management and resolution of crises but their creation. Crisis managers are the 'Typhus Marys' of stress. They are able to conjure up a crisis out of nothing. All setbacks or misfortunes are escalated into crisis. They become masters of hyperbole when discussing day-to-day business.

Cuckoo Management: Cuckoo managers offer help to close colleagues to overcome problems; most short-term targets take the longer view, then evict them from their own department. Cuckoo managers reap the benefit of watching the competent manager's carefully laid eggs hatch. Cuckoos love mergers and restructuring because it is an ideal time to discover a better nest.

Defensive Management: Defensive managers try to protect themselves from poor decisions by negating responsibility. Committees, panels and others are constructed with the prime purpose of taking the flak and blame if anything goes wrong.

Displacement Management: The idea of this style is to displace energies and focus from what you should be doing into more sexy and enjoyable activities that are easier than really managing. Training of all types is popular along with performance management and working parties.

Evangelical Management: This is management by mission statement, the latter being a set of vague but PC commitments to all sorts of moral, ethical and environmental issues currently in vogue. 'It should be clear to visitors who read this document that they have entered a corporate heaven in which those fortunate enough to gain admission will spend blissful hours, enviably occupied in bringing good things to more people' (McKibbin, 1998: 21).

Homoeopathic Management: As most people know, homoeopathic remedies are universal because they produce symptoms like those of the disorder they are intended to cure. Thus one calls in bureaucratically minded people to deal with problems of excessive form filling and time wasting; one hires others to help with problems of over-staffing.

Hostage Management: A hostage is someone willing to sacrifice his or her career for yours. This style involves managers putting other people in trouble spots rather than dealing with it themselves. If these 'plants' surprisingly succeed, the hostage manager can take the credit for strategic decision-making; if they fail, it must be put down to operational misjudgement by the hostage.

Inflation Management: This is the making-amountain-out-of-a-molehill approach. Everything is inflated – success and failure. Grand certificates are given after training courses. The training centre becomes the company university. The 100-volume library is an information centre and, most important of all, job titles enjoy massive inflation.

Lifeboat Management: This occurs when the organization is in crisis and appoints various committees to analyse the problem. Once the call for equal sacrificing occurs it is done so enthusiastically that too much and too many are thrown overboard. The remaining people are so obsessed by jettisoning for the future that they completely lose the sense of what they should be doing.

Meddle Management: A 'hands on' approach that involves 'compulsively and perpetually altering, fidgeting and tampering, a monstrous regiment of tinkers, meddlers and fiddlers whose ill-timed and misguided interference is ruining many a business' (McKibbin, 1998: 35). Gurus may be good meddle managers, advocating changes, relocations and restructuring again and again.

Narcissus Management: Management that is obsessively concerned with its own image. Focus is on PR image – portraying one and finding out what others think. Forget the real business, the product, the customers' needs. Managers are concerned more with their popularity than with their effectiveness.

News Management: This is management communication by news broadcast. Nothing is too trivial, irrelevant or obscure to be made newsworthy. There is an obsessive concern with blowing up all issues to make them important.

Obstruction Management: These managers rejoice in preventing others from doing anything. They always mention safety or discrimination, or other powerful words that allow them to obstruct any good idea or policy that may benefit the company as a whole.

Placebo Management: This is management via the 'boardroom lunch'; the 'staff committee' where people are made to feel better although nothing actually happens. These activities make both sides feel better because they believe that real communication occurs, although neither side talks honestly and nothing ever results.

Prosthetic Management: This is the replacement of intelligence by prosthetic electronic gadgets. Thus certain computers can help people who cannot spell or draw:

> All that now remains is for science to devise a prosthetic replacement for the ability to read, a machine that is able to scan and speak a printer text, eliminating at a stroke the unfair advantages currently suffered by those who cannot read. (McKibbin, 1998: 58)

Puppet Management: This is management through others, not unlike ventriloquists' dummies. They write speeches, feed ideas and ultimately pull the strings of others. This may suit both parties – puppet and puppeteer – until the former is required to mouth something that is deeply controversial.

Signal Management: Signal managers are more concerned with appearances than reality and are most concerned with sending the wrong kind of signal. They are concerned more with form than content; with the interpretation rather than the consequence of the signal.

Territorial Management: These managers are like fierce animals that adopt strange, aggressive tactics to warn and ward off trespassers: 'Within an organisation, savage inter-necine battles for territory are waged with memoranda, reports, position papers and incessant lobbying activities' (McKibbin, 1998: 25). The idea is to expand your department, take over another's territory.

Virtual Management: This is management by elaborate charade that is little concerned with better products or services. It is a collusion between manager and employee where meetings are held, jobs defined and evaluations performed, but little or nothing is done.

Zoological Management: This takes various forms:

- *Hamster Management*: Industrious, obstinate, energetic but unable to learn from experience.
- *Seagull Management*: Flying in from head office just long enough to crap over hard-working provincials and fly back to the nest.

- *Locust Management*: A technique to strip every asset of a company, leaving it picked clean of every morsel.
- *Peacock Management*: A proud strutting manager that appears sleek and complacent but suddenly flies off to loftier perches.
- *Rabbit Management*: The idea is to reproduce as much as possible: to copy parent company style all round the world; acquire subsidies and replicate oneself enthusiastically. All of us recognize the incompetent manager in these different styles. Some organizations favour one over another.

The joke, of course, is that each in their different ways is essentially incompetent. The tragedy is that not only are these incompetent manager styles common but that they are tacitly approved of and perpetuated in various organisations.

2.5. Under-employment: A Cause of Incompetence

All employees have a vested interest in pointing out how overworked and overstressed they are, and many managers believe that they have unique, chronic and acute work stress. They hope that if this is acknowledged, they will get more money, more staff (possibly both) and less work ... and perhaps sympathy from spouse, peers, colleagues and friends. However, this self-defined problem conflicts with another rarely discussed source of stress at work: boredom and the tedium of unemployment. Some jobs are just plain boring. Some organizations are simply over-staffed ... maintaining employment programmes for the indolent.

The under-employed are found in all business sectors and may not even realize their status. They can be a serious problem for people working at full capacity. Under-employed bosses in particular can threaten the profitability of their organizations. They call pointless meetings, send long and tedious emails, trap hapless colleagues by the photocopier, invent peculiar rules, and generally harass the hard-working people in the organization. They love faddish ideas and, as a result, attend lots of training courses. In fact, they are often out of the office because it makes little difference to their work output.

The worst possible combination is the relatively dim, compulsive attention-seeker in the role of an under-employed manager. While doing little themselves, they can seriously distract an office full of hard-working individuals. After having fought so long for promotion to a managerial job, the new incumbent may be surprised to discover that there is not much to do. However, a manager must seem industrious, hence the scenario of the bored bureaucrat bewildering the busy.

Like adolescent ennui, boredom through under-employment arises from a number of sources. Some jobs are inherently tedious. Consider two examples: attendants at museums and security guards. The first have to keep an eye on the public, try to spot lunatics before they slash works of art, and ensure that school children don't make off with a collection of Roman coins. The second group have to watch out for intruders, to try to stay awake while sitting slumped behind a desk in a warm room, and ensure that people don't break into the building and steal the computers while they (the guards) are asleep. The coping strategy in both cases seems to be self-hypnosis, producing a state of glassy-eyed semi-wakefulness. But imagine what their bosses do!

Another source of boredom is repetition. This comes from having to perform the same simple task over and over again. A favoured technique for relieving boredom is to break or sabotage the machine that one must operate. Modern Luddism has as much to do with easing the monotony of the job as the original form did with saving them.

Other jobs are dull because they are essentially all about monitoring. Pilots are required to monitor computers; so are security camera or X-ray staff, but because they have to be alert, their jobs are regularly rotated. Some people monitor machines, others monitor people. The favourite trick of the bored people monitor is to frustrate the public. Stopping someone driving a large, expensive car is even more amusing, because a little ritual humiliation makes the minutes fly by. Security people are masters in the art of spotting important people in a hurry and then demanding to be shown their personal identification. It is the revenge of the under-employed on the over-employed.

There is yet another psychological cause of boredom. It involves the use of 'attention-seeking' strategies by those who feel they have been overlooked, marginalized or sidelined. Security and safety guards may feel undervalued, but they know that, by randomly locking doors, changing entry codes and inspecting private spaces in the name of safety, they can underline their importance in the organization.

But what about the under-employed people manager? Yes, they do still exist. But how do they cope? Meetings are the favourite forum of the bored and under-employed manager. Shadowing studies of real managers show that many spend as much as two-thirds of their time in meetings. Some of these gatherings are genuinely used to canvass and share opinions, others to make decisions. But all too often, they call meetings in order to diffuse responsibility by making collective decisions on risky topics.

Re-engaging the under-employed is not easy. The number of meetings called or attended should be limited to three a week and the managers should be required to document the outcomes. The under-employed need their goals and targets to be re-evaluated and 'ratcheted up' in the performance appraisal system. Feedback from the work-stressed colleagues, subordinates or clients may help to provide evidence to the under-employed of how people actually see them and have developed resistance/survival skills.

Beware the under-employed. They are frequently well dug in and difficult to move. They squeal loudly when challenged and usually have a history of resistance to change. Paradoxically, they are often the ones who have survived previous restructuring efforts aimed at removing them.

Below is a guide for recognizing the telltale signs of the under-employed manager:

1. Meeting addicts: they attend, call and participate in two to three times as many meetings as properly employed peers.
2. Too eager to manage by walking about. This is really an excuse to stroll around and interrupt others in the so-called guise of a particular management style.
3. Involved with union or related affairs (welfare, health and so on). The fact that they don't work any harder than others, but can do all that other stuff is the key to their under-employment.
4. Excessive communicating by the chosen medium – emails, circulars, faxes and so on. Remember, they are bored and lonely and want others to talk to them.
5. Training enthusiasts: eager to go on a range of courses that get them out of the office. Frequently absent, but not through illness.
6. Slow to respond: paradoxically, they are slow to respond to requests (for example, providing data) and always complain about the effort involved. Remember that they have to keep up the appearance of being overworked.
7. Interested in development and planning – possibly interested in the past (archive obsessed), but more likely to love strategic planning and so on. Always better to plan than to do.

Five out of seven is a good indicator of serious under-employment.

2.6. Excusing Incompetence

Incompetent, ineffective and inadequate managers need no longer feel guilt or shame about their poor performance. Over the past 20 years management gurus have discovered a variety of mysterious syndromes designed to excuse rather than explain incompetence. Whether these themes are called diseases, disorders or syndromes, the idea is the same.

McKibbin (1998) has provided an insightful catalogue of these behaviours:

Feline Obesity Syndrome – or fat cat management where senior managers award themselves salaries, bonuses and special awards such that they may earn per week what the average work employee earns per year.
Motivation Deficiency Syndrome – the only cure for which is setting (modest) targets and rewarding the achievement of these out of proportion to their difficulty of being met.
Atlas Syndrome – where the chiefs begin to outnumber the Indians. Job title and rank inflation occurs and the top-heavy apparatus threatens to destroy the whole organization.

Counselling Dependence Syndrome – this is an unusual co-dependency syndrome where half the managers are addicted to giving counselling and the other half to receiving it. The net result is that neither side gets any work done.

Competitive Dedication Syndrome – the ostentatious display of dedication to work. This involves arriving very early, staying very late, working (and infecting others) when ill and refusing to take holidays.

Rogue Reflex Disorder – a set of dramatic, pointless but politically correct and media-grabbing reactions to a serious problem. The essential idea is that the reactions to the problem are bizarre, irrelevant reflex actions that do no good.

Corporate Disintegration Syndrome – the loss of skilled and experienced people after the introduction of well-intentioned but backfiring human resources schemes dreamed up by incompetent managers. It then may happen that a promotion from a written principle leads to a desperate management casting about for anyone with competence among a dwindling supply.

Pangloss Disease – named after one of Voltaire's characters, this is pathological complacency. It is the inability or unwillingness to recognize how bad things really are.

Delegate's Disease – this is a form of narcolepsy where sufferers find concentration more and more difficult.

Compulsive Prognosis Disorder – a drive to issue and revise forecasts. More effort and time are devoted to plans than to current achievements.

Obsessional Status Neurosis – job title inflation or the desire to give oneself and staff ever grander and misleading titles possibly in lieu of financial reward.

Reduced Consciousness Syndrome – this is an obsession with 'awareness campaigns' and 'is as much a disease of management as it is of society as a whole, calling for energetic prophylactic measures designed to raise management consciousness of risks and opportunities to at least the level found in hibernating bats' (McKibbin, 1998: 80).

Canute's Disease – the inability to accept reality. What looks like resolution and courage is in fact blind obduracy and obtuseness.

Compulsive Calling Disorders – an overwhelming and continuous urge to offer counsel and advice, by someone who is usually unqualified to speak. The advice is meddlesome and safely ignored.

Multiple Accreditation Disorder – this can be observed at the individual or organizational level and involves the accumulation (often in exchange for cash) of documents, fellowships, certificates of probity, competence, quality or training.

False Achievement Syndrome – the morbid attachment to symbols of achievement (and new computer system) rather than considering the attainment of the objective.

These syndromes are a joke at the expense of those psychologists who are eager to find a new problem to solve. These are often more like sin-drones than syndromes. Note that a syndrome is a set of concurrent behaviours or emotions that seem to form a pattern. Science usually begins with description, then taxonomization and then explanation. Describing a syndrome is little more than setting out a hypothesis about cause. Certainly it does seem that the search for syndromes is motivated by a desire to explain away a problem ... or at least to ensure that people do not have to take personal responsibility for their actions.

2.7. Conclusion

This chapter has explored some different ways in which popular management writers have described incompetence. Some focus on the common mistakes made by managers, others on why organizations seem to promote managers to positions in which they inevitably fail. The difficult people and the management-style approach lead to long lists of types and styles that amuse more than explain. To the trained psychologist they are clumsy: categories overlap too much and there is often too much emphasis on how to change or challenge the type rather than understanding how and why they originate in the first place.

Sometimes incompetence is easily explained. It may be that managers have too little to do. But to invent various syndromes does little to promote a real understanding of the causes of management incompetence. For that we need an understanding of personality and individual differences, which will be done in the second part of the book.

CHAPTER THREE

Paradoxical Incompetence and Management Madness

3.1. Introduction

Incompetent managers often have strong ideas about how to treat people but have no evidence to support them. Worse, they never look for evidence to evaluate their ideas. For example, they are often ritualistic. They learn and then perpetuate pointless ceremonies from other incompetent managers. These may be idiosyncratic meetings (Monday morning briefings), particular techniques (focus-group research) or other security-providing patterns. They often demand blind obedience and scrupulous observance of their rituals because the rituals give them a sense of familiarity. Indeed, the more turmoil and change they set in motion, the more they, and others, will need these pointless rituals. They create a craving for laws, rules and codes, all of which make their behaviour predictable if not productive.

Along with rituals go fetishes and pedantry. Things have to be done a particular way. Extra energy is invested in making sure that others follow the prescribed and proscribed behaviour. These fetishes come from many sources. Some business schools religiously advocate technical and numerical competence. Getting the bottom line right becomes more important than managing human capital. Again, incompetent managers never dream of modelling what they preach. They are secretive but talk about openness; they are individualistic while preaching teamwork; they are eager to empower but careful not to lose any power of their own.

Many are almost heroically ignorant because they avoid accurate feedback on their performance. This ignorance is often combined with arrogance, and is seen most frequently in self-confidence in the face of objective data. Some believe that they are visionary prophets of the future. Resisting the incompetent manager's ideas is seen as misguided and possibly insubordinate.

As we shall see, incompetent managers believe that there are standard solutions to problems. One is to merge one's way out of trouble, another is the precise opposite – to divest oneself of one's problems. But the most common fallacy held by incompetent managers is about other people's motives, particularly those of their staff. This is the source of the famous myth that people at the top respond best to reward (incentive, bonuses, share options) whereas people at the bottom respond best to threats (lay-offs, cuts). These clueless managers think that performance management systems alone will ensure that they get the best out of their people. This is the old techno-myth that 'systems' are more important than 'people processes'; the reality is that standardized and rigorously enforced 'systems' will reduce all innovation. Quality assurance assures neither quality nor quantity but rather roboticism.

But myths fulfil functions. They make the incompetent feel better about themselves. They function to devalue or help ignore disconcerting evidence. They serve to reduce guilt about their incompetence and the appalling way in which they treat others.

Myths help find acceptable alternatives to necessary work. Training courses, workshops and communication meetings all help the incompetent manager feel gainfully employed while doing nothing.

Incompetent managers learn a sort of double-speak. Thus, seriously inconveniencing and enraging motorists is called 'introducing traffic calming systems'. There is rhetorical, euphemistic and bold-faced double-speak, but it all amounts to the same thing. Sometimes these double-speak terms are attached to the beloved but ever-changing management mantras about 'customer focus', 'premier division' and 'cutting-edge technology'.

Furnham (2000a) has observed paradoxical incompetence. He notes:

> The paradox is that competence is held up as a model of excellence. Incompetence, not its opposite, leads to success in certain organizations. Stifling, inefficient, constipated bureaucracy is still modelled in certain companies and sectors. The bureaucratically competent (and, by definition, incompetent) manager can rise up the greasy pole precisely because their management style is approved of and culturally sanctioned.

So, what are the signs of paradoxical incompetence? How does one achieve this status? Consider the following dozen traits of this dubious style of management.

1. *Diffuse responsibility*: It is essential to ensure that should anything go wrong you personally cannot be held responsible. So, form a committee of those with little else to do – namely, aspirant incompetent managers. Send e-mails and memos requiring that ideas and proposals are received and therefore accepted. It is better to prepare for cock-ups than to ensure you can take unique credit for success.

2. *Delegate but don't empower*: Duties and responsibilities, particularly for dreary or risky activities, should be seen to fall clearly on others – other

departments, rival agencies, outside suppliers, even ambitious colleagues, and particularly one's own staff. The secret is to give them responsibility but without the actual power to do a good job.

3. *Expand your empire*: Grow your own department. There are many good reasons for this wasteful, self-aggrandizing strategy. First, the more people you have in your department (under you), the more elevated your title has to be according to the span-of-control principle. Second, in lean times, you can easily afford to cut a few out, so getting selfless hero-points but without any significant loss. Big is beautiful, powerful, successful.

4. *Never underspend your budget*, but pretend to be lean and mean. The essential principle here is to be modestly profligate while seeming to be the precise opposite. Remember that sending yourself on interesting conferences abroad is in the training budget, and buying an expensive computer for the home comes under innovative IT solutions. Spend highly but secretively while talking a good deal about under-funded, shoestring activities.

5. *Shun measurement around targets*: Never, ever set clear measurable targets or risk being objectively caught out by agreeing to have any 'objective' criteria of success measure. The favourite criteria are time, money and customer response, and they could include many things such as measures of quantity and quality. Remember that useful phrase: 'What can be measured isn't important ... what is important can't be measured.' But do not hesitate to impose measurement on others. Remember that what you do is utterly unique and beyond simple and misleading measurement systems.

6. *Make a virtue out of stability*: Praise continuity and tradition; avoid change and innovation. Remember the concept of precedent, the phrase 'an interesting but alas premature idea' and 'we tried that before and it failed miserably'. Devise and practise ways to humiliate young, bright innovators. Change is anxiety provoking and threatens the status quo – reason enough to oppose it.

7. *Pace yourself*: Eschew freneticism and any sense of urgency. As all good actors know, timing is everything. Although it is crucial to look busy, even stressed, don't accept deadlines, although you may quite happily impose them on others. Never concede to the obsessive desire to do things in shorter and shorter time, and of necessity have a string of stories about how impulsivity is a recipe for disaster. The hare and the tortoise, after all, is an excellent fable to recount on occasions when you are asked to 'speak up'.

8. *Never, ever, take risks*: Bureaucracy is not about celebrating success but about avoiding failure. The steady-as-you-go philosophy means never being first with an idea. Let someone else be the guinea pig. The risk-taking type might have occasional starbursts of success but may fizzle out, whereas the cautious, one-foot-at-a-time type rises slowly and inexorably up the organization. Learn a vocabulary of derogatory terms for the risk-

seeker, such as puerile sensation-seekers, dangerously deluded. Be cautious and guarded in all things.

9. *Put everything on paper, carefully and legalistically*: Cover your arse with good records. Remember to phrase delicate or difficult points very sensitively so that at a later time uncomfortable truths are not revealed. Records are power. If you keep better track of things than your peers, you win arguments and vindicate actions. This does not mean establishing smart IT tracking systems – God forbid – but rather taking minutes of all meetings, documenting sign-offs, and so on. Never agree anything without it being put on paper. And have a legal mind and turn of phrase on everything. Beware multiple meanings and serious commitments recorded on paper.

10. *Establish protocol, procedures, rules and systems*: Of course, this is at the heart of all bureaucracy, but don't use words such as rules and procedures as they merely come back and bite you. You must, however, ensure that everybody follows your systems and guidelines, which are designed for quite specific purposes, such as to put off enquirers, scare off critics and baffle outsiders. It is true that people like an orderly, stable and predictable world, and that is what systems are there for. For every new technology and activity, we need a system and a protocol to ensure that it is used uniformly and correctly throughout the organization.

11. *Communicate nothing of real importance.* Knowledge is power; secrets are a resource. Never explain, never apologize, but communicate constantly. There is an art to constantly saying little of importance and letting out important facts in ways that render them unrecognizable. Open communication is the deadly enemy of all Sir Humphreys (the arch-manipulator in *Yes, Minister*) because it opens the path to powerlessness and exposure. Remember all sorts of talk about official secrets, the importance of confidentiality and the power of secret societies. Talking of which, consider joining the most famous for extra influence in certain circles.

12. *Consult through and with committees*: Committees are wonderful devices to find out things. They may even be used as private focus groups. They can diffuse responsibility (see point 1) and create the illusion of industry (see point 7). They are deeply conservative and nearly always inefficient. The are ideal for social loafing while appearing moderately democratic. (Furnham, 2000a: xix–xvi)

The paradox is that these behaviours are modelled and rewarded in many organizations. Young managers see how their bosses become successful through using these techniques and then perpetuate them when they are in senior positions. This leads in turn to incompetent corporate culture – or the prototypical bureaucracy of old.

3.2. Managerial Madness

Turn a Freudian analyst loose in a business school and he or she will soon discover a great deal of evidence for management madness – not stupidity but pathology. Over the past 20 years Kets de Vries, a Canadian trained Dutch psychiatrist who teaches at a French business school, has traced business failure to managerial madness – or the *intrapsychic functioning of key organizational members*, as he more correctly puts it.

He argues that neurotic senior managers influence the organizational style in their image. Strategy, process, structure, selection, even advertising reflect their personal pathology. Powerful but disturbed leaders create businesses in their image in order to deal, often unsuccessfully, with their personal pathologies. Thus the whole organization takes on the pathology of the single manager. We shall revisit these concepts in Chapter 6. What Kets de Vries does is take selective categories of personality disorder and show how powerful leaders with these psychiatric disorders actually form companies in their own image sharing similar pathologies. Kets de Vries identifies five neurotic styles, although, to be accurate, some are actually psychotic (Kets de Vries and Miller, 1985).

1. The *Paranoid Organization*: When power is highly centralized in a leader with paranoid tendencies ('everybody is out to get me'), there will tend to be a great deal of vigilance caused by distrust of subordinates and competitors alike. This may lead to the development of many control and information systems and a conspiratorial fascination with gathering intelligence from inside and outside the firm. Paranoid thinking will also lead to a centralization of power as the top executive tries to control everything himself (no one can be completely trusted). The strategy is likely to emphasize 'protection' and reducing dependency on particular consultants, sources of data, markets or customers. There is likely to be a good deal of diversification, with tight control over divisions and much analytical activity. A leader who is obsessed with fantasies concerning distrust can set a very distinctive tone for the strategy, structure and culture of an organization.

   The characteristics of these organizations are easy to describe. Suspiciousness and mistrust of others; hypersensitivity and hyper-alertness; readiness to combat perceived threats; excessive concern with hidden motives and special meanings; intense attention span; cold, rational, unemotional, interpersonal relations. The paranoid organization is defensive and hypervigilant. It is pervaded by an atmosphere of distrust. But this can have benefits – certainly such organizations will be alert to threats and opportunities inside and outside the organization. A small advantage perhaps, and at a great cost.

2. An obsessive–compulsive manager leads to the development of a *compulsive organization*. A compulsive organization emphasizes ritual; it plans every detail in advance and carries out its activities in a routine, pre-programmed style. Thoroughness and conformity are valued. Such organizations are hierarchical and generally have elaborate policies, rules and procedures. The strategies of compulsive firms reflect their preoccupation with detail and established rituals. Each compulsive organization has a distinctive area of competence and specializes in this area, whether or not the area is related to the marketplace.

   For Kets de Vries and Miller (1985) these organizations are characterized by: perfectionism; preoccupation with trivial details; insistence that others submit to an established way of doing things; relationships defined in terms of dominance and submission; lack of spontaneity; inability to relax; meticulousness, dogmatism and obstinacy. This is the military organization Dixon (1981) talks about so eloquently.

   Compulsive managers are inward looking, indecisive, cautious and fearful about making mistakes. They are deeply involved in the minutiae of facts and figures and love promulgating rules and regulations to make their lives easier. They are often inflexible, oriented to the past and unwilling to change. They typically have excellent internal control and audit mechanisms and well-integrated procedures. But all too often they are anachronistic bureaucracies that seem out of touch with the flexible and adaptive companies of today. The faster the world changes, the more incompetent they are – change is an enemy not an opportunity.

3. The impulsive, creative, intuitive manager will also stamp his or her organization in characteristic ways. The *dramatic organization* is hyperactive, impulsive and uninhibited. In such an organization, decision-makers prefer to act on hunches and impressions, and take on widely diverse projects. Top managers reserve the right to start bold ventures independently; subordinates have limited power.

   Such organizations are characterized by: self-dramatization and excessive emotional displays; incessant self-displays organized around crises; a need for activity and excitement; an alternation between idealization and devaluation of others; exploitativeness; inability to concentrate or sharply focus attention. This is not only the world of 'Ad-land' but increasingly that of e-commerce.

   Dramatic managers are not risk averse. They often make rash, intuitive decisions, swinging company policy in radically different directions. They are impulsive and unpredictable. At their best they can revitalize tired companies and provide the necessary momentum at crucial periods in a company's history (merger and acquisition or start-up). But most of the time they simply create instability, chaos and distress. A major task of any manager is to bring order and predictability to business issues, not the opposite.

4. Many people are prone to depression or may experience periods of depression caused by stress or trauma. But some managers seem always to have depressive symptoms, and this can lead to *depressive organizations*. The depressive organization lacks confidence, is inactive, conservative and insular, and has an entrenched bureaucracy. The only things that get done are routine activities. Depressive organizations are well established and often serve a single mature market.

   The characteristics of a depressive manager and the organization he or she creates in his or her own image are feelings of guilt, worthlessness, self-reproach, inadequacy and a sense of helplessness and hopefulness – of being at the mercy of events; there is also a diminished ability to think clearly, a loss of interest and motivation, and an inability to experience pleasure. Depressives are negative, pessimistic and inhibited. Apathetic, inactive, hopeless managers are prevalent in these organizations. The gloom pervades all.

5. The fifth type of neurotic organization according to Kets de Vries and Miller (1985) is called schizoid. The *schizoid organization* lacks leadership. Its top executive discourages interaction. Sometimes the second level of executives makes up for the leader's lack of involvement, but often they simply fight to fill the leadership vacuum. In such organizations strategy often reflects individual goals and internal politics rather than the external threats or opportunities the organization needs to take into account.

   These organizations are characterized by: detachment, non-involvement and withdrawal; a sense of estrangement; a lack of excitement or enthusiasm; an indifference to praise or criticism; a lack of interest in present or future; and a cold and unemotional climate. These organizations are quite political and the resulting climate of distrust inhibits normal collaboration.

Kets de Vries suggests that the unconscious and neurotic needs of the key people in an organization lead them to do things to the organization that create incompetence. Observations suggest that neurotic managers choose, create and maintain dysfunctional work groups that have shared organizational myths, and that these myths often distract them from primary tasks. Their neuroticism means that they transfer their anxieties and odd imaginings on to their staff (superiors, subordinates, peers, and even shareholders and customers) and this frustrates and angers staff who may be somehow bound to or curiously abandoned by their neurotic managers.

Psychologists believe that much managerial neuroticism is a legacy of frustrating interpersonal experiences at earlier life stages. Pathological symptoms are seen as the result of the defensive reactions needed to preserve a sense self. The rigidity, apathy and defensiveness of some managers are, it is argued, defensive strategies devised to circumvent unknown or threatening situations. The defences are often unsuccessful, however, and they lead the entire organization to develop a neurotic culture or style of interaction. It is the personality of the manager rather than his or her ability or training that leads to these problems.

Adaptation to the world of work can cause some people to develop a sense of inadequacy; this is associated with frustration, disappointment and apathy. Frustrated aggression in the workplace can be turned either inwards or outwards. Turning aggression inwards leads to doubt, anxiety and guilt; turning it outwards leads to hostility and bad manners. Organizations must learn to expect and then to channel aggression because survival and adaptation are determined, in part, by the balance between inward-directed and outward-directed aggression.

The desire to be exceptional and the virtual impossibility of achieving perfection often lead to anxiety, feverish activity and hyper-vigilance. Persons in this state may never finish tasks, may be overly forgetful, or unwilling to follow up promises precisely because they fear negative feedback. It can also lead to 'workaholism' where work provides a structure that seemingly prevents emotional breakdown and self-fragmentation.

A neurotic manager may be exceptionally competitive, harbouring hidden fears of retaliation dating back to early childhood. On the other hand, the unstable manager may become dependent, identifying with, and internalizing the values of, power over others. The dependent manager may take refuge in idleness, ignorance, helplessness or irresponsible acts.

In a more recent paper Kets de Vries (1999) looked at two 'puzzling personalities' – the hypomanic and the alexithymic manager. This paper is another attempt to adopt insights and terminology from psychiatry to explain managerial incompetence. Kets de Vries chose these because they were at two ends of the 'emotional rainbow'. In view of the recent enthusiasm for emotional intelligence, this seems to be an important issue. The idea is simple: managers with either of these tendencies become, or are, incompetent and then cause mayhem, chaos and misery for all they deal with. Again, this theme is revisited in Part II, Chapter 6.

The hypomanic manager

These people are 'mildly manic' in the sense that they are not certifiable:

> Their behaviour with its recurring up- and downswing has a larger-than-life quality. On the upswings, hypomanics exhibit abundant energy, unbridled enthusiasm, thirsty gregariousness, intense feeling, a sense of destiny, a strong belief in themselves and their ideas (bordering on the grandiose), persuasiveness in convincing others of their point of view, a willingness to go

where others dare not go, optimism, heightened alertness and observational ability, courage, a willingness to take risks (bordering on the imprudent), unpredictable and subtle changes in mood, impatience, and shortened attention span. During their highs, hypomanics have a feeling of unlimited physical and mental energy, the expansiveness in mood state symptomised by grandiose thoughts and feelings. With their sense of exaltation and rapture, they may experience a heightened sense of reality. Hypomanics on the upswing enjoy feelings of ease, strength, buoyancy, financial omnipotence, and euphoria. (Kets de Vries, 1999: 10)

As managers they are enthusiastic and visionary with unlimited ideas about business possibilities, but they can easily become irritable, intolerant and unhappy with the work of others. They are sensitive and react badly to criticism.

Kets de Vries specifies 12 warning signs:

1. Does the person have grandiose ideas, make unrealistic plans, and exercise poor judgement?
2. Is the person over-talkative and given to aggressively seeking out others (to the point that those others feel intruded upon)?
3. Does the person verbalise feelings of excessive well-being?
4. Does the person seem to have an inflated sense of self-esteem?
5. Is the person unusually distractible, and jump from one subject to the next while exuding a physical restlessness?
6. Is the person easily irritated, becoming combative and argumentative when things do not go his or her way?
7. Is the person overactive, trying to do too many things at once?
8. Does the person appear to have unlimited energy and a diminished need for sleep?
9. Is the person sexually preoccupied and inclined to engage in sexual indiscretions?
10. Is the person engaged in irrational financial activities, including massive overspending and unwise investments?
11. On 'down' days, does the person obsess over past actions, berating him- or herself unduly?
12. Does the person have a problem with drugs or alcohol? (Kets de Vries, 1999: 12)

Kets de Vries offers various strategies for coping with these individuals. First, people need to build coalitions throughout the whole organization to keep the hypomanic out of harm's way. Next people can help the manager by creating a genuinely supportive environment. Third, one can help these managers by preventing them from making impulsive decisions. One can even get professional help from human resources directors. Members of the manager's family can help monitor and stabilize the manic and educate him or her about the disorder. They can, of course, also help the hypomanic get professional help. Indeed, with modern medication they can easily and quickly be stabilized.

Curiously some organizations seem to attract these people, and even reward them for their pathology. At best they forgive them rather than help them and all the others caught in the rollercoaster of emotion.

The alexithymic manager

These managers are emotionally detached and live in a world of formalities and ritual rather than emotional highs or lows. Kets de Vries calls them dead fish:

> In such people, the normal experience and expression of emotions has been subdued, removed from conscious awareness. These people are, in effect, emotional illiterates. Incapable of reflective self-awareness, they express little interest in their inner subjective lives. Their tendency to externalise, that is, to steer clear of emotion, is reflected in a cognitive style focused on external processes and activities. They seem to live in a world of concrete operations.
>
> Alexithymics are unable to symbolise their emotions as fantasies, dreams, images, or desires. They have marked difficulty verbally expressing or describing their feelings. They go to considerable effort, however, to mask this deficit, behaving like colour-blind people who have learned to infer, from indirect indicators, what they cannot see. Unfortunately, although alexithymics may use the right words to describe certain feelings, that is where the process stops; they cannot develop their personal reactions to emotionally charged issues any further. Their observations remain at a rather vague and general level. True alexithymics feel neither passion nor enthusiasm; they have no fire in their belly. (Kets de Vries, 1999: 14)

The alexithymic manager has low emotional intelligence and seems unmoved by the joys and crises of everyday business life. Some believe the problem originates in genetics, others see the problem as a response to childhood trauma. Certainly they are not fun to be around. They are mechanical rather than spontaneous, disinterested rather than empathic, and preoccupied with operational details rather than the big picture.

Kets de Vries (1999: 17) offers 12 warning signs:

1. Does the person have difficulty communicating with other people?
2. Does the person describe details ad nauseam but never mention feelings?
3. Does the person use actions to express emotion?
4. Does the person appear confused about the emotions he or she feels?
5. Does the person describe the circumstances rather than the feelings surrounding an event?
6. Is the person preoccupied with physical problems?
7. Does the person suffer from an absence of fantasy and imagination?
8. Do dreams and daydreams play little role in the person's life?

9. Does the person prefer movies with action to psychological dramas?
10. Is the person's thought content associated more with external events than with fantasy or emotion?
11. Does the person find life pretty boring most of the time, rarely exhibiting excitement?
12. When talking with such a person, do you yourself get bored and frustrated, eager to get away from him or her?

These managers lower morale, stifle creativity and exhaust those around them. They can be sent to places in the organization where their detail-oriented, mechanical approach is useful (for example, data processing). They need to understand that their emotional coldness is not desirable. They may even be encouraged to obtain professional help.

Kets de Vries argues that emotions are the lifeblood of the organization. Certainly the current enthusiasm for the topic of emotional intelligence supports this view. Those with too little or too much can seem superficially attractive but can create significant problems. What de Vries doesn't say is that organizations in some sense need both manics and alexithymics – advertising, PR and media relations need the former; data analysis and safety checking need the latter.

Studies of managerial psychopathology are important because they focus on the personality, needs and thought patterns of individual managers as the causes of incompetence. People in business, like the public in general, tend not to be very psychologically minded. Hence they do not always have the vocabulary or insight necessary to see that they are dealing with people who need help and who may need to be 'relieved of their responsibilities' before they do further damage to the organization. This issue will be considered in detail in the longest (and perhaps most important) chapter, Chapter 6.

3.3. Neuroticism, Balance and Incompetence

Is the incompetent manager bad, mad, sad – or some combination of the three? To imply that incompetent managers are bad is to imply that their incompetence is a moral issue, that they change, transgress or ignore ethical, legal and moral codes, or simply march to the beat of a different drum. This, no doubt, does occasionally happen.

To imply that incompetence is related to mental illness is not new but is probably half true. Most employees have seen and wondered about the apparently neurotic behaviour of their bosses. A central question refers to the direction of causality – do incompetent managers go mad or do 'mad' people become incompetent managers? This theme will be revisited in the second part of this book.

Paradoxically, psychology has always been more interested in the negative side of human behaviour than the positive side. There are probably one hundred books on depression for every one on happiness. The case is precisely the opposite in the management literature, which has attempted to accentuate the positive.

Somewhat belatedly, however, the 'dark side' of organizational behaviour has been explored (Mick, 1996). For example, as we have seen, Kets de Vries (1994) argues that the crucial management roles of charismatic, visionary and instrumental supporters depend on the single factor of personality called neuroticism and emotional stability. Kets de Vries is a psychoanalyst and he believes that:

> Clinical observation confirms that even the most successful organizational leaders are not exactly rational, logical, sensible and dependable human beings, but in fact are prone to irrational behaviour ... organizations cannot perform successfully if the quirks and irrational processes that are part and parcel of the leader's inner theatre are ignored. (Kets de Vries, 1994: 79)

Kets de Vries (1994) argues that there are powerful pressures on managers. Senior managers experience the *loneliness of command*. They have to maintain some distance and relinquish important social support networks. They become the *targets of envy* because of the extrinsic rewards of the job. They experience new *fears* like losing office or power. They may become *afraid of success*, believing themselves undeserving, and fulfil their fears through self-destructive behaviour. Some become paralysed (and depressed) by the demands of *decision-making* or deciding where to go after their success.

Managers are corporate figureheads but, as psychologists are happy to point out, we respond to them not only in terms of what they do or say but also in terms of significant authority figures from our past, particularly our parents. Many people *transfer* to their management superiors the emotions, needs and experiences that they developed in response to other powerful, significant figures in their past. This explains why many employees feel a strong need to do anything to please their incompetent manager (parent) who will treat them well until something goes wrong, and then they have a temper tantrum.

The key to understanding the neurotic manager, according to Kets de Vries (1994), is narcissism, where the problem lies in having either too much or too little self-esteem. He distinguishes between *constructive narcissists* who, despite the term, are well balanced and have sufficient positive regard and self-esteem, and *reaction narcissists* who continually try to protect their defective sense of self-esteem and are preoccupied by feelings of envy, spite, revenge or vindictive triumph. It is the reactive narcissists that are most dangerously incompetent for the following reasons: they seem to have a grandiose sense of self-importance. They habitually take advantage of others in order to achieve their own ends. They live under the illusion that their problems are unique. They have a sense of entitlement, deserve especially favourable treatment and rules-for-all do not apply to them. They seem addicted to compliments and never seem to get enough. They lack empathy and are unable to take the role of the other. Their envy of others and rage when prevented from getting their way can be formidable.

Kets de Vries (1994) posits various 'neurotic styles' labelled paranoid, schizoid, passive–aggressive, histrionic and compulsive. He believes that the characterological problems of powerful senior executives can lead to neurotic organizations:

> the 'irrational' personality characteristics of principal decisions makers can seriously affect the overall management process. At the head of a neurotic organisation (especially one in which power is highly centralised) one is likely to find a top executive whose rigid neurotic style is strongly mirrored in the nature of inappropriate strategies, structures and organisational cultures of his or her firm. If this situation continues for too long, the organisation may self-destruct. (Kets de Vries, 1994: 86)

For psychoanalysts, managerial incompetence is based in unconscious, irrational processes that originate in the past. But others have argued that it is possible to conceive of the organizations themselves, especially those in decline, as being neurotic. Merry and Brown (1987) claim that there are seven telltale signs of neurotic organizations:

1. *A failure of self-image*: Where employees see their own organization as 'sick' or a 'mess', unable to cope with problems or even be responsible for itself. They also have 'failure scripts' which are self-fulfilling and ensure that every attempted project will result in failure, decline and disintegration.
2. *A low energy climate*: Lethargy, low levels of energy, hopelessness and low morale, and often talk about discontent, frustration, unhappiness and dissatisfaction.
3. *Breakdown of communication*: Considerable interpersonal and intergroup mistrust, hostility and suspicion characterized by critical, hurtful and sarcastic daily information. Communication is guarded, filtered, coded and edited.
4. *Disagreement on goals and values*: Expression of different priorities and the inability of leaders to define goals and values, and commit to them. More important normative behaviour – acceptance of ways of doing things (rites, traditions) – are undermined by giving contradictory signals.
5. *Organizational dysfunction*: Characterized by slowdown and shrinking outputs; by an inability (and unwillingness) to deal with everyday problems; by an inability (and reluctance) to plan ahead; and by an obvious neglect of physical facilities.

6. *Deteriorating conditions*: Seen as a breakdown of leadership (because capable people have long left) and recurring intensifying periods of crisis.
7. *A difficulty in changing these patterns*: In a sense this is the neurotic paradox because, although neurotics are fully aware of their condition, they seem powerless to do anything about it.

It is the self-defeating nature of the neurotic lifestyle, caused by a poor representation of reality, that is at the heart of the problem. Merry and Brown (1987) offer the following definition:

> Neurotic organisational behaviour will be defined as (1) repetitive patterns of (2) pathologic (3) seemingly unchangeable (4) organisational behaviour, (5) involving a distortion of reality. In this definition 'Organisational' refers either to the organisation as a whole or to one of its parts, such as a management team or a department. (Merry and Brown, 1987: 20)

The concept of balance is also related to the concept of stability, where unstable means neurotic. However, the word balance nearly always refers to the conscious or deliberate apportioning of time and energy between such things as family life versus work and leisure time versus work.

Kofodimos (1990) argues that many managers respond to implicit and explicit organizational norms that demand long hours, repeated relocation, frequent travel, weekend/holiday homework and business entertainment. Such dedication to work, which by definition yields occupational rewards, comes at the expense of family and personal life. Work becomes a substitute for an impoverished or unhappy personal life and the workplace may then be used to meet relationship (affairs) and leisure (sport conferences) needs.

Dedication to work can be satisfying because working develops and exercises abilities that then define one's identity and enhance self-esteem. Kofodimos (1990) calls this *striving for mastery* in which

> the individual relies on intellect and rationality, takes an active posture, focuses on future goals, seeks productivity, exerts discipline over self and others, maintains distance from others and values individuality. The expansive person is likely to take the approach not only in his job but also in his personal life. Frequently, the consequence is an inability to relax and enjoy leisure; there may be a consequent health risk. (Kofodimos, 1990: 63)

This obsession with developing work skills and rewards is often associated with an *avoidance of intimacy*. Workplace relationships are rarely intimate and allow the unbalanced manager to ignore or hide natural feelings for love, nurturing and intimacy. Work can be a source of self-worth and a refuge from pain. According to Kofodimos, avoiding intimacy serves the purpose of protecting your ideal self-image. Intimacy encourages the confrontation of fears, facts and feelings you would rather forget or repress.

It is interesting that the subordination of your needs to those of an organization means that loyalty, obedience and duty become paramount and valued, especially in others.

Of course, organizations have a vested interest in encouraging striving for mastery and avoidance of intimacy. They value intellect, know-how and problem-solving abilities but pooh-pooh sensitivity, empathy and emotional awareness:

> To compete and win, he must be detached from compassion for the losers. To devote himself to career success, he must be insulated from loneliness, guilt or regret, regarding sacrifices in his personal life ... people who want successful careers are faced with a dilemma: To succeed, they may have to adopt the necessary mastery type values, attitudes, and behaviour, even though doing so might involve compromising themselves and subordinating some of their needs and values to those of the organisation. (Kofodimos, 1990: 69)

The answer to this dilemma, according to Kofodimos, is to reallocate time and energy, tempering mastery strivings, coming to appreciate intimacy and coming to greater self-awareness and compliance. The costs of not doing so may ultimately be too high:

> An executive who is uncomfortable expressing feelings might fail to provide positive feedback, encouragement, or appreciation. An executive who denies doubts or vulnerabilities might not seek advice or help when it is needed. An executive who is reluctant to own up to weaknesses or mistakes might resist critical feedback and delay taking corrective action. An executive who needs to be perfect and therefore to handle and control every issue facing his unit might be unwilling to delegate responsibility to others. An executive who is overly demanding of others (as he is of himself) might intimidate them into hiding their problems from him. An executive who fears failure might be reluctant to take risks and therefore be overly slow and analytical in his decision-making. So inner imbalance can compromise the very success and achievement it was intended to further. (Kofodimos, 1990: 72)

Although business magazines are full of hagiographic stories of heroic visionary business leaders, there are a few curious case studies that show visionary leaders plunging their organizations into disaster. Conger (1990) identifies *failed vision* as a key source of leaders' incompetence. One form of failure involves confusing one's own needs with the needs of the market. Leaders who do this are often so personally driven that they ignore the costly implications of their strategic aims. This is often the result of experiencing early success and then developing an exaggerated belief in one's ability. Problems also result from an unrealistic assessment or distorted perception of the market or from a failure to recognize the changes that occur within it.

Conger (1990: 50) argues that leaders deny flaws in their vision and presents half a dozen typical problems (Table 3.1).

Table 3.1 Potential liabilities in the leader's communications and impression management skills

- Exaggerated self-descriptions
- Exaggerated claims for the vision
- A technique of fulfilling stereotypes and images of uniqueness to manipulate audiences
- A habit of gaining commitment by restricting negative information and maximizing positive information
- Use of anecdotes to distract attention away from negative statistical information
- Creation of an illusion of control through affirming information and attributing negative outcomes to external causes

(Conger, 1990: 50)

He also stresses that incompetent visionaries inappropriately manipulate others by impressive management and poor communication skills (Table 3.2).

Table 3.2 Potential liabilities of a leader's management practices

- Poor management of people networks, especially superiors and peers
- Unconventional behaviour that alienates
- Creation of disruptive 'in group/out group' rivalries
- An autocratic, controlling management style
- An informal/impulsive style that is disruptive and dysfunctional
- Alternation between idealizing and devaluing others, particularly direct reports
- Creation of excessive dependence in others
- Failure to manage details and effectively act as an administrator
- Attention to the superficial
- Absence from operations
- Failure to develop successors of equal ability

(Conger, 1990: 52)

These management practices inevitably become liabilities.

One of the themes of this book is that incompetent managers are often psychologically disturbed. Their personal history, their coping styles and their personality often play a central role in the way they conduct their lives. Not all are classic neurotics. Some are stressed out by the particular circumstances of their lives. But many of them make their beds and then lie in them.

3.4. Organizational Dysfunction and Misbehaviour

As has been noted, difficult people are often bad, sad or mad or some devilish combination of all three. Some incompetent managers are bad in the sense that they perform illegal acts such as sabotage and pilfering or 'cooking the books'. Others may be classified as sad in the sense that they have little ability or seem unwilling to apply the ability that they have. The third group are often the most dangerous; although not clinically certifiable, such matters as their narcissism or their tenuous contact with reality can mean that they make very bad decisions. Rather than concentrate on individuals and the way their personal inadequacies lead to group, departmental or even company failure, some writers have examined issues from a wider perspective looking at organizations as a whole. In doing so they have focused on the consequences of management incompetence.

Jones (1999) lists 20 dysfunctional behaviours that are associated with individual incompetence (Table 3.3).

Table 3.3 Dysfunctional behaviours checklist

- Communication is indirect
- Conflicts are not stated openly
- Secrets are used to build alliances
- Gossip is used to excite and titillate
- Corporate memory is lost or forgotten
- Requests for policy clarification are ignored
- The open expression of true feelings is absent
- The search for the cause of a problem is personalized
- People look for direction on how to act and react
- Friendship between professional colleagues is lacking
- Complex procedures are initiated by memorandum
- Meetings have long agendas and end up going in circles
- Inconsistent application of procedures is not challenged
- Mundane announcements are given too much time at meetings
- Promises of better times ahead seduce people into a status quo
- Dualistic (us versus them) thinking creates conflict and sets up sides
- Perfection creates an atmosphere of intolerance for mistakes
- Judgements are made about people being 'good' or 'bad'
- Isolation keeps management from seeing what is happening
- Management isolation is used as a basis of decision-making by cliques

He argues that there are developmental stages in organizational dysfunction. First, ambiguities are not questioned, then inconsistencies are ignored and, finally, neither ambiguities nor inconsistencies are discussible. Thus, 'Undiscussibility is undiscussible'.

He also describes the characteristics of functional and dysfunctional employees in groups (Table 3.4).

Table 3.4 Characteristics of employees in groups

Functional characteristics	Dysfunctional characteristics
• Helping others to understand	• Criticizing others for not understanding
• Sharing beliefs and assumptions	• Telling others what they should do
• Clarifying what is meant	• Challenging what is said
• Being concise and to the point	• Being vague and changing subjects
• Focusing on positive behaviours	• Focusing on negative personalities
• Providing objective descriptions	• Passing subjective judgements
• Opening up to positive change	• Defending the way things are
• Offering studied observations	• Fabricating baseless inferences
• Moving towards the future	• Dwelling on the past
• Providing useful specifics	• Making confusing generalities

Authors, consultants and managers who are concerned with reducing dysfunctional and incompetent behaviours tend to concentrate on cure rather than cause. Arguably, cure is more important than cause because correct diagnosis is essential for determining cause. To continue the analogy further, it is essential to admit that not all cases are curable.

There is a substantial literature examining organizational misbehaviour. Furnham (1998) has argued that group norms (rules about what it is acceptable to steal, how much and under what conditions) are powerful determinants of behaviour in groups. Some managers turn a blind eye to stealing and pilfering, seeing it as a part of the invisible wage structure. The practice of permitting theft as a 'side payment' is often considered quicker, easier and more direct than getting promotion approved.

Open, non-bureaucratic organizations tend to have less theft than rigid, over-administered organizations. Thieves may have a whole series of techniques for rationalizing their clearly unacceptable behaviour:

• Minimization – 'it's only a pen; the company can afford it and won't miss it'.
• Externalization – 'the boss made me do it; I was framed'.
• Normalization – 'everyone does it; this is what we do round here'.
• Superordination – 'they owed me; it's only fair repayment'.

It is important, indeed necessary, to take an organizational, as well as an individual, perspective on misbehaviour. Lying, deceit and subterfuge are more characteristic of some organizations than others because of the nature of jobs and organizations. Consider the following hypotheses:

• The more skilled the jobholder, the less he or she will be likely to cheat.
• Flexibility in time keeping will be negatively associated with lying.
• Higher performance expectations on the part of the boss or company will be associated with more lying.

- People having more than one formal role will be more likely to try to deceive.
- People with considerable demands (for example, parental demands) outside the organization are likely to be more deceitful.
- People reporting to more than one boss are more likely to be deceitful.

Each of these hypotheses has received empirical support, and they suggest that workplace deviance is created by certain job factors and by certain bosses. Cheats at work gravitate to, and operate in, different organizations. Mars (1984) described them in terms of four animal types:

Hawks: Individualistic entrepreneurs, small businessmen, fairground buskers, taxi owner–drivers and wheeler–dealer 'Mr Fixits'. The people involved all possessed a high degree of autonomy from group control and job definition and this meant that they could bend the rules to suit themselves. These are not high taxpayers.

Wolves operate in 'wolf packs'. They pilfer according to agreed rules and through a well-defined division of labour. Like a wolf pack, they possess a group hierarchical structure, with a leader giving orders and with informal rules that control the behaviour of members through sanctions. Gangs of dockers, teams of miners, refuse collection gangs and airline crews fall into this category.

Vultures operate on their own when they steal, but need the support of a group in order to do it. They are typically in jobs that involve a large amount of moving around and where performance success depends, to a certain degree, on an individual's flair and ability. Hence travelling salesmen, waiters and driver–deliverers operate vulture fiddles. Some even boast of their behaviour.

Donkeys: People who are constrained by their jobs and are isolated from other workers. Transport workers, machine minders and supermarket cashiers are all in donkey occupations. Donkeys can either be very powerful or powerless; they are powerless if they passively accept the constraints placed on them but powerful if they exert power through rejecting constraints, breaking the rules and thus causing temporary disruptions.

When there is a lack of fit between people's actual and ideal jobs, they react in various ways. They can resign (withdrawing mentally from this personal conflict), they can experience a nervous breakdown, or they can experience a sense of alienation. Such alienation in an organization often appears as above-average absenteeism, employee turnover, sabotage and fiddling. Thus, fiddling represents only one of a number of possible responses to work alienation. Furthermore, the fiddles of donkeys are not motivated primarily by the desire for monetary gain. Instead, organizing and operating fiddles provide these workers with some degree of individuality and an element of creativity that is missing from their jobs.

The lack of fit between a person's actual and ideal job may also result from a lack of contact with reality. The nature of a working life is, to mis-quote Hobbes, 'short, nasty and brutish'. The reality of work for many people is that the change is relentless, the work is hard, and companies are more concerned about profit for their shareholders than the quality of life of their staff. And it was ever thus.

3.5. How and Why Disordered People are Selected as Managers

Psychologists and psychiatrists maintain that personality differences are sta-ble over time. Interview the 'young adult' and 'what you see is what you get'. If you are extravert at 20, you are likely to be extraverted at 60, though with less energy. A person prone to antisocial behaviour patterns at 18 may grow out of them but is unlikely to do so. The obsessive–compulsive in their early 20s is likely to remain so, as is the narcissistic personality.

A major explanation for management incompetence lies in the personal-ity (and to a lesser degree the ability) of managers. Their make-up – their strongly preferred behaviour patterns – leads them to maladaptive behav-iour that strongly influences all those they work with.

The question is, why do they get selected in the first place for either a job promotion or a senior position? Are they skilful impression managers? Are selection boards naïve and lacking in insight? Again and again, retrospective case studies show that many signs and signals of disorder are apparent right at the beginning of a manager's career. So why are they ignored?

The answer to the question is twofold and is mainly concerned with the way traditional selection and appraisal is done.

Select in and select out. In essence, the business of selection is pretty straightforward and can be described as in Figure 3.1.

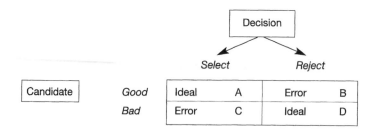

Figure 3.1 The business of selection.

For most people involved in selection the task is almost exclusively con-cerned with box A: describing (through job analysis) and finding the ideal candidate. It may be expressed in terms of job fit or compromise, but it is seen as a *hunt for the best or ideal candidate*.

But errors are made that everyone can attest to – namely, selecting 'bad' candidates. They come in many forms: people who turn out to be very different from what they say in the interview; those with insufficient talent and ability to do the job; those who are quite frankly very demotivated. They are all to be found in box C and everyone can (or should) admit to it when they have made one of these poor decisions.

A second error we often never find out we have made is found in box B. It refers to good candidates who were rejected. It is often amusing to read stories of famously successful writers whose manuscripts were turned down time after time, of famously successful captains of industry turned down for a job. There are lots of good and bad reasons why these errors occur. The problem is learning from them.

However, perhaps the most interesting is box D, because most people in the selection business see themselves as trying to select in, not select out. This is precisely opposite to the person involved in *quality control*. The job of the quality controller is quite specifically and objectively to spot faults, to detect poor quality, to monitor standards. Those in quality control have different temperaments from those in selection, which at times is a pity.

The issue is this: *rejecting is as important as selecting*. But it seems like a passive act. All those not accepted are rejected. However, it could profitably be seen as a positive act such that all those not rejected get accepted. In some very high-security jobs, the business of selecting out is taken very seriously. You cannot have a neurotic pilot or bomb disposal person; you should not have lazy or careless people running power stations, and so on.

Many organizations have been tempted to look back to their decision-making processes after they have made a seriously bad selection decision. An employee lied, cheated, embezzled, even killed others: why? Were there no signs at the interviews that he or she had these tendencies? What did they miss?

Often the reason is that organizations do not have a profile of incompetencies or unacceptable characteristics that are used positively to select out. Some people fail and derail because they are emotionally unstable: but is neuroticism considered a select-out variable? Some managers can't hack it because quite simply they do not have a developed moral conscience and find devious, immoral and illegal activities to their liking. The more senior, the more important, the more skilful the job, the more effort should be put into both processes of selecting in and selecting out. Organizations are now loath to admit select-out factors because of the possibility of litigation, although all good ones engage in the process.

Management incompetence and derailment may be a result of stress on the job. But more often it is both predictable and preventable by looking for early signs of traits that may lead to dysfunction in the workplace.

Organizations concerned with security are often very good at 'selecting out'. Where a person has serious responsibility (for example, being a pilot) or has to have a strict lifestyle (for example, being a monk) organizations put in place many different and varied tests to attempt to detect suitability. Also in some jobs – ministry, counselling, psychiatry – that are known to attract unstable types, there is often a concern with looking for signs of traits that exclude individuals.

The idea of the probationary period is also used to select out. In theory, it is an extended 'job try-out', where the employer and employee have the opportunity to see how well they are suited. Selection errors can be corrected in the period when hopefully the characteristic working patterns of individuals are clearly manifest. Alas, because of fear of litigation, few organizations use the probationary period for what it is primarily designed for.

The answer to part of the question of why incompetent managers are selected relates to biases in the business of selection. The second is perhaps more common and explains why pathology is overlooked.

3.6. Too Much of a Good Thing

Most people think more in linear terms than in curvilinear terms. That is, when considering two things, they speak as if both move in unison: the more attractive you are, the happier you are; the richer you are, the more content you are; the healthier your lifestyle, the longer your life.

However, we all know that sometimes the relationship between variables is curvilinear. Consider music: very familiar music *and* very unfamiliar music are rated as moderately appealing whereas music that is partly familiar is most appealing. The same is true of most names: John and David and Peter (very familiar) are rated as modestly appealing, as are rather unfamiliar names such as many foreign names. Lower-frequency names are most liked, then become more popular and inevitably then go out of fashion.

The concept of optimality is relatively common in psychological research, but often seems to be ignored in the workplace. Consider the idea of intelligence and success at work (Figure 3.2).

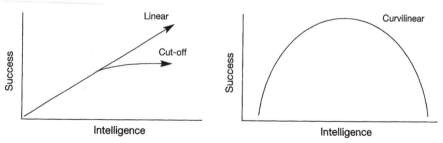

Figure 3.2 The relationship between intelligence and success.

Is intelligence related to job success? The answer is indeed yes. In fact, one of the best predictors of job success is intellectual ability. However, what is the relationship? It can be expressed in at least three ways:

1. *Linear.* This suggests that the brighter a person is, the more successful they are at work. This may be true in certain jobs – the academic physicist for instance.
2. *Cut-off.* This suggests that intelligence is linearly related to work success up to a point, but beyond that point it carries no advantage. The idea is akin to minimum height requirements in certain jobs. As long as you attain the standard cut-off point there is no advantage to be gained in being taller. Naturally, one could conceive of the cut-off differing for different jobs.
3. *Curvilinear.* Figure 3.2 suggests that both low *and* high intelligence lead to poor job success but that average intelligence is best. The idea is of an optimum amount.

Managers are selected and promoted on all sorts of criteria, often called competencies (see Chapter 4). They are frequently meant to have almost superhuman qualities; some of them are almost contradictions. But can too much competence lead to incompetence? Can a strength become a weakness? Can one simply have too much of a good thing?

McCall (1998) has a clear theory of management incompetence and derailment. Essentially, there are three important themes. The first is that in any business divided along traditional lines – finance, human resources, marketing, operation – people are *likely to be good at certain things and less likely to be good at others.* Thus marketing people are action oriented, entrepreneurial, resourceful and risk-takers, *but* they are less likely to be consistent, self-disciplined team workers who go through the appropriate channels and use company systems. Operation managers, on the other hand, often have considerable strengths in efficiency, teamwork, maintenance and the use of systems. They are, however, less concerned about the big business issues and poor at responding to customers or initiating change. People in finance are good at analytical detail, strategic thinking and cost control but they are often poor at influencing the managers and turning clever ideas into appropriate actions.

There is nothing unusual or surprising about these assertions. Indeed it is the very essence of the stereotypes that people hold. However, the second theme is that of *organizational complicity.* In essence, this means that organizations recognize individual manifest strengths but they forgive, overlook or suppress evidence of weakness. Thus, the brilliant, technically sophisticated young manager is promoted frequently as reward and soon discovers that he or she is attempting to manage others with little or no ability – that is, they get analysis paralysis or bogged down in process, unable to inspire others or get things done.

Equally, the marketing manager with a strong track record of getting things done and delivering profit is forgiven the fact that he or she is perhaps a little egocentric and refuses to use the accounting or performance management systems. The organizational complicity is to reward rather than punish rule breaking and to promote the person to senior roles where they are overwhelmed with complexity and have no strategic perspective.

Once the golden-child, Wunderkind manager begins to derail, organizational complicity turns into unforgiveness, leading to total derailment. Be successful and the organization overlooks flaws; fail and they get magnified.

The third theme to this 'theory' is that all competencies have their *dark side*. And this is very much a compensations theory (consider the eight examples suggested by McCall in Table 3.5).

Table 3.5 The dark side of competencies (McCall, 1998).

Competency	Potential dark side
Team player	Not a risk taker, indecisive, lacks independent judgement
Customer-focused	Can't create breakthroughs, can't control costs, unrealistic, too conservative
Biased towards action	Reckless, dictatorial
Analytical thinker	Analysis paralysis, afraid to act, inclined to create large staffs
Has integrity	Holier than thou attitude, rigid, imposes personal standards on others, zealot
Innovative	Unrealistic, impractical, wastes time and money
Has global vision	Missed local markets, over-extended, unfocused
Good with people	Soft, can't make tough decisions, too easy on people

Many organizations have as competencies the eight specified in the left-hand column. However, what McCall is suggesting is that you need an optimal amount of each. Consider this: integrity and innovativeness. All managers need to have integrity: it refers to honesty, morality, incorruptibility and adherence to a code of ethics and behavioural standards. Indeed, the quality that people *most* want in their boss is honesty. But can one have too much integrity? McCall suggests that it is possible to be over-zealous in your morality, imposing inflexible, possibly unattainable standards on others. There are many examples from literature of the rigid moralist, many of whom are portrayed as hypocrites partly because they try to impose on others standards that they personally do not live by. These are often the characteristics manifest by authoritarians (see Chapter 1).

There are many good reasons why being over-zealous is potentially a handicap. Moral and ethical standards have to be adaptable to different times and conditions. Standards of integrity can also be both egocentric and ethnocentric in the sense that they can be very particular to an individual and a culture. They are 'imposed' on others. People with very strict standards also tend to be too dismissive and rejecting of those who do not hold their particular views. They are prone to absolutist 'black-and-white' thinking. They can be too fundamentalist in their thinking and acting. These characteristics – morality, intolerance, zealotry – can be a source of derailment in any manager. They are often unattractive to customers, shareholders, bosses and subordinates.

Managers need integrity, to follow rules, codes and laws, and to have ethical standards. But they must know how to apply them sensitively and to be flexible where appropriate. A manager without integrity is a serious handicap and their lack of honesty is one of the most important sources of distrust at work.

The message is simple. Integrity, like height and intelligence, can be described on a linear scale. There are degrees of integrity. And there is probably an optimal amount. There are some rules that may very rarely be broken, whereas others are much more flexible. The trick is to know which. There is also the distinction between the spirit and the word of the law. Wise leaders know when to turn a blind eye and when to admonish, when to set examples and when to bend the rules.

The same applies to innovation. Initiating and adapting to change are very important features in work today. Managers need to know when, what and how to innovate. The anti-innovative, anti-change, 'if-it-ain't-broke-don't-fix-it' school of management is a recipe for disaster, especially in high-tech, fast-moving sectors. But so is the restless change-phile eager to introduce all sorts of new practices and procedures for their own sake. There is often a great cost to change in terms of time, money, goodwill and managerial 'work'. With all such things there is a trade-off. Is the expense of not changing (yet) greater than the cost of changing?

Managers in some sense need to be dreamers. They need to have a clear vision of where they and their company are going – and how to get there. Many learn the hard way how difficult it is to 'drive' change, so they give up. Others 'rock the boat' all the time, trying to keep up momentum.

Innovative people tend to be attracted to marketing, research and development (R&D), and IT, although they tend to have very different visions and approaches. R&D people innovate products; IT people innovate systems; marketing people innovate campaigns. They have different budgets, time frames, and influence strategies. In all these areas you can find the impractical, unrealistic, dreamy time wasters. Hopefully they are spotted early enough.

The message is the same. The Duchess of Windsor said you can never be too thin or too rich. She was wrong on both counts: anorexics are too thin and there is evidence that beyond a certain point wealth has no effect on a person's contentment and quality of life. Indeed, having too much of a quality – a trait, an attitude, an aptitude – can lead to derailment. Behind every silver lining there is a dark cloud!

3.7. Conclusion

This chapter suggests that what some managers believe is 'best practice' is in fact deeply misguided. The fact that these practices may be beneficial to their careers in the short term is in part a condemnation of the organization in which the practices are successful.

Although managers can become incompetent by following the advice they are given by gimmick-peddling charlatans, management consultants and business gurus, the fact remains that neurosis is at the basis of much incompetence. In addition to imbalance and disorder, some managers are simply bad – they are incompetent because they are immoral. Their incompetence arises from their selfishness, cheating, lying and stealing, which can actually bring a company down.

Much management incompetence borders on the absurd. Although few people believe it, there is plenty of evidence that the behaviour of 'serious grown-ups' is often irrational. One of the great attractions of psychology is the discovery of counter-intuitive facts. For instance, we know that groups often make riskier decisions than individuals. We know that brainstorming groups nearly always produce fewer and lower-quality ideas than people working alone and we know that extrinsic rewards such as money can quash morale. So it is with management common sense – it is often wrong and frequently misleading. No wonder, then, that the average manager is prone to becoming incompetent.

CHAPTER FOUR

The Concept of Competence

4.1. Introduction

For nearly two decades people in human resources have been talking about competencies. Half, if not all, of British companies use competency frameworks to guide how people are recruited, selected, trained, developed and even paid. Despite all the talk about competency, very little is heard about its absence or its opposite. This chapter explores the topic of competence to see what it tells us about incompetence. Although psychologists tend to think about individuals in term of ability, motives and traits, human resource people talk about capability, competency, experience, know-how, potential and proficiency. The term incompetence thus lies squarely in the practitioner's camp. It is not a psychological concept. But this does not mean that psychological theories, concepts and insights might not help explain it. Indeed, that is a central thesis of this book.

The word competent, like the word satisfactory, has a pleasant ring to it, but its current meaning is somewhat different from its dictionary definition. Business language has been so overloaded with inflationary superlatives that to call somebody competent now sounds almost pejorative. It seems to imply average or mediocre; everyone wants their staff and their service to be not competent but excellent, outstanding or exemplary. Competence sounds like the 50th percentile and what one really wants is the 80th.

Jacobs (1989) observed that the term competence, with its allusion to mere sufficiency and adequacy, sounds dated in a world that demands excellence and outstanding performance. Some have argued that people can only infer competence from seeing incompetence (Waibel and Wicklund, 1994). On the other hand, dictionary definitions stress that competence is an ability, skill or know-how: something done in an efficient and effective or adequate way. Interestingly, English dictionaries are more likely than American dictionaries to define the word as synonymous with merely adequate.

Although there may be difficulties with the technical definition of competence, there are even more difficulties when it comes to incompetence. Consider the following half-dozen alternative meanings:

1. *Not having the competencies*: This involves not having the abilities, traits or motivation to behave competently. Whether these are learned or inherited is, of course, crucially important, but the salient point for the definition is that the crucial, specified (core) competencies are missing.
2. *Not applying the competencies*: The definition suggests that a person has the necessary skills, abilities and traits needed for competence but chooses not to exercise them. This may be an individual act or a collective one. For instance, 'work to rule' is a possible sign of volitional incompetence. On the other hand, it is possible, but unlikely, that people have latent competencies but do not 'apply' them through lack of awareness, lack of self-confidence or lack of opportunity.
3. *Having irrelevant or redundant competencies*: People may have been recruited and selected for a particular set of competencies that are now redundant. Jobs change, as do the skills and attitudes required to do them. It is therefore possible that a person who was once competent becomes less so over time.
4. *Being too competent for a job*: Most people have experienced being 'overqualified' for a job. Jobs that are dull, routine, tedious or repetitive can wear down talented and skilled individuals who then perform them badly.
5. *Being deliberately incompetent*: There are reasons why individuals or groups choose to behave in ways that are less than competent. There are often feelings of anger, vengeance or inadequacy resulting from some perceived inequality at work. Individuals may perform poorly in order to demonstrate the importance of their job (when competently executed) to customers, colleagues or superiors.
6. *Not practising the competencies*: Because competencies are related to abilities and skills, they require practice. If not exercised, they can become rusty and hence a competency becomes an incompetency.

The English-speaking management world has been concerned with defining, delineating and selecting for management competencies for almost 20 years. The popularity of the concept of competency is usually attributed to Richard Boyatzis' 1982 book, *The Competent Manager*. The concept of competency seemed to offer a new way to think about performance by getting away from the literal-mindedness of behaviourism – for example, what competencies are needed versus what behaviours are displayed? It also seemed to offer a *neutral* term to evaluate work-related performance. Despite the popularity of the idea, there are various problems in defining it, or indeed in distinguishing it from other concepts. However, the term has, in fact, made the job for the manager *more* rather than *less* difficult because it has confused the various characteristics that are necessary for efficient management.

The confusion was partly created by Boyatzis himself. He defined a competency as 'an underlying characteristic of a person'. It could be a 'motive, trait, skill, aspect of one's self-image or social role, or a body of knowledge which he or she uses' (1982: 6). This definition covers almost anything, but it doesn't define the common denominator of all these things and raises the question of whether the term is simply a piece of jargon.

In an interview with Boyatzis, Adams (1997) notes that the competency movement (reflecting the number of human resources people who have jumped on the competency bandwagon) is a fad with too many people putting old wine in new bottles, simply repackaging their materials in a 'competency surround'. Adams feels that competency is trivialized and that it has become, in effect, 'proficiency'. He disapproves of using competencies in selection or pay because they are broader than the capabilities that can be reasonably specified for a job. Furthermore, many people never use their competencies:

> Take consultants. For years I've watched them with clients – they're very charismatic, sensitive, empathetic – then they'd come back to the office and behave like jerks. Now, should I pay them for the competencies they're demonstrating in the office, or for the competencies they're demonstrating with clients? And if I only see them in the office, how do I know what competencies they're demonstrating with clients? (Adams, 1997: 20)

Competency assessment often ignores the capacity for change and a person's potential for self-development. Boyatzis believes that competencies, like skills, can be developed, although the usual questions about which, how and how much are ignored.

All researchers have acknowledged that it was probably McClelland's (1973) paper that really popularized the concept of competency. Like many others before (Mischel, 1968) and after (Sternberg, 1996), McClelland was dissatisfied with the ability of personality and ability tests to predict job success. He hoped to develop tests to measure competencies primarily through the *behavioural event interviews* and *critical incident method*. These techniques compare above-average, average and below-average managers to understand how they do their job (based on critical incidents of good and poor performance) and then use these comparisons to detect competencies. There is therefore a dictionary of behaviours behind each competency. A decade later McClelland and his colleagues tried to find generic competencies – this resulted in Boyatzis' (1982) fundamental nine competencies – and allowed them to be motives, traits, skills, self-image, knowledge set or whatever. But behind each competency was a clear, specific behavioural description. McClelland seemed ambivalent about traits. He rejected the usefulness of single traits (conscientiousness) or abilities ('g') to predict performance in all or most jobs; yet he almost always found achievement motivation (his favourite trait) to be a major determinant of managerial performance.

McClelland argued that the term competency should replace the term skill, which was too narrow. Thus one may have the skill to drive a bus, but lack the competency to deal with passengers. He argued that the only comprehensive way to identify competencies is through behavioural event interviews, which are expensive but effective. Furthermore, standard job analysis methods, which focus on minimum competencies, leave things out, particularly how outstanding individuals work. Thus, strategic planning, as a competency, needs to be backed by a competence for influencing so that plans can be 'sold' to others.

According to McClelland, the core competencies of an organization are embedded in the organization's systems, motives, mechanisms and processes. Core competencies may represent unique sources of an organization's competitive advantage.

McClelland's ideas have been criticized for various reasons. Competencies concern past, not future, behaviour and they concern success in the past, not necessarily in the future. Also behavioural interview methods are often unfair to minorities or women who have not had the same developmental experiences as white males. And it is very expensive to transcribe long interviews.

There seem to be as many definitions of competency as there are people who talk about them. The British define competencies in terms of something that managers can do – a demonstrable behaviour or an outcome. Some American writers believe that a competency is a 'higher-order' trait, skill, motive or disposition that distinguishes between average and superior managers. Competency has been used as an adjective and as a noun. Thus one can be a competent strategic planner or have marketing competency. Supposedly, one can also draw up a definitive list of required competencies – a discrete set of knowledge, values and skills. One may have areas of competence – that is, parts of a job (or skills) – that one does well.

Mansfield (1999: 14; emphasis in original) defined the term as meaning 'people who are *suitable for work, sufficiently skilled* for the work they do, *fit* for work and *efficient* in their work!'. He suggests that the term implies a barely acceptable level, or threshold, of ability (suitable, sufficient) but also rather more than that (fit, efficient). In short, competent people are efficient and effective, incompetent people are not.

But there is confusion over the term for various reasons. Consider the following three issues:

1. *Singular or plural*: Nouns are divisible into counted nouns and uncounted nouns. The former have simple plurals: manager – managers; article – arti-

cles. But the latter do not have simple plurals: asparagus and furniture have to have other nouns such as head and piece to make them plural – hence four pieces of furniture. Competence is an uncounted noun. Thus we have *the* competence of managers, not a competence, which confuses a task performed or any underlying trait or ability. It does not mean a set standard of behaviour.

At present, competence is taken to mean what people are like, how they do things and what they can do – all of which are conceptually distinct. Thus some supposedly competency-based assessments look at the *former* two factors to decide whether people have the 'competencies' needed to do the job well, whereas others use the *last* two factors to decide whether they have the ability or potential to do the job.

2. *Adequate or excellent*: There is some confusion about whether the term refers to barely capable or extremely good. One approach focuses on abilities and characteristics that may have good comparative norms; hence, it is easy to talk about levels of excellence. A second approach looks at what people should be able to do in order to execute the job competently, not what they are like. A good manager has the skills/knowledge to complete the job and characteristics for a particular team. Having particular characteristics will not ensure success nor will a job analysis say much about personal characteristics. Thus the adequate/excellent debate needs to be dropped.

3. *Inputs and outputs*: Most competency approaches have focused on how things are done; on outcomes of activities rather than on the underlying state or disposition that determines the activity. The emphasis is on the resultant behaviour not on traits or processes:

> To *have* a degree is still taken to be an important signal of general capacity. To *be* experienced is a valued characteristic in selection for employment. In some cultures, to be white or male – or both – is taken to be sufficient evidence of capability. The competency movement seeks to change the tradition by asking a simple question. People may have degrees, they may be experienced, they may be thought reliable – but what can they actually do? How they learned to do it, how long they have been doing it, and what kind of person they are, are seen as subordinate. (Mansfield, 1999: 28; emphasis in original)

The last point illustrates a major problem with the entire competency discussion – it focuses on consequences not causes. Unless you know why a particular person can or cannot do a job, you have no idea what else that person may be able to do and whether he or she can ever be taught. And it illustrates a great deal about the incompetent manager who, for one reason or another, simply cannot do those tasks that are fundamental to the job.

Matthewman (1997) surveyed 50 British organizations and found that, of the companies who used the competency approach, about 50% specified between 10 and 20 essential competencies. More than half used the original McClelland behavioural approach to define competencies, less than 10% defined them in strictly functional terms, and the remainder were in between. Competencies seemed to be used fairly extensively in recruitment, selection, training and development. However, only one-fifth of those surveyed used competencies as a major factor in calculating compensation.

4.2. A Question of Competency

Managers are now being encouraged to list the competencies that any employee in the organization needs in order to perform successfully. These competencies are then used in selection, promotion, performance appraisal, counselling and vocational guidance. The lists of competencies that managers believe are needed in their organizations are derived in a variety of ways. Sometimes an autocratic chief executive simply sketches the points on the back of an envelope; sometimes all the directors go through a 'focused' interview and the results are collated; other methods include group discussions, using repertory grids, job analysis and simply adapting someone else's list.

Once organizations have defined their 'unique and comprehensive' list of competencies, they then need to devise ways of measuring them so that applicants and employees can be compared and contrasted. How well this is done is another matter; competence, like truth and beauty, is in the eye of the beholder and hence very difficult to determine.

So, what are competencies? Are they just traits or aptitudes, or are they skills that decay if they are not practised? A wealth of theories attempts to specify the basic traits and abilities that are common to everyone wherever they work, including the work of Jung and Cattell, and there is a large body of research on the subject that could be tapped. But the question of what precisely competencies are remains unanswered.

How are competencies related to each other? A list of competencies is nearly always just that, a list, but human abilities are related. Depending on intelligence, thinking styles (for example, convergent or divergent thinking) and temperament, certain human factors are clearly related. For example, extraverts tend to be more socially skilled, more likely to be 'evening people', more likely to excel in brief, timed tests, and more likely to be involved in accidents than introverts. Some competencies will be related to each other and some unrelated, but which is which? In short, what is the *structure of competencies*? This is the first thing an organization should investigate after deciding on its competency profile.

Are competencies learned or inherited – or both? This question has important implications; if they are primarily learned, then they can be taught; if they are inherited, then they have to be selected. If they are learned, are they best learned at a particular age and in a particular way? Do some people simply learn competencies more effectively than others? Are some teaching methods more appropriate than others? The training industry works on the promise that competencies can be acquired in short courses, but this may not be true.

It is also possible that some competencies are found more often among certain demographic, racial, linguistic or religious groups than among others. Certainly some groups excel at sports and others at science; so it may reasonably be supposed that organizational competencies are unevenly distributed. What is the effect of this, and how can organizations square a competency-based selection policy with equal opportunities? Organizations need to look at this point very carefully.

Are competencies an all-or-nothing phenomenon, under which people can be categorized into types, or are they dimensional with a continuum from high to low competence? Most organizations talk about types of people but measure people along dimensions. The very concept of a competence certainly implies that people fall into types, with an implicit idea that someone is either competent or not.

Is there a finite, exhaustive, universal list of competencies from which subsets can be devised, or are competencies so varied and subtle that no such list could ever be derived? In our experience, every organization thinks it is unique, but organizations then specify that they need the same competencies. If competencies are organization specific, they cannot be compared.

Personnel professionals are interested in whether competencies can be reliably and validly measured. The whole point of establishing competencies is to be able to assess people, compare them, track them over time, rate them before and after they go on training courses, and so on. But how are they measured? What sort of test should be used: behavioural observation, questionnaire, rating (and, if so, by whom)?

Each assessment method has problems associated with it, and they lead to systematic bias and error. Furthermore, not all competencies are likely to be measured in an equally valid way. It is easier to measure some traits, such as linguistic skills, than others, such as intelligence. There are valid tests available to measure certain abilities, traits and beliefs, but competencies such as 'forward planning' and 'coping with change' are difficult to measure. Comparing people on unreliable measures is highly problematic, and it seems to be impossible reliably to measure common sense, ability to motivate and many other bland terms that are considered to be competencies.

Some people assume that competencies are the major determinant of behaviour in an organization. Presumably organizations value competencies because they represent the fundamental abilities and capabilities needed to do a job well. But does having a competency mean that it will be used? Impersonal factors may prevent competent people from performing and allow incompetent people to perform adequately. Organizational factors can clearly override the contribution of individuals, irrespective of their level of competency. Anxiety, obsessionality, phobias and poor ability to cope with everyday stress may prevent competencies from ever manifesting themselves in behaviour.

Is it possible to compensate for the lack of a particular competence? Can people function well in an organization when they do not have a particular competence or set of competencies? This may be possible through hard work, delegation or redefinition of their job. People with specific handicaps have been able to triumph over considerable difficulties, so it is possible that the absence of some competencies is not necessarily a problem.

Is the opposite of competency no competency or incompetency? What tasks can be done effectively if a particular competency does not exist or is insufficient? There is quite a difference between knowing how to do a job and doing it badly, which is incompetence, and not knowing how to do it, which is no competence.

People-related competencies are different from 'thing-related' competencies, such as computing or finance skills. Some people are attracted to computers or accounting systems because they are logical and predictable, whereas others shun them because they prefer to deal with people using their intuition and sensitivity. Managerial jobs usually demand both kinds of competencies, but is it possible to find both in equal measure? It is perfectly possible for personnel managers to have more of the former and engineering managers to have more of the latter.

Organizational competencies necessarily change over time. All organizations live in volatile environments that demand adaptation and innovation. Does the selection of a homogeneous workforce (in terms of salient and non-salient competencies) mean that an organization will be better able to handle change, because there are bound to be people in the organization who have the competencies needed to deal with the new environment? From this point of view, the most salient competency may be the ability to deal with change or even seek it out, and the one competency to avoid is resistance to change.

Psychologists interested in personality, individual differences, organizational behaviour and psychometrics have studied extensively the importance of personality traits, intelligence and other abilities for occupational success. The term competence is new and fashionable, but the concept is old. The questions raised are neither trivial nor simple, and they should not be dismissed as solely of academic interest. The answers to them are crucial for any organization in search of competencies.

4.3. Competencies Lists

Boyatzis (1982) listed 10 different competencies, and described a pro-gramme of research conducted in a variety of different private-sector and public-sector organizations to discover the competencies related to mana-gerial effectiveness. The competencies included motives, traits, skills, self-image and knowledge. One method used to identify competencies was the 'behavioural event interview' (similar to the critical incident technique). Incidents of effective and ineffective behaviour were obtained in interviews with managers who were preselected on the basis of their effectiveness. The sample included 253 managers from all levels, some rated low in effective-ness, some rated medium and some rated high. Incidents were classed into competency categories, and traits and skills were inferred from an analysis of behaviour in relation to the manager's intentions and the situation. A sta-tistical analysis defined nine competencies with a significant trend, such that the average competency score was highest for effective managers and lowest for ineffective managers. These nine competencies were as follows:

1. *Efficiency orientation*: Demonstrating concern for task objectives, high inner work standards, and high achievement motivation, with behaviour such as setting challenging but realistic goals and deadlines, developing specific action plans, determining ways to overcome obstacles, organizing the work efficiently, and emphasizing performance when talking to others.
2. *Concern with impact*: Demonstrating a great need for power and concern for power symbols, with behaviour such as acting assertively, attempting to influence others, seeking high-status positions, and expressing concern about the reputation of the organization's products and services.
3. *Proactivity*: Demonstrating a strong belief in self-efficacy and internal locus of control, with behaviour such as initiating action rather than waiting for things to happen, taking steps to circumvent obstacles, seeking informa-tion from a variety of sources, and accepting responsibility for success or failure.
4. *Self-confidence*: Demonstrating belief in one's own ideas and ability by behaviour such as taking decisive action rather than hesitating or vacillat-ing, and making proposals in a firm, unhesitating manner, with appropriate pose, bearing and gestures.
5. *Oral presentation skill*: Ability to use symbolic, verbal and non-verbal behav-iour and visual aids to make clear and convincing presentations to others.
6. *Conceptualization*: Ability to identify patterns or relationships in informa-tion and events (inductive reasoning), and to convey the meaning of developing a concept, model or theme, or by using appropriate metaphor and analogy; also the ability to develop creative solutions and new insights into problems.

7. *Diagnostic use of concepts*: Deductive reasoning, using a concept or model to interpret events, analyse situations, distinguish between relevant and irrelevant information and detect deviations from plans.
8. *Use of socialized power*: Ability to develop networks and coalitions, gain cooperation from others, resolve conflicts in a constructive manner and use role modelling to influence others.
9. *Managing group process*: Ability to manage group processes, and to build member identification and team spirit by creating symbols of group identity, emphasizing common interests and need for collaboration, and providing public recognition of member contributions.

In summary, Boyatzis inferred competencies from descriptions of effective and ineffective behaviour, based on incidents distinguishing more effective from less effective managers. The competencies included motives, personality traits, cognitive skills and interpersonal skills. In general, his findings were quite similar to those from earlier trait studies using different research methods.

The quest for the definitive, comprehensive, universal 'periodic table' of competencies has continued. For instance, Dulewicz (1989, 1992, 1994) is convinced that there are 12 'totally independent' dimensions of performance or key supra-competencies derived from 49 primary competencies. He argues:

> The Supra-Competencies constitute 12 independent dimensions of middle management performance, based on self and boss ratings from a wide range of organizations, which account for more of the total variance in performance. They could therefore form the basis of generic personnel selection specifications, dimensions for performance appraisal systems and as a development needs analysis tool. At a minimum, the model could be used as a template against which to check if company systems are exhaustive, and if not, where possibly gaps exist. (Dulewicz, 1989: 56)

Supra-competencies

The following are short definitions of 12 independent performance factors:

Intellectual

1. *Strategic perspective*: Rises above the detail to see the broader issues and implications; takes account of wide-ranging influences and situations *both* inside and outside the organization before planning or acting.
2. *Analysis and judgement*: Seeks all relevant information; identifies problems, relates relevant data, and identifies causes; assimilates numerical data accurately and makes sensible interpretations; work is precise and methodical,

and relevant detail is not overlooked. Makes decisions based on logical assumptions that reflect factual information.

3. *Planning and organization*: Plans priorities, assignments and the allocation of resources; organizes resources efficiently and effectively, delegating work to the appropriate staff.

Interpersonal

4. *Managing staff*: Adopts appropriate styles for achieving group objectives; monitors and evaluates their work; shows vision and inspiration; develops the skills and competencies of staff.

5. *Persuasiveness*: Influences and persuades others to give their agreement and commitment; in face of conflict, uses personal influence to communicate proposals, to reach bases for compromise and to reach an agreement.

6. *Assertiveness and decisiveness*: Ascendant, forceful dealing with others; can take charge; is willing to take risks and seek new experiences; is decisive, ready to take decisions, even on limited information.

7. *Interpersonal*: Shows consideration for needs and feelings and takes account of them; is flexible when dealing with others.

8. *Oral communication*: Fluent, speaks clearly and audibly, with good audience levels of understanding.

Adaptability

9. *Adaptability and resilience*: Adapts behaviour to new situations; resilient, maintains effectiveness in face of adversity or unfairness. Performance remains stable when under pressure or opposition; does not become irritable and anxious, retains composure.

Results orientation

10. *Energy and initiative*: Makes a strong, positive impression, has authority and credibility; is a self-starter and originator, actively influences events to achieve goals; has energy and vitality, maintains high level of activity and produces a high level of output.

11. *Achievement motivation*: Sets demanding goals for self and for others, and is dissatisfied with average performance; makes full use of own time and resources; sees a task through to completion, irrespective of obstacles and setbacks.

12. *Business sense*: Identifies opportunities that will increase sales or profits; selects and exploits those activities that will result in the largest return.

Source: Dulewicz (1989).

Woodruffe (1993) points out the similarities between the exclusive and 'unique' competencies of various companies. He drew up a table of the competencies used by five major British companies and showed how similar they

were (Table 4.1). The fact that different organizations end up with very similar wish-list competencies implies either that competencies are universal or
that the companies that specify them have almost identical models.

Table 4.1 Comparison of the competency lists from five different organizations.

Cadbury Schweppes	WH Smith	BP	Manchester Airport	National Westminster Bank
Strategy	Written	Personal drive	Critical reasoning	Information
Drive	communication	Organizational	Strategic	search
Relationships	Oral	drive	visioning	Concept
Persuasion	communication	Impact	Business	information
Leadership	Leadership	Communication	know-how	Conceptual
Followership	Team	Awareness of	Achievement	flexibility
Analysis	membership	others	drive	Interpersonal
Implementation	Planning and	Team manage-	Proactivity	search
Personal factors	organizing skills	ment	Confidence	Managing
	Decision-making	Persuasiveness	Control	interaction
	Motivation	Analytical power	Flexibility	Developmental
	Personal strength	Strategic thinking	Concern for	orientation
	Analytical	Commercial	effectiveness	Impact
	reasoning skills	judgement	Direction	Achievement
		Adaptive	Motivation	orientation
		orientation	Interpersonal	Self-confidence
			skills	Presentation
			Concern for	Proactive
			impact	orientation
			Persuasion	
			Influence	

(Woodruffe, 1993)

Adding to the misery of the bewildered personnel officer is the fact that
other quite different systems exist. Thus Evers and Rush (1996) listed 18
skills (sort of primary competencies), which they categorized into 'four base
competencies'. They were:

1. Mobilizing innovation and change: Ability to conceptualize, creativity,
   risk-taking, visioning.
2. Managing people and tasks: Coordinating, decision-making, leadership/
   influence, managing conflict, planning and organizing.
3. Communicating: Interpersonal, listing, oral communication, written
   communication.
4. Managing self: Learning, time management, personal strategies, problem
   solving.

Despite the fact that so many lists and 'models' exist, they are characterized more by their similarity than by their differences. This implies that
there is a set of traits, abilities and motivations that is related to success in

all jobs. Personality psychologists believe that these can be summed up in terms of a set number (3–7) of specific, clear, unrelated personality traits (such as stability) and general intelligence (see Chapters 5 and 6). The central and important question remaining is: are people without these competencies, or is the presence of some other factor, such as mental instability, the real cause of incompetence?

4.4. Identifying Competencies

According to Adams (1998), there are three key methods for identifying competencies, although they share many common features and only one of these methods was specifically designed to be used in competency analysis.

1. *Critical Incident Techniques (CIT)*: The idea is to identify how employees behaved during complex, sudden, unforeseen, difficult events. Questions include: the specific nature of the problem/situation; who was involved; what were the objectives; what the person actually did and with what effect – therefore, which behaviours were least and most effective. The focus is on behaviours that were successful; these are then grouped into categories, dimensions or 'competencies'. This is an expensive method that depends on the insight and honesty of the employee and the skill of the interviewer, in both the chat and writing up the data. Furthermore, the method overlooks the many tedious, humdrum, but important tasks that have to be done.

2. *Behavioural Event Interviews (BEI)*: This is similar to the CIT but focuses more on the person – his or her thoughts, feelings and motivation. The method also seeks to compare the responses of good, average and weak employees in an attempt to find discriminating and predictive behaviours. Again, interviews are analysed and coded for competencies. The interview also considers 'folklore' values – namely, job incumbents' ideas about the things needed to do the job effectively. Reliability is evaluated by having two coders rate the taped interviews. Validity is evaluated by determining whether the competencies differentiate between known groups in the organization and predict superior future performance. The method inevitably generates a huge amount of data. However, like biodata, it may be too historically focused. Furthermore, if known groups – high-flyers/average performers/weak performers – cannot be clearly identified, then the whole system may fail.

3. *Repertory Grid (RG)*: Derived from clinical psychology, this method uses people to generate constructs. Thus, people (managers, employees) are given the names of three colleagues and asked to specify a dimension (construct) that differentiates one from two others (for example, confident versus nervous). Once a list of constructs is generated, they are put

into an array, which is a process of explaining who is more effective, confident or nervous, and why. Finally, experts are asked to describe the typical behaviours of confident people that differentiate them from nervous or anxious employees. This last step yields the competencies. The analysis also yields insights into personal values. However, the people who complete the RG may not fully understand the demands, pressures and role requirements of others at work.

But just as competencies may be derived using different methods, they may also be differently conceived. The competency movement has become so popular that it has inspired various reviews. Berman (1997) compared the way competencies are conceived in the United States, Britain and France. In the United States three issues seem unresolved: no single agreed-upon method of assessing managerial competency; uncertainty as to whether competencies encompass the actual responsibilities of managers; and whether competencies even define the role of managers in a useful way. In France, according to Berman (1997), competency is a cognitive concept – know-how, not performance. Work is defined in terms of acquired knowledge. Yet many French companies still believe that formal qualifications are the best criteria for selection and development. The British either follow the US tradition or follow the functional route, which focuses on acceptable performance and adequate knowledge rather than excellent performance. A major problem is that once people have been 'certified competent' there is little motivation to check whether their subsequent performance is competent.

Moloney (1997) argues that you need to distinguish between capability and performance when considering competencies. The former refers to skills, knowledge and understanding while the latter refers to achieving targets. The application of capability leads to performance. Competency consultants try to identify clusters of behaviours that are specific, observable and verifiable, and can be theoretically or empirically classified together. Note the emphasis on observable behaviours, which suggests that those skills/abilities (such as creative thinking) that are hard to observe may be ignored.

Ziyal (1997) pointed out that most competency specifications and ratings are categorical not continuous. By that she means that one can determine that people either do or do not have them, or that they could be judged to have (or not have) the potential to acquire them. But competency analyses typically say nothing about the level and range of competencies needed or whether different business contexts demand different competencies. Her solution is not new although it is expressed in the language of competencies: identify critical performance (competency) demands of the typical situations associated with a job and then select and train for them.

Drakeley and White (1999) argue that the term competency is an all-purpose umbrella word that means all things to all people. The two most commonly confused issues are 'things' at which people are competent versus 'things' that competent people possess. Drakeley and White further argue that 'the evidence strongly suggests that whatever assessment centres measure, they are not measuring competencies with any degree of precision. If anything they measure exercise performance rather than enduring traits or competencies' (1999: 7). Rather cynically they point out that organizations have competency lists, frameworks, models or architecture ... and the term they use depends on how much they pay their consultants!

Drakeley and White argue that it is crucial to distinguish between:

- competence – an individual capacity to perform a task competently, and
- competency – a particular skill, ability, knowledge or quality possessed by an individual.

Furthermore, it is relevant to distinguish between the task that people need to perform and the qualities that they need to perform it and which competencies are needed in order to carry out a task with competence. Thus a competence task is preparing a budget, and conscientiousness is a competency.

Roberts (1998) attempted to introduce personality measures into a system using four categories of competencies. These include a *natural* cluster (essentially four big personality traits), an *acquired* cluster (experience, professional/technical education), an *adapting* cluster, which includes motivational variables, and a *performing output* cluster, which includes the observable behaviours resulting from the other two.

To complicate matters further, Losey (1999) provides the following 'equation':

$$intelligence + education + experience + ethics + interest = competency$$

It is precisely these sorts of 'equations' that have given competencies a bad name. This equation does not specify what type of intelligence (verbal, spatial, mathematical, crystallized/fluid) nor does it specify how many types there might be. It is even possible to have too much or too little intelligence. The equation does not weight intelligence or the other four factors, nor does it distinguish between education and experience. In being 'all things to all men' competence ends up being a hopeless concept.

4.5. Current Research

Furnham (2000b) found that the scattered literature on competency in the HR world yielded 10 interesting questions.

1. Should we use the term 'competency'?

Although this may be a relatively minor point, for some non-human resources people it remains an important and contentious issue. Because the whole competency movement has moved on since the 1990s, the 'competency' term is not as widely used as it was. Now the term 'capability' is becoming popular.

Those who have chosen not to use the term have done so for various reasons. To many people, 'competency' sounds mediocre. Furthermore, not *having* competency or not being *competent* implies incompetence, which is a serious issue in business.

Others have preferred to use their own terms such as *high performance behaviours*, *management practices* or *standards*, with which they can identify. They argue that these labels are better understood by line managers, and have the individual stamp of their company. They're genuinely unique to them. Note that most companies specify the competencies that they want to select for; they never speak of incompetencies they want to reject.

More recently, companies seem to have become interested in 'selecting potential'. In essence, this means that the organizations are future oriented rather than past oriented, and they want a language to reflect this. Somehow, 'competency' does not fit well, and they are seeking clearer synonyms. This issue of language is important in communicating ideas to line managers. For some organizations, it may be wiser quietly to drop the term in favour of something more easily understood and containing less 'historical baggage'. Equally importantly, it is desirable to specify 'select out' or reject characteristics.

2. How many competencies do we need?

Whatever research methods organizations use, most end up with a framework typically having between 8 and 15 competencies, although some organizations may have as many as 30 general or core competencies (each with a number of behavioural indices). One lesson that many companies report is that a list of 10 or 15 competencies is probably too long. It becomes unwieldy for the managers, and adds much to the bureaucratic burden. However, others who are tied into industry standards find that they can cope quite adequately with as many as 20 supposedly unique competencies.

If there is a pattern for organizations in the number of competencies in their general list, it is *curvilinear*. At first, competencies increase in number to be comprehensive and all inclusive, but then they are reduced in number because they simply become unwieldy. Later on in the process, it is quite common for there to be two lists: general competencies and job-specific competencies. Human resources (HR) specialists feel most comfortable with the former type of list and line managers with the latter.

Most organizations start with two approaches: (general) competencies and (specific) behaviours. Thus, one may have 10 competencies with four or five behaviours for each criterion. This yields a 50-item assessment form. If one has 20 competencies and each, in turn, has six behaviours/criteria/levels, the list expands to 120 items. It soon becomes apparent that the search for comprehensiveness leads to an unwieldy assessment form, and a frighteningly bureaucratic exercise for the line manager.

There is always a trade-off between comprehensiveness (with its down-side of bureaucracy) and the best, most parsimonious, level of description. The systems that work best are short, simple and *comprehensible* rather than comprehensive. This is, and has been, an important issue in explaining why frameworks have failed: even those practitioners in HR complain about the time taken to complete documentation and the perceived lack of benefit from the exercise.

3. How is a competency framework derived?

There are a number of issues here: should one do the research in house or use consultants? Is the initial research essential to the buy-in process? How important is it to do research across all sections or departments of the organization? How long should this phase last? Is any one methodology more helpful than another in generating a useful, and unique, framework?

It is probably unwise to rely entirely on consultants for the work involved in developing competencies, as they tend to provide lists they have used before and are comfortable with; and it is particularly unwise to use more than one consultancy at the same time, because they will tend to compete and over-engineer solutions. Having a small, bright, dedicated and multi-functional working party for early research works well.

Where the team responsible for introducing competencies has done extensive pilot work on the organization, the introduction has tended to be more successful. Line managers like to be consulted – often individually rather than in focus groups and meetings – and taken seriously. Failure to listen to specialist groups, particularly in engineering/finance, has often led to later problems.

Many organizations attribute their problems with the competency approach to the time taken to generate the framework, from deciding to go down that route to producing agreed and finalized documentation. It seems usual for it to take two to three years between announcing the initiative and the documentation appearing. Expectations have often been badly man-aged, and this has often led to cynicism and scepticism.

The critical issue lies in timing and managing expectations about when the framework will be finished and how it will help line managers in particular, and the organization in general. Communicating clearly about purpose and progress right from the beginning can solve many of the problems.

4. When and how to use consultants

To a large extent, this depends on the consultants used, the relationship between HR and the particular consultants involved, and the general practice of use of consultants in the organization. Consultants can be used at various stages, typically:

- conducting early research as part of designing the framework;
- launching the project;
- providing training associated with the framework;
- auditing the process; and
- redesigning and updating the project.

Naturally, consultants have different specialities and approaches, and hence are used differently. The most common uses are in research and training; organizations have tended to be happier with the latter rather than the former. Outside trainers are often valued for their skill and impartiality. Furthermore, even some of the biggest organizations seem to have 'outsourced' the training department. Some line managers resent consultants, and it can become an issue in the initial stages of the project. Without doubt, the nature of the final competency framework is more a function of the consultants used (if so) than the uniqueness of the organization itself.

5. Should the framework apply across the whole organization?

Most organizations start with the explicit aim of trying to devise a framework that is generally applicable across all departments, sections and regions for those at or above a specific level of seniority. Thus, for instance, part-time or support staff are not initially included and may never be so.

A universal framework such as this is thought to be important to ensure that a common language is used in organizations, and that the managers and HR specialists at all levels use and understand the same terms.

After a period of time, however, it is quite common for organizations to start to distinguish between general and specialist competencies. This occurs after technical specialists complain that they cannot work with the framework. It might meet the managerial business needs of the organization but not the clear and specific requirements of technical specialists. This situation then presents the organization with a dilemma. What often occurs is that the number of specialist competencies grows, while the general competencies get reduced in number or fall into disuse. The overall effect is ultimately for each department to have its own competency framework, thus significantly defeating the whole point of the exercise.

Again, this is an issue of balance. Allowing specialists to have a small number of three to four competencies to add to a short but manageable list of six to eight general competencies works well. This is the 'compromise position' that many organizations find themselves in. By contrast, those that resist introducing specific competencies often have the use of the whole framework threatened.

6. Who needs to champion the project?

The issue of an organizational champion or organizational support is not unique to the problems of introducing competency frameworks. However, the issue seems more crucial when considering the design, introduction and maintenance of HR projects.

Where competency frameworks have failed, research has frequently noted two related things: the loss of the champion and/or the withering of board-level support.

Just as importantly, if the board does not endorse the introduction of the framework, it seems doomed to failure. This includes going on training courses, attending early research meetings and being seen to use the system. This support is needed not only at the initial phase but also right through the process.

7. How often and why do competency frameworks need updating and revising?

There are three phases to the successful implementation of all frameworks: planning/creating, implementing/launching and maintaining. Typically, the money and energy are exhausted in the first phase, which takes longer and proves more difficult than expected. Although there is, of necessity, money and energy left for the launch and the training support of the competency framework, this can easily evaporate in the really important phase: maintaining the system and ensuring that it is used in the organization.

Typically, there is a call for changing and revising the system a few years after launch. This is a normal and healthy reaction. However, it is not easy to reproduce or adapt the manual. Hence, it is rare to see frameworks thoroughly revised and updated as much as they should be. Indeed, there seems to be a negative relationship between the amount of work done on the initial 'manualization' and the desire to change the system,

It seems to be the case that, like all systems, there needs to be a balance between continuity and change. Competency frameworks clearly need revisiting every 2–3 years to ensure that they are still relevant. Resistance to updating is a common source of failure. Many people report that, when frameworks were introduced, they were all concerned with the *current* rather than the *future* needs of the organization.

8. For what function should the competency framework/architecture be used?

One of the initial attractions of the competency framework idea was that it would help integrate a variety of people management functions, specifically, recruitment and selection, development and training, and performance appraisal. The idea was that the system would generate both the concepts and the data bank for each of those systems.

Different companies began at different points: some started investigating the idea of introducing competencies because they had problems with retention, others with development and still others with appraisal. The research seems to suggest that implementation through personal development programmes (either 360° feedback at senior level or certificates at the junior level) works best.

Most companies use the frameworks for training, some for selection and fewer for appraisal. The last nearly always has serious problems associated with it. Most line managers need to be introduced to the language of the competency by first applying it to themselves and understanding their own behaviour. The language of general management competence helps managers focus on what they should be doing and also provides company-wide consistency around these issues.

9. What training is required around competency frameworks?

There are three types of training that need to be done to support all and any competency frameworks:

1. *Individualization of work plan*: Many companies find that frameworks need to have two parts to them – that is, those that apply to everyone, at their level, and those that apply to them only (generic vs personal). These may be called 'key objectives', 'key result areas', 'key practices' and so on, but require personal specifications. Individuals need training in writing their own work plan, particularly in specifying success criteria. Although it is not difficult to list competencies and behaviours, people frequently find it problematic to come up with measurable criteria to evaluate each competency. Training and facilitation are needed around this issue.
2. *Progress/interim reviewing*: Most managers are poor at, and fundamentally neglect, giving staff feedback on their performance. This is not in the context of final, end-of-year appraisal but an interim discussion about

progress on specific competencies. They need to be taught how to structure and conduct these sessions so that they feel confident in giving both positive and negative feedback to their staff.
3. *Rater training*: Where competencies are rated by line managers for selection appraisal, it is most important that they know the pitfalls of rating and do not fall into one of the many traps, which seriously undervalues the numeric (or even verbal) feedback generated. Rater training courses are about the measurement and assessment of competencies to ensure that measurement is accurate and reliable.

10. What are the problems of linking competencies to pay?

This is an enormously complex and sensitive issue and explains why so few competence frameworks drive performance-related pay systems. The issue revolves predominantly around the reliability of the ratings of competence, who rates (boss, peers, subordinate), comparability of ratings across raters (soft, tough, boss), the size of the pay reward relative to base rate of pay, and so on. Certainly, the evidence suggests that the introduction of competency frameworks other than through developmental issues raises expectations that performance/competence will be rewarded (possibly by pay). Although competency frameworks in appraisal are sold on their ability to improve consistency and equality, the opposite is often the case. Both managers and staff are deeply sceptical, even cynical, about all appraisal systems. Introducing a competency framework in the hope that it will cure all the problems of appraisal and performance-related pay is to expect too much.

So what are the characteristics of a good competent framework? In essence, they need to be:

- *Simple*: Parsimonious, not overcomplex, and more understandable than fully comprehensive competency frameworks
- *Salient*: They must be relevant to line mangers, staff, senior managers, and the business objectives and plan.
- *Supported*: They have to be fully supported in terms of staff and money and, most importantly, morally championed consistently from the top.
- *Flexible*: It must be recognized that all systems are temporary and in need of updating regularly, based on changed circumstances.
- *Rewarding*: The application of the system must be rewarded, particularly for line managers and staff. The former need to see that it helps the process of good management and the latter need feedback, qualifications and so on.
- *Developmental*: The idea that the system needs to be initially linked to developmental opportunities for senior managers.
- *Communicated*: The aims, deadlines and benefits of the project need to be spelled out clearly, regularly and simply – and are best not oversold.

- *Adaptable*: The system must allow for certain individual departments to add specific or technical competencies. Departments can have both unique and shared competencies.

Furnham reached several conclusions. He suggested dispensing with the concept of competency because of its associations and ambiguities. He also proposed that 7, plus or minus 2, were enough competencies and that the competency list for any organization should be derived from consultants or focus groups.

Furnham also noted six interesting omissions in the literature:

1. *Succession management and manpower planning*: Although it is easy to see that competencies are useful for succession planning, they tend not to be used exclusively to drive the process. It seems as if the competency framework 'informed' persons responsible for succession planning but did not constrain or limit them to this. Part of the problem seemed to be that the competencies did not take sufficiently into account specialist competencies. Other reasons included not having a succession management strategy, but perhaps the most important problem is that few companies have good databases on the current competencies of their staff.

2. *Filling critical jobs*: It is always nice to show how useful a system/framework is for solving particular problems such as filling critical jobs. Inevitably, these tend to be either highly specialist jobs or very senior middle management jobs. Ironically, most companies' frameworks seemed unsuited for either, particularly the former. Again the language of competencies helped clarify discussions when such posts were filled but seemed not to drive the process.

3. *Predicting future competencies*: Some organizations become aware that frameworks are either too static or too backward looking to be useful. Hence some focused on the issue of potential and the competencies that seemed to predict it. This was not the same as attempting to predict how the competency might have to change to respond to new and different organizations. Thus, for instance, few organizations attempt to do future-oriented strategic planning and to link the anticipated future needs and structure of the company to future frameworks. There seemed little evidence that any one competency would become more or less important over time, let alone which would disappear altogether and which others would emerge over time.

4. *Competencies and leadership*: The success of introducing a competency framework depended heavily on it being championed by high-profile organizational leaders, preferably the CEO and members of the board. However, few talk about the leadership style in the organization (for example, authoritarian, democratic) and how this itself may have helped or hindered the whole process of introducing a competency framework.

Moreover, leadership styles differ in different parts of an organization, and this may have accounted for why the competency framework approach was embedded so easily and quickly in some parts but resisted so much in others. Furthermore, it was never clear whether leadership (as opposed to management) was one of many competencies or super-competencies, or the sum of all (or most) of the competencies put together. The competency movement has in some senses usurped the concept of leadership. There was, for instance, no talk of the different competencies required for transactional versus transformational leaders.

5. *Corporate culture*: In the 1990s there was a great deal of interest in the concept of corporate culture and many attempts were made to assess or categorize culture. It was argued that corporate culture had a very powerful and often 'subliminal effect' on organizations that influenced all aspects of the business, such as structure, systems and processes. Thus one could use various models of corporate culture to predict which organizations would embrace and which would resist the introduction of competency frameworks. The idea of corporate culture was, however, hardly ever mentioned to describe organizational processes or to attempt to explain why they succeeded or failed.

6. *The link between the business plan and the competencies*: Although the textbooks point to the idea that competencies must be derived and driven from the business plan, this seemed more rhetoric than reality. When competency frameworks were being planned, there seemed to be some concern with the linkage, but after that the idea seemed to have been dropped. It is obviously difficult to translate business/strategic plans and concepts to the language of competency. The former is about strategy and process and the latter is about people. Not only is the linkage difficult but also business plans can change radically over the course of a year and from year to year. Thus, even if the link was well established in the first place, it would have to be reforged at least on an annual basis. Because it took companies two or three years to put their initial competency frameworks in place, the process of subsequently updating the plan seemed to slip.

Other researchers have also come to interesting conclusions. Strebler, Robinson and Heron's (1997) findings have clear implications for best practice:

1. Introducing competencies without a clear business purpose raises staff suspicion.
2. The perceived job fit and relevance of competency frameworks influences users' satisfaction.
3. Competencies have made the process of performance review more open.
4. Interpersonal skills are perceived to be the most difficult to assess and develop.

5. Competencies are perceived to improve the consistency and fairness of the assessment and measurement process, but not the outcome (e.g. competency measures).
6. The outcomes of the performance review (e.g. link to pay and/or training) impact on users' confidence with their use of competencies.
7. Competencies raise the expectations that improved performance will be rewarded.

4.6. The Competent Organization

Some writers have talked about competent organizations. Burn and Dearlove (1995) argue that the effectiveness of a competency approach depends on its ability to raise the performance of an organization by improving the performance of everyone in it. They believe that a competent organization will measure and then manage the 'hard' and 'soft' competencies for each job as they follow from the business plan. Burn and Dearlove (1995: 1) describe organizational competencies and associated critical competence indicators and propose the following measurement model:

> We can now pull together the measurement model for the competent organization into six basic steps as follows:
>
> 1. The senior management team identifies the organizational competencies required to support the business strategy and the crucial competence indicators that determine the measurements necessary to validate the competency programme.
> 2. The competency task force translates what is required and cascades this information to managers.
> 3. Changes in individual behaviour and competence are measured by managers and reported to the competency task force.
> 4. Components of the competency development programme are monitored by feedback from participants and task force assessments.
> 5. Results of each of the measures are fed into the competency programme to improve the quality of content and delivery.
> 6. The process is audited continuously at each stage to improve standards of assessment.

One important cause of organizational incompetence is that organizations select managers for particular skills and characteristics that they believe are needed to meet current business demands. But when these demands change, and they can do so very quickly, the skills and characteristics of managers must change. Thus, it is not uncommon for senior managers to discover that they are not as well suited to the new conditions as they were to the old. Some individuals are ideally suited to start-up operations, others to maintaining existing operations and still others to rebuilding.

Gerstein and Reisman (1983) argue that managerial selection should be linked to business strategy. They define various different business situations – start up, turnaround, rationalizing existing business, divesting people (downsizing), maintaining existing business, and making new acquisitions; then they specify the major job thrusts. Following this, they specify the traits or ideal characteristics of managers for each particular phase. Thus, for the situation of liquidation they suggest that managers need the following characteristics – callous, highly analytical, risk taking, low glory seeking, and wanting to be respected but not necessarily liked.

Strategic selection, according to Gerstein and Reisman (1983), involves six steps: specifying business conditions and strategic direction; getting an appropriate organization structure; developing a description for each key managerial job in the structure; assessing key personnel; matching individuals with positions; and implementing the plan.

In this strategic staffing model, incompetent managers are essentially misfits. They have been retained and rewarded by people who believe in the concept of the universal manager – the notion that a good manager can handle any problem, regardless of its peculiar demands. The assumption is that really good managers can adapt to any conditions. Although this may be true of a few talented younger managers, the evidence suggests that it is less true of most managers.

The lesson here is that some managerial incompetence is caused either by poor selection – that is, not getting a good fit in the first place – or by changing circumstances in which a different mix of dispositions and attitudes becomes necessary.

4.7. Reputational Competencies: References and Testimonials

So many organizations think about managers in terms of competencies that reputations have also become organized in these terms. Organizations can then make decisions about people using references and assessment centre performance, because this information is all about reputation. This raises the question of whether traditional references are useful or valid for making decisions about the real competence of managers.

One can obtain information about people's competencies through three sorts of data: self-reports or asking people about themselves, observational data or what others (observers) say about people they have had an opportunity to study, and test data, which may show what people can actually do. Case studies of incompetence in a sense provide test data, but more usually test data come from assessment centres where actual knowledge/ability is measured. Valid test data are expensive to obtain, so most organizations rely on references.

Many business people believe that the best way to find out something about a person is to ask him or her. This presupposes that people both can and will give accurate and honest information. There are many reasons why neither presupposition is necessarily true. Some people cannot tell others about their competencies simply because they do not have sufficient insight. They may exaggerate, understate or distort information about themselves. For example, most people believe that they have a sense of humour and they also believe that they are brighter than their school record shows; neither statement is true for most people. We know that people (neurotics aside) usually process information so as to put themselves in a good light and to maintain positive memories about their past. It is difficult for most people to report on their needs (achievement, abasement, affiliation, dominance, submissiveness), let alone where the needs came from.

Equally, there are good reasons why people will not give honest responses to straightforward questions. Everyone knows about the possible negative consequences of saying what everyone is thinking but no one has the courage (gall) to mention. We are all taught how to say things so as not to hurt other people, and how to market ourselves. The consequence is that, through errors of omission and commission – that is, leaving out things or distorting things – people do not always give factual information.

It is interesting to note that those managers who doubt the utility of personality tests do not doubt the utility of interviews. Somehow they believe that people will 'lie through their teeth' when filling out personality tests but tell the truth in interviews. The data suggest otherwise. It is very difficult to catch fakers in interviews, and the distortions that occur in 'self-reports' occur no matter how you ask people about themselves. Indeed, a mountain of evidence shows that the traditional job interview is the least valid way to select employees.

A second method for evaluating people is to get observational data on them. In business this is called taking up references or getting testimonials. References, as they are typically used, are often a complete waste of time, although, curiously, most organizations spend considerable effort obtaining them.

Despite all we know about the shortcomings of employment interviews and letters of recommendation, these remain the two most prevalent methods of evaluating prospective employees. We have said enough about the employment interview, but what of the hallowed custom of requesting letters of reference and testimonials? Why do we call for them? Are they at all useful or valid? How does one spot lies or attempts to fudge or obfuscate?

Nearly 90% of companies take up references, in part to check the accuracy of information provided by individuals, and in part in the hope of learning something new. Some search references for evidence of negative traits such as absenteeism, dishonesty or maladjustment, but most claim that they are looking for evidence of typical behaviours or personality. Very few are structured in the sense that they ask specific questions with set answers/ratings. Most reference checks ask for a couple of written paragraphs about a person using any preferred format.

Research evidence suggests that the information contained in most references is unreliable in the sense that different referees say very different, possibly opposite, things about a person. The upshot of looking at the sort of qualities (traits, competencies) referees write shows that the 'free-form reference appears to tell you more about its author than about its subject' (Cook, 1998: 69). The only time people agree is at the extremes – when they are describing very good or, more likely, very bad (incompetent) employees.

A reference is defined by the *Shorter Oxford Dictionary* as 'a structure of the qualifications of a person seeking employment or appointment given by somebody familiar with him'. A testimonial is very similar and is defined as 'a written statement of a person's character, abilities or qualifications'. When giving a reference, it is not fair to recommend an employee whom you would not employ yourself. On the other hand, it is essential to remember the importance of good references to someone seeking a household post, so even if you are smarting with annoyance you must be scrupulously fair and explain the good points of the applicant as well as the bad.

Why does the practice of requiring letters of recommendation, requested in numbers roughly proportional to the status of the job, remain so prevalent? When people ask for references, what they are usually doing is trying to increase the size of the selection committee; by adding to the number of people making a judgement on a candidate, they can spread the blame or at least diffuse the responsibility for bad decisions. Furthermore, reference writers are supposed to know the candidate extremely well and be able to comment on his or her behaviour, skills, abilities and temperament, on, as well as off, the job. In this sense, they represent what one might call in medical circles an expert second opinion. From this point of view second opinions seem to be highly desirable, especially given how hard it is to fire people who were mistakenly appointed, or indeed to find out anything that a candidate is trying to hide. And as Cook (1998: 72) has shrewdly noted, 'But references do have one great advantage – they're very cheap, because someone else does all the work, and doesn't expect to be paid'.

Requests for references come in many forms, as indeed do testimonials, although we don't receive as many of the latter. Some requests simply tell the referee that a person known to them (and presumably nominated by them) has applied for a certain position and would they be so kind as to state the extent to which they feel the candidate is suitable. Other requests require one to comment on a range of features of job-related behaviours of the candidate, such as the extent to which they are punctual, socially adept, computer literate, hypochondriacal and so on. More commonly, references ask one to fill out rating scales going from outstanding to poor, using schoolmaster phrases like satisfactory and average. The rating scales resemble those seldom-completed questionnaires used by hotel chains that boast complete homogeneity of decor and cuisine, irrespective of the country in which they are located. And, of course, they include a stamped addressed envelope to encourage compliance.

There are three factors that render references pretty worthless: the referees are nominated by the candidate and so are biased; there are unwritten, implicit and hence ambiguous rules for writing references in code; and one cannot be sure of the motives of the writer who completed the reference.

The first problem lies in the source of the references. Some interview panels are non-specific and request letters from 'two people who know you well'. Others specifically request letters from your boss, immediate superior, former lecturer – but these often give the candidate pretty extensive leeway to choose another. For instance, if your immediate superior will not write a good (and possibly dishonest) reference, you simply go up the ladder or along the 'organogram' to find somebody who will. It is comparatively rare that candidates are required to obtain a reference from someone mentioned by name, and hence the exact choice of reference writer is open to potential abuse.

The second problem is that references are written in a sort of code of their own, and the code is often hard to crack. References are, in our experience, a bit like low-church funeral eulogies, containing only praise. They are dreadfully one-sided and it is, on occasion, difficult to recognize either the dearly departed or the refereed, however well you knew them. Some nationalities are worse than others – they write as if every student is an Einstein, every worker a Stakonovite, every leader a Churchill. These references are worthless because they fail to discriminate the able from the unable, the competent from the incompetent, the efficient from the inefficient.

The final problem lies in the motives of the reference writer. The loss of any employee has consequences – some good, others bad – and it is difficult to see how these might not influence the writer of a reference.

Studies in the area of organizational behaviour and personnel psychology show that letters of reference on applicant competence do not predict future job performance. This is mainly because they are too homogeneous with respect to the evaluation of applicant attributes and qualifications, because everyone is characterized as 'somewhat desirable'. However, some negative comments among the positive may be seen as a sign of honesty on the part of the referee. Often references have been shown to be invalid because of the unreliability of what they were attempting to predict – that is, supervisors' ratings. What is clear is that references are never as good as ability tests.

Many intelligent and sceptical employers and educators believe that, with a modicum of common sense, the process of selection is straightforward. This is far from being the case, as people who have studied the issue know, even to their own cost. Outdated, invalid and corruptible methods are still used to select staff and students, and misplaced faith is invested in them. Letters of reference are, in general, too susceptible to bias of one form or another to be of any real value in assisting the generally difficult process of selection, appointment and promotion.

References can be useful, however, under particular conditions:

A. *Forced Choice Format*: Where the referee has to decide between pairs of equally good (soundly desirable) or bad (undesirable) characteristics:

Works fast and accurately   Frequently absent
Comes up with novel solutions   Disliked by work colleagues

B. *Key Word Counting*: Studies have shown that lay people tend to use words that fall into natural groups. Thus agreeableness or cooperative is written as congenial, good-natured and accommodating; intelligence is described as mental agility, ingeniousness, imaginativeness; extraversion as urbane, talkative, bold; conscientiousness as dependable, persistent, tenacious; and so on. The more words in one category, the more accurate the trait descriptor.

C. *Referee Credibility*: It helps if referees are bright, articulate and observant, but it is more important that referees be critical in the best sense of the word and that they are accurate. Perhaps the best way to ensure accuracy is to let them believe that their credibility is at stake. In that way, accuracy is rewarded and the opposite is punished, in the sense that it affects your reputation.

4.8. Conclusion

The competence concept brought both advantages and disadvantages to practitioners of human relations. It brought a common, shared descriptive language to talk about individuals at work and their unique performance. However, it also brought a lot of meaningless psychobabble such as 'take the helicopter view' or 'think outside the box'. It also stressed the need for the measurement of performance and the benefits of giving people regular and specific feedback on that performance. Watson-Wyatt (1998), an international consultancy, noted six benefits of the competency system:

• Articulating what the organization values.
• Providing a common language for employees and managers to describe value creation.

- Establishing a new paradigm for HR programmes (organizational levers).
- Focusing on the development of the individual instead of on the organization structure.
- Linking pay, promotions and growth directly to what the organization values as successful.
- Guiding employees and managers to what is expected and how value is defined even in times of dramatic change and restructuring.

If HR specialists brought in competence frameworks that were simple, salient, flexible, rewarding and adaptable, and that stressed the need for personal development, they were usually successful. However, they often failed. The most common reasons were not having enough or the right 'champion' to introduce the competency framework from the start – that is, senior managers did not really believe in it. The development phase was too long and drawn out, and was out of date by the time it was introduced. Then the framework itself was too complicated and inclusive to be easily understandable and usable. Some companies would have 35 competencies, which is far too many when we know that people have only 5–7 clearly identifiable unique traits. Next, line managers received confused messages about the use and purpose of the system, and they felt they were 'oversold' on it early on, and then experienced it as a bureaucratic burden. Another problem concerned not understanding the need for flexibility, in that frameworks require constant updating. As organizations and jobs change, so do the competencies of the people within. Another failing is not allowing for a distinction between general vs specific/technical frameworks and not ensuring that the business plan and the competency framework remain aligned as the former changes over time.

Your reputation in organizations matters greatly in organizational life. Reputations have to be nurtured, protected and given 'spin'. The idea of collecting references and testimonials on people's competencies is fraught with problems. Unless it is done thoughtfully, the reputation of a person as manifest in references about him or her may be extremely misleading, and may tell more about the writer of the reference than the competency of the subject of the reference.

PART II
THE CAUSES OF
INCOMPETENCE

CHAPTER FIVE

The Causes of Incompetencies: Personality Traits

5.1. Introduction

As noted before, this chapter starts the second and core part of the book. The next three chapters are concerned with the psychology of individual differences. Chapter 5 deals with what psychologists call (normal) personality traits. Chapter 6 deals with what psychiatrists call (abnormal) personality disorder. Chapter 7 deals with what sociologists call teamwork.

An understanding of 'what makes people tick' is essentially the psychology of personality and individual difference. It is the branch of psychology that is concerned with the cause and consequence of individual differences.

In this chapter we shall consider the concept of personality and that of personality–job fit. At first normal personality will be considered but in the next chapter abnormal psychology will be considered. The argument is this: the wrong personality type in the wrong job clearly leads to incompetencies. Second, a manager with a personality disorder is a disaster waiting to happen.

For a hundred years psychologists have tried to describe as parsimoniously, as non-tautologically and as scientifically as possible the nature of personality. There are almost 20,000 trait words in English. Some are used by psychologists in a 'technical' sense, and others are almost ignored by trait researchers. Words such as stoicism, fortitude and integrity are strangely missing from many personality systems. Lay people describe and explain behaviour that they see (in others) by the use of trait words – for example, 'He is an extravert', 'She is impulsive', 'They are neurotic', even 'He has no personality'. However, because these words are used to describe behaviour, this does not mean that they are always scientifically useful.

Even some psychologists never escape the tautological loop of, for example, saying that an extravert is impulsive and sociable, and that sociable and impulsive people are extraverts, but never offering an explanation for the origins of traits and the mechanisms and processes whereby they influence behaviour. The central question is what leads extraverts to behave in a particular way that seems consistent across situations and stable over time. Most scientist and lay people believe in the *causal primacy of traits*. Although it is agreed that this works at many levels, and can be indirect, it is assumed that traits shape and structure (and hence predict) behaviour. Furthermore, most agree that traits are fundamental (biologically based and stable over time), not simply a superficial mask that is negotiable in different social encounters. Deary and Matthews (1993) argue that the trait approach is not only 'alive and well', but is flourishing. They highlight various 'bright spots' in current trait theory:

- growing agreement concerning the number, character and stability of personality dimensions;
- a greater understanding of the heritability of personality traits, and hence a greater appreciation of the role of the environment;
- a growing sophistication of research which aims to describe the biological and social bases of trait differences;
- an appreciation of the extent to which personality differences predict outcomes, or act as moderators, in cognitive and health settings.

They assert, as many others have done before them, two fundamental points:

1. *The Primary Causality of Traits* – the idea that causality flows from traits to behaviour and that, although there is a feedback loop, it is less important. Personality leads to both competent and incompetent management behaviour.
2. *The Inner Locus of Traits* – the idea that traits describe the fundamental core qualities of a person that are latent rather than manifest. That is, traits are the essence of personality.

The causes of personality traits have always been acknowledged to be both biological *and* social. The evidence for the former is primarily based on behaviour genetics. The fact that there were so many competing theories, typologies and measures of traits did not serve the trait position well. There is growing consensus over the emergence of the 'Big Five' as fundamental higher-order orthogonal factors. The 1980s and 1990s have been dominated by the five-factor model (FFM) of traits. What this means is that many personality psychologists have accepted that there are five fundamental (higher-order), orthogonal (independent of one another) personality traits (these will be described later).

Traits psychologists aim to develop a comprehensive but parsimonious and powerful theory of personality. For nearly 100 years the psychometric approach has been characterized by the construction and refinement of questionnaires through multivariate statistics. The fundamental aim is to develop reliable and valid measures that accurately measure the fundamental traits. Some theories attempt to combine measures of ability, motivation, personality and mood, but most stick to traits alone. Perhaps the most celebrated of all traits is extraversion. This construct can be found in the writings of Hippocrates and Galen, Wundt and Jung, and Eysenck and Cattell. It can be measured by self-report (questionnaire) and by ratings by others, as well as by indirect or objective measures such as salivation after receiving 'lemon drops' in the mouth, colour preference or speed of reaction.

Moods, by definition, vary – traits do not. Thus you can distinguish between trait and state anxiety. Even people with very low trait anxiety can be measured in the same way, but they are psychometrically different. Therefore trait anxiety should correlate with neuroticism (another trait), whereas state anxiety does not. Equally, state anxiety should correlate with other concurrently assessed negative mood measures, whereas trait anxiety does not. Usually, trait factors are better predictors of behaviour than state factors, but, in extreme situations, various state factors can have very powerful effects on behaviour.

State factors, like trait factors, can be measured by questionnaire, and it is possible to try to determine the fundamental dimensions of mood. Experimentalists find that mood is fairly easy to manipulate through films, music or drugs, to test their effects on behaviour. Yet moods are a mix of biological, cognitive and social influences.

It is also important to distinguish between traits and types. *Types* (for example, gender) are regarded as categories of membership that are distinct and discontinuous. People are either the one or the other. Most people think in terms of types. In *trait* theories, people differ along a continuum. Trait theorists see the difference between individuals quantitatively rather than qualitatively. Typologies are out of fashion academically because assignment has often proved to be too arbitrary and unreliable. After all, even gender is not absolutely perfect. Trait theories often talk in typological terms, but think of traits as continuously (often normally) distributed. One way to contrast the two is shown in Table 5.1.

Table 5.1 The differences between traits and types

Trait theory	Type theory
Concerned with universals possessed in different amounts	Concerned with preferences which are perhaps inborn or learned
Involves measuring	Involves sorting
Extreme scores are important for discrimination	Midpoint is crucial for discrimination
Normally distributed	Skewed distribution
Scores mean amount of trait possessed	Scores indicate confidence that sorting is correct

We shall consider three types of theories in this chapter. First, typological theories without any theoretical base will be looked at. These remain remarkably popular among lay people. Next, we shall look at typological theories with a theoretical base, primarily because some are the most well known in the world. Third, we shall examine evidence-based trait theory, which is state-of-the-art, good science. And thus the last part of the book, which examines fit and misfit, will concentrate specifically on trait theory.

5.2. Typologies without theories

As noted in Chapter 2 (section 2.3) under 'The difficult people approach', a number of books adopt a typological approach to attempting to understand people. Essentially they fall into two groups: theory driven and not theory driven. The latter tend to be 'wise and witty', and books that adopt this approach sell well. Consider as an example of this work a book by John Wareham (1986) entitled *Basic Business Types: The Characters You Need to Know about to Succeed in Business*. The author describes 21 types, which he says are useful in analysing a potential spouse as well as friends and work colleagues. He claims the list is not exhaustive and that you may have problems identifying your type. He suggests you may build a new profile for yourself.

Wareham admits that some of his business types are 'partly or wholly negative' but believes that 'apparently wonderful people can also be incompetent and foolish, vainglorious and vexing, vicious and vindictive' (1986: 20). He is, however, very concerned about the stability of his types. He notes: 'I was also amazed at the way in which people stay in the character of the type' (1986: 19) and later, 'The bright side in all of this is that some people can change when the darker side of their own nature is held up to them. Not many alas. But some' (1986: 21).

Various features of each type are presented. Twelve of these are shown below in the order in which they appear in the book.

1. Emperor

Basic type:	Founder and/or creative force behind a business empire.
Façade:	Charming, no-nonsense, realistic, pragmatic.
Favourite saying:	'Let's *do* it.'
Apparent objective:	To lead a successful business empire to ever greater heights.
Real objectives:	To fulfil high familial expectations. To compensate for a sense of inferiority relative to forces outside his family.
Underlying emotions:	Aggressive, steely, guilt free, untroubled by self-doubt but still driven to 'prove himself'.
Management style:	Benevolent autocrat.
Strengths:	Energy, acumen, creativity, negotiating ability, charm, strength under pressure.

Weakness:	Not always understanding of insecurity in others, so can sometimes be a poor judge of people – thinks they are as well adjusted as he is. No major flaws, though.
How to spot:	Father is or was a successful businessman, often highly so.
	Extremely ambitious.
	Usually eldest child.
	Record of success in practically everything he touches.
	Quick learner.
	Many interests, and can turn his hand to virtually anything.
	Strong understanding of the technical side of his industry.
	Usually shows a record of election to leadership roles.
	Charming but unctuous.
	Possesses genuine presence or charisma.
	(Wareham, 1986: 33–4)

2. Queen Bee

Basic type:	Outstanding female executive or entrepreneur.
Façade:	Charming, warm, confident, poised.
Favourite saying:	'My father always used to say anything's possible if you give it your best shot.'
	'Frankly, I'm very glad to have been born a woman.'
Apparent objective:	To achieve, to be the best.
Real objectives:	To achieve, to be the best, thereby making good on the subconscious psychic understanding reached with her father.
Underlying emotions:	Ambition, aggression, steely determination to dominate.
Management style:	Benevolent autocrat.
Strengths:	Energy, industry, judgement, cool head.
Weakness:	No major flaws. Minor flaw might be lack of a stable domestic support system.
How to spot:	Only or eldest child.
	Outstanding history of achievement in most phases of life.
	Charming but not overtly manipulative.
	Tactful.
	Often mentions father, clearly as role model.
	Feels confident in her success.
	Has almost always been in line management.
	First-class presentation. Discretely well dressed. Does not wear imitation of male uniform.
	Likely to have been divorced.
	Current husband or partner often either passive or drone, or altogether a totally well adjusted person, happy to share Queen Bee's success.
How to manage:	Give her all the responsibility she can handle – then get out of her way. (Wareham, 1986: 38–9)

3. Sidekick

Basic type:	In theory, the boss's closest associate and most loyal aide.
Façade:	Dedicated, loyal, hardworking, 'crisp'.
Favourite saying:	'Don't do anything till I check with the boss.'
	'The boss says we should ...'
	'You said it yourself, Boss, we should ...'
	'Yes, Boss.'
Apparent objective:	To be the loyal servant to his boss.
Real objective:	Right hand:
	To be the loyal servant to his boss and the organization.
	Left hand:
	To gain personal power, status, and security by serving a powerful chief executive.
Underlying emotions:	Right hand:
	Basically a well-adjusted person.
	Left hand:
	Feelings of inferiority, high power needs, strong ambivalence towards authority.
Strengths:	Right hand:
	Rationality, organizational ability, clear-headedness, fundamentally sound emotional adjustment.
	Left hand:
	Political skills, detail orientation, subtle persuasive skills, manipulative abilities.
Weaknesses:	Right hand:
	Lack of creativity, lack of charisma.
	Left hand:
	Basically impotent, indecisive, bureaucratic, considers virtually all tasks in light of own survival needs, chronic yes-man.
How to spot:	Right hand:
	Administrative but not leadership success. Lacks sharp cutting edge, creative accomplishment. Most roles 'assistant to'.
	Left hand:
	Mentions devotion to the Chairman, highly deferential to him, likely ever to have held only staff positions, seldom makes a clear-cut position (except to support his boss), subtly isolates chief executive, attracted to autocratic bosses.
How to manage:	Right hand:
	Nurture, involve, reward.
	Left hand:
	Shun. (Wareham, 1986: 48–9)

4. Gatekeeper

Basic type:	Screener of the chief's incoming telephone calls and scheduler of his or her appointments.
Façade:	Professional, arm's length relationship.
Favourite saying:	'Let me just see if the boss is in conference.'

	'I'm not sure that the boss will be available.'
	'Perhaps *I* might be able to help.'
	'I'm sorry you feel that way.'
Apparent objective:	To be the loyal servant to the boss.
Real objectives:	Often to build own status, or to manipulate or mother a father figure.
Underlying emotions:	Often highly ambivalent towards people seeking to contact chief executive.
Strengths:	Inside knowledge of the boss.
Weakness:	Can become hindrance to communication.
How to spot:	Solicitous of authoritative figures.
	Likely ever to have held only staff roles.
	Apparently highly trusted by the chief executive.
	Cool and detached yet authoritative manner.
How to manage:	Establish honest professional relationship. (Wareham, 1986: 56–8)

5. Wiseman

Basic type:	Idealized adult and mysterious sage.
Façade:	Wise, clever, witty, adult, a little mysterious.
Favourite saying:	'I think the key issues here are ...'
	'In my experience, this kind of thing ...'
	'It might be wise to ...'
	'In this kind of situation it's best to ...'
	'My feel for this kind of thing is ...'
Apparent objective:	To help and save the MD, the entire company, or both.
Real objectives:	To earn a living and win status.
Underlying emotions:	Status conscious, fearful, money and power hungry.
Management style:	Charismatic autocrat.
Strengths:	Certitude.
	Intellectual and verbal skills.
	Creativity.
	Specific industry knowledge.
Weakness:	Not as knowledgeable as he seems.
	Despite aura of authority, doesn't really know all the answers.
	Can be totally wrong.
	Often impractical.
	Not a team player.
How to spot:	Impressive or unusual appearance, often including facial hair.
	Speaks with apparent great authority.
	May wear attention-getting garb.
	Interested in cerebral pleasures.
	Has been or talks about being published.
	May have been in the services, the church or prison.
	Politically attuned.
	Has earned a living by his wits.
	Seeks advisory role.

	Promulgates a pet theory.
	Good fun to be with.
	Wants to work on retainer.
	Has absorbing part-time interest(s).
How to manage:	Heed but never become dependent upon.
	Entirely self-absorbed.
	Not truly interested in accomplishment. Self-destructive.
	(Wareham, 1986: 68–9)

6. Gonnabee

Basic type:	Status-seeking reactive–dependent.
Façade:	Aggressive, tough, macho, highly confident.
Favourite saying:	'When the going gets tough, the tough get going.'
Apparent objective:	To become a tycoon, or a mini-tycoon.
Real objective:	To compensate for feelings of inferiority by becoming a 'Big Shot'.
Underlying emotions:	Anxious, insecure, fearful, hostile, angry in the extreme.
Management style:	Angry autocrat.
Strength:	Highly manipulative.
Weaknesses:	Inherently unsuited to the role to which he aspires.
	Emotionally weak, highly dependent.
	Poor judgement.
	Overprotected upbringing.
	Living beyond personal means.
	Broken marriage(s).
	Speaks lovingly of his mother.
How to manage:	Place only in sales role.
	Organize his work and hours.
	Structure role carefully.
	Build in checks to prevent customer abuse.
	Give high status for high performance.
	Focus hostilities in sales competition.
	Let go rather than promote. (Wareham, 1986: 76–8)

7. Wooer

Basic type:	Male, reactive–dependent, compulsive salesman, star of the sales team.
Façade:	Loving, warm, sincere, dynamic. A sales 'magician'. Vitally happy, not a care in the world.
Favourite saying:	'Say, *you're* looking great.'
	'Nothing happens till someone sells someone something.'
	'Before you sell anyone anything, you've gotta sell yourself.'
	'Can I be honest with you?'
	'Trust me.'
Apparent objectives:	To overcome all obstacles and consummate sales.
Real objectives:	To punish his father and seduce his mother.
	To win status, attention, love. To compensate for anxious feelings of inferiority, hostility and frustration.

Underlying emotions:	Guilt, anxiety, hostility, sense of inferiority, wish to 'get even' and to be centre of attention.
Management style:	Manipulative abdicator.
Strengths:	Compulsion to find and sell to new prospects. Immense charm.
Weaknesses:	Poor judgement. Very little self-discipline. Unrealistic, a wishful thinker. Antipathy to authority. Emotional dependence. Self-destructive tendencies.
How to spot:	Quickly on first-name terms. Dress calculated to win approval. Takes command of interview. Strongly empathetic. Boasts achievement. Critical of politicians, police, past employers. Expelled from school or college. Signs of underlying frustration. May drink heavily. Running to fat. Status conscious. Dominant, well-bred wife. Sales experience with large corporation. Higher education uncompleted.
How to manage:	Place only in sales role. Nurture, build esteem. Structure role carefully. Award status. Let go rather than promote. (Wareham, 1986: 92–4)

8. Footie

Basic type:	Salesperson and aspiring local business leader. Former jock, of sorts.
Façade:	Hale and hearty good fellow.
Favourite saying:	'It used to be that ...' 'When I was at school I remember ...' 'When I was the captain of the football team ...' 'Can you believe they've made that wimpy bastard executive president?'
Apparent objective:	To be an achiever and family man.
Real objective:	To retrieve and maintain the level of status achieved at high school.
Underlying emotions:	Insecure, worried, extremely anxious. Frightened of wimps.
Management style:	Sports coach.
Strengths:	Strong achievement needs. Affable, outgoing. Useful sales skills.

	Fairly practical.
Weaknesses:	Poor performer under pressure.
	Modest intellect.
	Unimaginative.
	Basically dependent.
How to spot:	Imposing appearance, thick build, tall.
	Former high school sports star.
	Uses heartiness to impose viewpoint.
	Unimaginative.
	Basically dependent.
	Dull.
How to manage:	Nurture, build esteem.
	Structure role carefully.
	Provide all possible training.
	Award status.
	Pay for results achieved. (Wareham, 1986: 100–2)

9. Boxer

Basic type:	The workhorse of the sales team.
Façade:	Dedicated, loyal, hard-working company man.
Favourite sayings:	'For the good of the team we might try to ...'
	'Have you looked at my long-term contribution?'
	'I'm not sure you're hearing me ...'
Apparent objective:	To be a professional salesperson.
Real objective:	To gain status and self-esteem by serving others, and being 'on the team'.
Underlying emotions:	Feelings of inferiority.
	Extreme frustration with the company.
	Internalized anger.
Strengths:	Strong need to attain results.
	Hard working.
	Useful sales skills.
	Practical.
	Highly persevering.
Weaknesses:	Poor presentation. (Wareham, 1986: 109–10)

10. Maverick

Basic type:	Small- to medium-sized entrepreneur.
Façade:	Confident go-getter.
Favourite sayings:	'They can't do that to me.'
	'I'll show them.'
	'Get that interfering son-of-a-bitch out of here.'
Apparent objective:	To be an entrepreneur and mini-tycoon.
Real objective:	To win autonomy, thereby beating out his father to earn his mother's favour.
Underlying emotions:	Optimistic to one level of business success.
	Fearful of building a larger business than he can handle personally.
Management style:	Autocratic, domineering, impatient.

Strengths:	Innovative, strong drive, good people skills, highly motivated.
Weaknesses:	Antipathy to authority impairs growth potential.
	Unable to cope with major success.
	Perfectionist.
	Opinionated, difficult to work with.
How to spot:	Profit-oriented youthful activity.
	Aversive to authority figures or institutions.
	Somewhat zealous in pursuit of own goals.
	Self-employed (of course).
	Father self-employed.
	Smouldering resentment of father (often masked).
	Warm feelings towards mother.
	Restless spirit.
	Egotistical, opinionated.
	Difficulties with own children.
How to manage:	Best not to hire.
	Not a good prospect for partnership.
	If hired, then define clear area of responsibility and leave alone, holding accountable only for final results.
	(Wareham, 1986: 116–17)

11. Smallshot

Basic type:	Son of the founder of a medium-sized successful business. A reactive–dependent.
Façade:	Arrogant, tough, macho, highly confident.
Favourite sayings:	'Business is much more sophisticated these days.'
	'I'm not gonna get mad, I'm gonna get even.'
Apparent objective:	To become a tycoon.
Real objectives:	To prove he's better than the 'old man'.
	To compensate for feelings of inferiority.
Underlying emotions:	Anxious, insecure, fearful, extremely hostile.
Management style:	Autocratic.
Strengths:	Manipulative, driven.
Weaknesses:	Extremely poor judgement.
	Unrealistic, a wishful thinker.
	Refuses to accept authority.
	Highly dependent.
	Self-destructive.
How to spot:	Black sheep of well-to-do family.
	Father a successful businessman.
	Highly ambitious.
	Critical of politicians, police, past employers.
	Expelled from school or university.
	Overindulged upbringing.
	Living beyond personal means.
	Broken marriage(s).
How to manage:	Place in high-status low-supervisory role.
	Get him professional help.
	Let go rather than promote. (Wareham, 1986: 124–5)

12. Boy scout

Basic type:	Overqualified clerk or bureaucrat.
Façade:	Dedicated, loyal, hard-working, go-getting company man.
Favourite saying:	'What is the game plan, exactly?'
	'The book says we have to ...'
	'Surely we cannot make exceptions?'
Apparent objective:	To serve a great company or a fine master.
Real objective:	To be saved from an apparently threatening world.
Underlying emotions:	Fearful, insecure, pious, extremely low tolerance for ambiguous situations.
	Resentful in later life.
Management style:	Missionary or scout leader.
Strengths:	Strong achievement needs.
	Technically well qualified.
	Highly educated.
	Wants to be a 'team player'.
Weaknesses:	Impotent.
	Neither a leader nor possessing leadership material.
	Naïve in the extreme.
	Cannot really think for himself.
How to spot:	Overeducated.
	Works for a large, highly structured organization.
	Religious, pious.
	Attracted to punishing athletic sports.
	Spouse the dominant partner.
	Spouse older than Boy scout.
	Highly perfectionist.
	Conformist upbringing.
	Parents lower-middle class.
How to manage:	Structure the job tightly.
	Put into staff role.
	Exploit technical expertise. (Wareham, 1986: 134–5)

There are, however, major problems with this approach if one is to take it seriously. Inevitably the first question refers to *the evidence* on which the whole façade is built. How good is that evidence? Is it open to public scrutiny? Are different interpretations of it possible?

The second question refers to the *parsimony* of the types. Are there 12 uniquely identifiable types or, as the author suggests, can we go on adding others? On those grounds, is one permitted or advised to do so? Can people belong to more than one type at a time and, if so, does that not really threaten the whole concept of type? A good typology is like the periodic table in chemistry. It describes unique, unrelated elements and how they 'fit logically'.

Third, the descriptions do not say anything about *aetiology*: how did people come to be that way? Are the types 'hardwired', by biology or the result of experience at or before work? What critical experiences lead to what outcome? We are not told but aetiology is important because it tells us about progression.

Fourth, the typology provides *no insight into mechanism or process* – that is, it does not explain how the 'real objectives' and the 'underlying emotions' influence behaviour. The basic question is what leads a person to become a type: what biological and social processes define the cause type?

Finally, the typologies are *silent on change*. Can people change types? Who, when, how? Are some happy not to change while others are desperate to do so? Are some relatively easy to change and others well nigh impossible?

It is all very well being amused but there can be as much amusement as frustration resulting from this approach.

5.3. Types with Theories

The most well-known personality test in the world is a type indicator based on a theory. It has been suggested that it is completed every minute somewhere. The test is called the MBTI or the Myers Briggs Type Indicator. Academic psychometricians are puzzled by the test's success given its problems but tend to interpret it in terms of the aggressive marketing of test publishers and the use of it by trainers and consultants who find it difficult to keep up with new developments. Moore (1987) has noted that the use of personality tests in industry is wide, and Haley and Stumpf (1989) have pointed out, quite correctly, that the popularity of the MBTI in executive circles affords researchers tremendous opportunities for research. Moore (1987) noted that most companies use the MBTI to help managers understand better how they come across to others who may see things differently. Other applications include team building, improving customer service, smoothing out group differences, working on projects, adapting to change, analysing troubles, behaviour between employees, and between employees and their jobs, and facilitating competitive strategic thinking.

The test results in a four-letter typology. Thus you may be an ENTJ or an ISFP or any one of 16 combinations. Hirsh and Kummerow (1989) have looked at work style preferences of the four type dimensions:

- *Extraversion–introversion:* The extraversion (E) and introversion (I) preferences are applicable to the work that people choose, the work setting that maximizes their strengths, and the kinds of workers with whom they feel most congenial and productive. Extraverts enjoy a work setting that is activity oriented, has variety, and allows for frequent interactions with others. Introverts enjoy a work setting that is quiet and private, and that allows for concentration on the task.

They further note:

Extraverts frequently choose occupations that encourage activity and interaction with others on a regular and frequent basis. Introverts frequently choose occupations that encourage reflection and in-depth concentration on concepts and ideas.

While extraverts can and do enter all occupations, some are more appealing to them than others. According to available research, some occupations (in alphabetical order) seem to be especially attractive to extraverts: consultant, dental assistant, food service worker, home economist, insurance agent, marketeer, receptionist, restaurant manager, sales manager, sales clerk, and other occupations in which they can put their energy to active use. These occupations are not meant to be an exhaustive list but serve to illustrate some areas that an extravert might enjoy.

While introverts can and do enter all occupations, some are more appealing to them than others. According to available research, some occupations (in alphabetical order) seem to be especially attractive to introverts: chemist, computer programmer, electrical engineer, lawyer, legal secretary, librarian, maths teacher, mechanic, surveyor, technician, and other occupations in which their energy is focused internally on facts or ideas. These occupations are not meant to be an exhaustive list but serve to illustrate some areas that an introvert might enjoy. (Hirsh and Kummerow, 1989: 20)

I am more likely to work like an extravert and:	*I am more likely to work like an introvert and*:
Become impatient and bored when my work is slow and unchanging.	Become impatient and annoyed when my work is interrupted and rushed.
Seek a variety of action-oriented tasks.	Seek quiet to concentrate.
Be focused equally on what is going on in the work site as well as with my work.	Be focused more on the work itself than on what is going on in the work site.
Respond quickly to requests and spring into action without much advanced thinking.	Think through requests before responding, even to the point of delaying action.
Enjoy the phone calls as a welcome diversion.	Find phone calls intrusive, especially when concentrating.
Develop my ideas through discussion.	Develop my ideas through reflection.
Use outside resources to complete my task.	Use myself as my basic resource to complete my tasks.
Need frequent changes in pace and seek outside events.	Get caught up in my work and disregard outside events.

(Hirsh and Kummerow, 1989: 17–18)

- *Sensing–intuition*: The sensing (S) and intuition (N) preferences are applicable to the work that people choose, the work setting that maximizes their strengths, and the kinds of workers with whom they feel most congenial and productive. Sensors generally choose a work setting that produces practical, useful products or services for people or organizations. They are likely to be where they are able to use their sensing preference to work carefully with people, things and data. They tend to prefer work settings that allow them to learn a skill and practise it to the point of mastery. Intuitives are likely to choose a work setting that produces new products or services. They like to be where they are able to use their intuition preference to meet future need or to find new possibilities for people, things and data. They tend to prefer work settings that allow them the opportunity to learn continually to do new things:

I am more likely to work like a sensor and:	*I am more likely to work like an intuitive and:*
Use my previously acquired work experience.	Do things differently than my previous work experience may dictate.
Appreciate standard ways to solve problems and reach solutions. Apply skills that are already developed, rather than take the time to learn new ones.	Use new and different ways to solve problems and reach solutions. Enjoy learning new skills for the challenge and novelty involved.
Distrust and ignore my inspirations.	Follow my inspirations regardless of the facts.
Like things to be concrete and seldom make errors of fact.	Like things to be generally stated and seldom worry about specific facts.
Prefer work that has a practical aspect to it. Want to understand how the details of my work make up a complete picture. Prefer to continue with what is tried and true and make adjustments for fine tuning.	Prefer work that has an innovative aspect to it. Want to see what is involved in the overall picture first and then fill in the details. Prefer change, often with major readjustments, to continuing on with what is.

(Hirsh and Kummerow, 1989: 31–2)

Hirsh and Kummerow (1989) note:

Sensing types frequently choose occupations that require more hands-on experience and direct experience dealing accurately with problems. Usually the jobs sensors enjoy call for attending to and mastering detail. Intuitives frequently choose occupations that call for seeing relationships and patterns and dealing with them. Usually the jobs that intuitives enjoy call for attending to underlying meaning and anticipating future possibilities and needs.

While sensors can and do enter all occupations, some are more appealing to them than others. According to available research, some occupations (in alphabetical order) seem especially attractive to sensors: accountant, bank manager, cleaning service worker, dentist, farmer, food service worker, law enforcement officer, mid-level manager, secretary, steelworker, and other occupations that allow for specific experience. These occupations are not meant to be an exhaustive list but serve to illustrate some areas that sensors might enjoy.

While intuitives can and do enter all occupations, some are more appealing to them than others. According to available research, some occupations (in alphabetical order) seem especially attractive to intuitives: artist, attorney, clergy, consultant, counsellor, entertainer, journalist, psychologist, social scientist, writer, and other occupations that allow for generalisation. These occupations are not meant to be an exhaustive list but serve to illustrate some areas that intuitives might enjoy. (Hirsh and Kummerow, 1989: 35–6)

- *Thinking–feeling*: The thinking (T) and feeling (F) preferences are applicable to the jobs that people choose, the work settings that maximize their strengths, and the kind of workers with whom they feel most congenial and productive. Thinkers are likely to choose a work setting that is more impersonal and governed by logic. Feelers tend to prefer a work setting that is personal, focusing on relationships between people and meeting people's personal need:

I am more likely to work like a thinker and:	*I am more likely to work like a feeler and*:
Orient myself toward the tasks.	Orient myself toward my relationships.
Like harmony, but can get along without it and still be effective at work.	Need harmony in order to work most effectively.
Use logic and analysis as a basis for my work.	Include others' opinions in addition to my personal values as a basis for my work.
Hurt people's feelings without being aware of it.	Pay attention to others' feelings and enjoy pleasing them even in unimportant things.
Decide impersonally and sometimes overlook others' wishes so I can get my work done.	Allow others' likes and dislikes to influence my decisions, sometimes taking precedence over getting my work done.
Manage and deal firmly with others.	Manage and relate sympathetically with others.
Readily offer criticisms or suggestions for improvement.	Avoid and dislike giving and receiving unpleasant feedback, even when well deserved.
Factor in principles and truths when making work-related decisions.	Factor in underlying values and human needs when making work-related decisions.

(Hirsh and Kummerow, 1989: 46–7)

As regards career information, Hirsh and Kummerow note:

Thinking types frequently choose occupations that encourage the use of logical and impersonal analysis. Feeling types frequently choose occupations that have a values basis and involve people relating personally.

While thinkers can and do enter all occupations, some are more appealing to them than others. According to available research, some occupations (in alphabetical order) seem especially attractive to thinkers: attorney, auditor, bank officer, chemist, computer systems analyst, engineer, farmer, manager, police officer, systems researcher, and other occupations that allow them to be logical. These occupations are not meant to be an exhaustive list but serve to illustrate some areas that thinkers might enjoy.

While feelers can and do enter all occupations, some are more appealing to them than others. According to available research, some occupations (in alphabetical order) seem especially attractive to thinkers: child care worker, clerical supervisor, clergy, counsellor, dental hygienist, librarian, nurse, physical therapist, secretary, school teacher, and other occupations that reflect their values. These occupations are not meant to be an exhaustive list but serve to illustrate some areas that feelers might enjoy. (Hirsh and Kummerow, 1989: 49)

- *Judgement–perception*: The judgement (J) and perception (P) preferences relate to the work that people choose, the settings that maximize their strengths, and the kinds of worker with whom they feel more congenial and productive. Judgers are likely to choose a work setting that is structured and organized, with plans in place. Perceptives tend to prefer a work setting that is spontaneous, flexible and open to change. Perceptives like gathering information as part of their work:

I am more likely to work like a judger and:	I am more likely to work like a perceptive and:
Do my best when I can plan my work and work my plan.	Do my best when I can deal with needs as they arise.
Enjoy getting things settled and finished.	Enjoy keeping things open for last-minute changes.
Like checking items off my 'to do' list.	Ignore my 'to do' list even if I make one.
Overlook new things that need to be done in order to complete my current job.	Postpone my current tasks to meet momentary needs.
Narrow down the possibilities and be satisfied once I reach a decision.	Resist being tied down to a decision in order to gather more information.
Decide quickly and seek closure.	Put off decisions to seek options.
Seek structure in scheduling myself and others.	Resist structure and favour changing circumstances.
Prefer to regulate and control my work and that of others.	Prefer to free up my work and that of others.

(Hirsh and Kummerow, 1989: 61–2)

Finally, as regards careers information, Hirsh and Kummerow noted:

To perform well at work, individuals may need to use all of the eight preferences at the appropriate time and when required by the situation. Knowing this, people tend to select occupations that allow them to use the preferences that are most natural to them.

Judgers frequently choose occupations that have requirements for organization and closure. Perceptives frequently choose occupations in which they can define their own schedules, be flexible, and remain open to new information.

While judgers can and do enter all occupations, some are more appealing to them than others. According to available research, some occupations (in alphabetical order) seem especially attractive to judgers: accountant, administrator, bank officer, dentist, elementary school teacher, guard, judge, manager, nurse, police supervisor, and other occupations that allow for closure. These occupations are not meant to be an exhaustive list but serve to illustrate some areas that judgers might enjoy.

While perceptives can and do enter all occupations, some are more appealing to them than others. According to available research, some occupations (in alphabetical order) seem especially attractive to perceptives: artist, carpenter, counsellor, editor, entertainer, journalist, labourer, researcher, surveyor, waiter and waitress, and other occupations that allow for flexibility. These occupations are not meant to be an exhaustive list but serve to illustrate some areas that perceptives might enjoy. (Hirsh and Kummerow, 1989: 64)

According to McCrae and Costa (1988), the MBTI is unusual among personality assessment devices for three reasons: it is based on a classic theory; it purports to measure types rather than traits of continuous variables; and it is widely used to explain individuals' personality characteristics not only to professionals but also to the individuals themselves, and their co-workers, friends and families. But they also point out its limitations: the original Jungian concepts on which it is based are distorted, even contradicted; there is no bi-model distribution of preference scores; studies using MBTI have not always confirmed either the theory or the measure. Yet Devito (1985: 1030) has described MBTI as 'probably the most widely used instrument of personality testing'. The criticism of the typology theory is also cogently put by Hicks (1984). He points out that even the evidence in the manual provides less evidence for type than for continuous trait-like measurement, which is against the spirit of the test. However, after careful evaluation, he argues that the MBTI merits serious consideration by psychologists.

In an extensive review of the instrument, Carlson (1985) pointed out that the MBTI has been used somewhat unsystematically in a wide range of areas, but generally with favourable validity assessment. The limited reliability research shows satisfactory internal (alpha) and test–retest reliability, but is limited by student samples and short test–retest intervals. He reviewed criterion-related studies in treatment and research settings and noted that 'it is to the credit of MBTI that the instrument successfully predicted

behaviours as far apart as personal problems to imagery and group conformity' (Carlson, 1985: 364). However, he does note that the introvert–
extravert dimension of the scale has shown most validational evidence,
which is perhaps not surprising given that this dimension is perhaps the
most well established in all personal testing.

There are many criticisms of the MBTI. It does not measure one of the
fundamental dimensions of human personality – namely, neuroticism or
emotional stability. Perhaps most fundamental are two issues. First, as
Garden (1991: 13) notes, 'empirical support for the distinctive typological
features of Jung's theory is equivocal at best'. In other words, the theory on
which the measurement is based has problems. Next there are psychometric problems with the MBTI. Garden (1991: 13) states: 'the MBTI has been
simplified in order for its absorption or easy applicability into the "real
world" but remains problematic. Perhaps it is better not to use the MBTI at
all if its use will be counterproductive'. In short, it is based on a poor
theory. Its popularity does not relate to its validity.

In academic psychometric circles types have been out of fashion for
decades. Traits are in. They explain the behaviour of others in terms of their
personality.

5.4. Personality Traits

Lay people, like most modern personality theorists, are trait theorists. Trait
theory, like psychology in general, has a long history but a short past. The
ancient Greeks, and before them the Chinese, both had clear trait theories
of personality. Most people are familiar with Galen's theory (AD 200) of
humours or bodily fluids leading to four temperaments – choleric, melancholic, phlegmatic and sanguine. Clear dimensions of extraversion–
introversion and neuroticism–stability can be traced through many philo-
sophical speculators until the very turn of this century. In fact Galen was,
strictly speaking, more a type theorist, although it is possible to consider
being more or less sanguine, more or less choleric.

Another way nineteenth-century thinkers pondered personality was in
terms of the strength and speed of emotional reaction of other people and
events. Those who have quick and strong reactions may be thought of as
choleric but those with slow and strong reactions may be thought of as
melancholic. Equally, those who have reactions that are quick and weak may
be described as sanguine whereas those who have slow and weak reactions
may be thought of as phlegmatic.

For more than 100 years trait theorists have had two quests, best thought
of as the search for the periodic table of personality. They have been trying
to establish:

- The most parsimonious, complete description of the structure of personality. This means finding the 'higher-order' traits and describing how they are related to each other. It is like finding the double-helix structure of DNA.
- The psycho-social and physiological–anatomical processes that explain how traits arise, how they are maintained and how they cause behaviour.

To a large extent the second quest is dependent on the first. And there have been many arguments during the past 100 years about the structure of personality. There are essentially two issues that divide the trait theorists. The first is whether you should attempt to find and describe the essential number of traits that are *orthogonal or unrelated to each other*. As Figure 5.1 shows, extraversion and neuroticism are unrelated. Just as one can be a neurotic extravert, so one can be a stable introvert or extravert.

This idea can be described thus: for Europeans height and eye colour are probably unrelated. One can be tall or short with blue, green, brown or black eyes. But height and weight are related. Short people can be fat or thin but taller people 'normally' proportioned tend to be heavier.

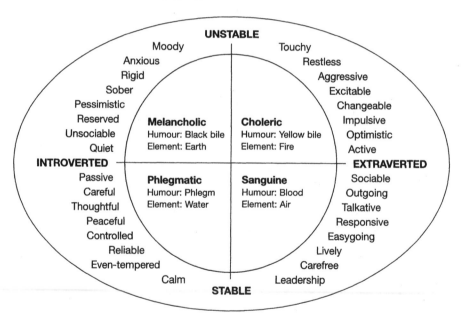

Figure 5.1 The four humours.

A consensus has been reached over these arguments, however. And that is that we can and should, for conceptual clarity as well as parsimony, describe fundamental personal traits that are independent of one another. They are sometimes called superfactors, and inevitably the argument is what are they? How many are there and how should they be labelled?

However, there is also consensus about *levels of description*. Thus you can take a superfactor that really is beyond dispute and describe it in more detail one level down. These can be called primary factors. One theorist (Hans Eysenck) listed several primary traits for extraversion, labelled: activity, sociability, risk-taking, impulsiveness, expressiveness, lack of reflection and lack of responsibility. On the other hand, two well-known US researchers (Costa and McCrae) listed six primary traits, labelled: warmth, gregariousness, assertiveness, activity, excitement seeking and positive emotions. It is self-evident that there is a lot of overlap. At the next level down you have behavioural dispositions. Thus you ask people five or six questions about their desire for stimulation, activity, doing things. These yield a score on activity, which forms part of the overall score (Figure 5.2).

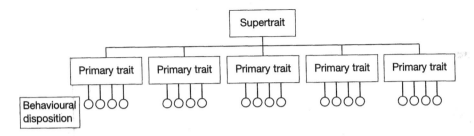

Figure 5.2 The structure of traits.

The central question remains: how many supertraits are there? Some researchers say three, others seven, but there is broad agreement on five. In the US Costa and McCrae, working in the psychometric trait tradition, settled on three and then five dimensions of personality. Now called the 'five factor approach' (FFA) or 'five factor model' (FFM), many sources now broadly agree with this model, including those who adopt the lexical approach – namely, they look at natural language and the relationship between everyday terms for personality traits. There are vigorous critiques of the FFM, but these have not reduced its popularity among personality researchers.

Costa and McCrae (1989) argue that there are five basic unrelated dimensions of personality (Table 5.2).

There are different synonyms for the big five:

1. Neuroticism: Emotionality, emotional control, affect.
2. Extraversion: Social adaptability, surgency, assertiveness, power.
3. Openness: Enquiring intellect, culture, intelligence, intellect.
4. Agreeableness: Conformity, love, likeability, friendly compliance.
5. Conscientiousness: Will to achieve, responsibility, work.

Table 5.2 The big five traits

High	Average	Low
1. Neuroticism		
Sensitive, emotional and prone to experiencing feelings that are upsetting	Generally calm and able to deal with stress, but you sometimes experience feelings of guilt, anger or sadness	Secure, hardy and generally relaxed, even under stressful conditions
2. Extraversion		
Extraverted, outgoing, active and high-spirited. You prefer to be around people most of the time	Moderate in activity and enthusiasm. You enjoy the company of others but you also value privacy	Introverted, reserved and serious. You prefer to be alone or with few close friends
3. Openness to experience		
Open to new experiences. You have broad interests and are very imaginative	Practical but willing to consider new ways of doing things. You seek a balance between the old and the new	Down-to-earth, practical, traditional and pretty much set in your ways
4. Agreeableness		
Compassionate, good-natured and eager to cooperate and avoid conflict	Generally warm, trusting and agreeable but you can sometimes be stubborn and competitive	Hard-headed, sceptical, proud and competitive. You tend to express your anger directly
5. Conscientiousness		
Conscientious and well organized. You have high standards and always strive to achieve your goals	Dependable and moderately well organized. You generally have clear goals but are able to set your work aside	Easygoing, not very well organized, and sometimes careless. You prefer not to make plans

These are fully described in Table 5.3.

Research clearly suggests that personality variables correlate differently with different job performance constructs. Current research on the relationship between personality and job performance has involved the integration of personality measures with the five-factor model. This method was used in two reviews of criterion validity (Barrick and Mount, 1991; Tett et al., 1991).

The first, Barrick and Mount (1991), was a large-scale meta-analysis using 117 validity studies and a total sample that ranged from 14,236 for

Table 5.3 Description of the big five

Factor		Factor definers	
Name	Scales	Adjectives	Q-sort items
Neuroticism (N)	Anxiety Hostility Depression Self-consciousness Impulsiveness Vulnerability	Anxious Self-pitying Tense Touchy Unstable Worrying	Thin-skinned Brittle ego defences Self-defeating Basically anxious Concerned with adequacy Fluctuating moods
Extraversion (E)	Warmth Gregariousness Assertiveness Activity Excitement seeking Positive emotions	Active Assertive Energetic Enthusiastic Outgoing Talkative	Talkative Skilled in play, humour Rapid personal tempo Facially, gesturally expressive Behaves assertively Gregarious
Openness (O)	Fantasy Aesthetics Feelings Actions Ideas Values	Artistic Curious Imaginative Insightful Original Wide interests	Wide range of interests Introspective Unusual thought processes Values intellectual matters Judges in unconventional terms Aesthetically reactive
Agreeableness (A)	Trust Straightforwardness Altruism Compliance Modesty Tender-mindedness	Appreciative Forgiving Generous Kind Sympathetic Trusting	Not critical, sceptical Behaves in giving way Sympathetic, considerate Arouses liking Warm, compassionate Basically trustful
Conscientiousness (C)	Competence Order Dutifulness Achievement Self-discipline Deliberation	Efficient Organized Planning ability Reliable Responsible Thorough	Dependable, responsible Productive Able to delay gratification Not self-indulgent Behaves ethically Has high aspirational level

openness to experience to 19,721 for conscientiousness. The study showed that there are differential relationships between personality dimensions and occupational performance across five different occupational groups. Performance measures in these groups were classified into three broad criteria that included job variety, training, proficiency and personnel data. The researchers reported that conscientiousness was consistently found to be a valid predictor for all five occupational groups and for all performance criteria, and that the other personality factors only generalize their validity for some occupations and some criteria. For example, extraversion was observed to be a valid predictor (across criterion types) for two occupations: manager and sales. Emotional stability is a valid predictor for the police; agreeableness is a valid predictor for the police and managers, whereas openness to experience did not show validity for any occupational groups. In terms of performance criteria extraversion was found to predict the training proficiency criterion relatively well, as did emotional stability and agreeableness. Similarly, openness to experience was found to be a valid predictor of training proficiency, but not for the other two criterion categories, job proficiency and personnel data. In a follow-up study Mount and Barrick (1995) found that the overall validity of conscientiousness had been underestimated, with the overall validity conscientiousness score and both of its dimensions (dependability and achievement) predicting specific performance criteria better than global criteria (for example, overall rating of job performance).

Tett et al. (1991) used only confirmatory studies – that is, studies based on hypothesis testing or on personality-oriented job analysis. The most notable finding was that mean validities derived from results generally supported the results reported by Barrick and Mount (1991), but are distinctly more positive. In essence, Tett et al. (1991) found that all personality dimensions were valid predictors of job performance. However, extraversion and conscientiousness had lower validity coefficients, whereas neuroticism, openness to experience and agreeableness had higher validities.

A third review of the relationship between personality measures and performance criteria was reported by Hough et al. (1990). Hough et al. (1990) investigated the relationship of nine personality dimensions and a range of performance criteria, specific to military settings. As developed by Hogan (1983), six construct categories were used and a seventh labelled 'miscellaneous', which Hough et al. (1990) later divided into three separate categories: achievement, masculinity and locus of control. Results indicate that adjustment (emotional stability) and dependability (conscientiousness) are valid predictors for the two most used performance criteria: training and job proficiency; and that the Big Five are predictors of training criteria. Therefore, the findings of Hough et al. (1990) were partly convergent with those of

Barrick and Mount (1991) but also provided evidence of some divergence. Each of the nine personality constructs correlates with important job and life criteria and constructs have a different pattern of relationships with those criteria. On the basis of Hough's data it has been suggested that Barrick and Mount overemphasized the broad dimensions of conscientiousness at the expense of other personality traits. The fact that other personality variables are not correlated with all occupational categories or criterion types does not necessarily mean that they are unimportant. Different jobs make different demands on employees and may contribute to a pattern of job-dependent validity coefficients.

In a further contribution to the debate, Salgado (1997) undertook a meta-analytical integration of the validity coefficients of the FFM for the prediction of job performance. This meta-analytical review differed from previous studies in that it included only studies conducted in the European Community. Previous studies by Barrick and Mount (1991) and Hough et al. (1990) had used studies carried out in the United States and Canada. Salgado (1997) found that the overall validity of personality constructs is small, excepting emotional stability and conscientiousness, even when the effects of measurement error in predictors and criteria and range restrictions have been corrected. In this respect the results show a great similarity to those of Barrick and Mount (1991) and Hough et al. (1990). Again, conscientiousness shows the highest estimated true validity and can be generalized for all occupations and criteria. The third finding of Salgado (1997) was that the estimated true validity for emotional stability was comparable to that for conscientiousness. Moreover, as with conscientiousness, emotional stability could be generalized across jobs and criteria. This finding is contrary to Barrick and Mount (1991) but is consistent with Hough et al. (1990). Openness to experience was found to be a valid predictor for training proficiency, thus consistent with Barrick and Mount (1991) and Hough et al. (1990). Other results support the suggestion that individuals with high scores in openness to experience may be those who are most likely to benefit from training programmes. A positive correlation was found between extraversion and two occupations in which interpersonal characteristics were likely to be important, confirming the findings of Barrick and Mount (1991) and Hough et al. (1990). However, extraversion did not seem to be a valid predictor for training proficiency. Finally, the results for agreeableness suggest that this factor may be relevant to predicting training performance.

What is clear from this literature is that, although some personality dimensions are good predictors of job proficiency, not all are. First, quite logically, different traits relate to different behaviours and, if a trait is unrelated to a particular occupational behaviour, it is unlikely that the two are correlated. Thus, neuroticism seems related only to 'negative' behaviour at work, such as absenteeism, but not to such things as productivity. If there were good theoretical reasons to suppose that certain specific traits (from a large battery) were related to specific measurable work outcome variables, the validity coefficients were around 0.20 but could rise to 0.30.

Second, not all personality measures were equally sound psychometrically. Third, and perhaps most important, the most common reason for the poor correlation between personality and occupational behaviour is because of the weak measurement of the latter. Measures of occupational behaviour, including training and selection criteria, often have problems because the measures are badly skewed, not aggregated or unreliable. Where efforts are made to obtain reliable and valid measures of job performance, the results suggest the utility of personality tests as predictors of job performance. Because of the poor reliability of individual measures, most researchers recommend that a battery of tests is used.

It would not be difficult to underestimate the popularity of the FFM and the quantity of research that is emerging of relevance to the work psychologist. The traits of extraversion and conscientiousness seem very important, particularly if the job involves people contact. Neuroticism, or 'negative affectivity' as it is sometimes called, is also a useful negative predictor of work success.

5.5. Misfits: Incompetent Personalities

It seems inappropriate, at least to a psychologist, but probably not to a manager, to talk about personality incompetence. Personality differences are about needs and preferences and therefore, in turn, about behaviours and values. The more extreme one is at one end of a personality trait continuum, the more likely people are to be inflexible in their needs, preferences and behaviours. The extreme extravert, like the extreme introvert, is easy to spot because their drives and needs are so strongly and constantly manifest. Ambiverts, or people more in the middle of the continuum, seem more flexible and adaptable because they have less strong drives and preferences.

While it may be that there are ideal personality types for the oddest of jobs, it is equally true that there are few ideal jobs for the oddest personality profiles. What sort of person does it take to be a pathologist, a forensic dentist or a steeplejack? It often takes an unusual combination of abilities, traits and motivation to succeed at extremely lonely, dangerous or morbid jobs.

Equally it may be very difficult to find a job for an obsessive–compulsive or someone far too easygoing. In fact, obsessives can do very well at safety and security jobs or those involved with quality control. Similarly, the easygoing individual might be very happy in jobs with little responsibility – if they exist.

One cannot have an incompetent personality but one can be incompetent in a job because of poor fit. People make poor selection decisions in that the abilities, motives and traits certain people have are either ideally/optimally suited to a job or not. Selectors can make errors but jobs change, which means that people appropriately selected become incompetent over time because what they are required to do differs from what they are selected for.

Other factors, other than selection error and job change, lead to an incompetent misfit. The first is *inappropriate promotion*. People can be promoted to levels and jobs not at all suited to their profiles. They may lack the ability, tenacity or even courage to do managerial jobs. Next, an organization can change relatively rapidly in terms of its values. A crisis in the industry, a buy-out or a merger/acquisition can relatively easily lead to a new value system and with it required managerial behaviours. A perfect fit between personal and organizational values can easily turn into the opposite.

People can, however, improve the fit by changing the job to fit their particular preferences in predictions better. This may be ideal for the individual – if indeed it is possible to change the job. However, changing the job to suit personal needs may mean that the job is inefficiently and ineffectively executed.

Possible types of misfit will now be described. However, it is important to note a number of caveats. First, a fit is dependent not only on personality but equally crucially on ability and motivation. Not having either the skills for the job or indeed the desire to do it renders one immediately incompetent. Next there is an important issue as to who defines and measures the incompetence: the job holder, the customer, the boss, the shareholders? Each could and does have quite different definitions. Third, the question as to who is responsible for the incompetence needs to be answered. Should we blame the job holder for a poor job selection decision, or indeed the people who chose him or her?

The definition of incompetence is essentially that of misfit. What this implies is that the demands of the job (well done) are not easy or natural for the job holder. This can mean either that the job is not well done or that the job holder suffers discomfort, even stress – or both.

Inevitably the concept of fit/misfit is linear – that is, there is a degree of fit or misfit. Furthermore, you can fit one feature or facet of a job but not another. However, for illustration purposes, we shall consider only personality job misfits in general terms.

The incompetent extravert

Extraverts are stimulus seekers. They seek variability and novelty. They trade off accuracy for speed. They are relaxed and refreshed by others. They are sensitive to the promise of reward and motivated by social events. Extraverts are attracted to sales and marketing for good reason. Every day is different; there are lots of opportunities to meet new people; the environment is one that exudes fun and optimism. Extraverts are happy people people. They seem socially skilled and self-confident. They are characterized by being friendly and warm, cheerful and sociable, affectionate and spontaneous. They tend to be jolly, pleasure seeking, rather daring and adventurous types. They are also characterized by being active, quick, hurried, impulsive and energetic.

People like extraverts because of their charm and easygoingness. So how could there be incompetent extraverts? The answer lies in what they do not like doing, but what in some jobs they need to do.

Extraverts are *not reflective*. They can speak before they think and tend to want to 'get going' too soon: to want to do something before analysing either the problem or indeed their plan of attack. Extraverts *get bored easily* and cannot easily sustain long periods of concentration without stimulation. Extraverts are *prone to accidents* and make lots of mistakes because of their need for excitement.

There are certain jobs that are not at all well suited to extraverts and at which they would be probably seriously incompetent. They would be characterized by:

- Solitariness – extraverts are gregarious so 'solitary confinement' is indeed a punishment.
- Little activity – extraverts are action people – they hate quiet, solitary, monitoring jobs.
- Monotony – being prone to boredom, extraverts hate regular day-to-day, predictable activities.
- Criticism – extraverts are optimistic – they are naturally cheerful, jolly and optimistic and shun a world where they are required to be hypercritical, pessimistic or gloomy.

The incompetent introvert

Introverts get a bad press in a world that is dominated by loud, happy extraverts. Introverts are reserved and serious but their critics call them aloof, shy, withdrawn – and boring.

Unlike extraverts, introverts are more self-contained and do not need to be around people. They are much less sociable, outgoing and talkative because they prefer not to be around too many people at once. They are not stimulus hungry like extraverts but the opposite – cortically overstimulated. Thus they shun sources of stimulation – parties, loud music, crowded shops – because they overstimulate the already overstimulated.

Introverts prefer to think before they speak; to be slow in their reactions; to take time to warm up. Introverts have a rich inner life and enjoy reflection. They are characterized by focus and depth rather than breadth of interests, skills and preferences.

Introverts seem *slow and hesitant* in large groups. They can easily feel overwhelmed by every discourse. Introverts *prefer cool media* for communication: they would prefer to write rather than speak. They may loathe traditional brainstorming, favouring the electronic version. Introverts may be particularly sensitive to, and even perhaps *over-observant* of, rules and procedures.

There are many jobs that introverts are particularly ill suited to and would make them unhappy and incompetent. They would be characterized by:

- Contact – introverts make unhappy and inefficient sales and service people. These jobs exhaust them.
- Stimulation – introverts can easily become overstimulated in, for instance, an open-plan office or an environment that provides Muzak.
- Speed of reaction – some jobs require quick decisions; introverts prefer to ruminate.

Stable incompetents

It is difficult to think of instances where it is not advantageous to be non-neurotic or stable. Stable individuals are calm and even-tempered. They tend to be optimistic and contented. They are also likely to have social poise and confidence. Stable individuals are not over-excitable and have good self-control. Moreover, they tend to be self-reliant and stress resistant.

In a word, they are mentally healthy. They are therefore particularly good under stress and valuable for their calmness and predictability. They are also well suited to particularly dangerous jobs like aeroplane pilot or bomb disposer. They cope well in business situations, such as when there are great changes because of a merger and acquisition or a re-engineering project.

Stable individuals seem both mentally and physically healthy. They do not suffer guilt and feel good about themselves. They also feel autonomous and non-obsessive.

There can be few instances when stability makes one incompetent. Stable people can be seen as too cool, too stoical – having too much sangfroid. They may underestimate the reactions of others and be too stoical in the face in adversity. It is often difficult for people who score high on a trait to understand their opposites. They may be seen as too analytical rather than sympathetic, too tough rather than tender-minded, too reasonable rather than compassionate.

Nevertheless, even for jobs such as counselling, being an actor or working with volatile creative people, it remains important to be stable. Perhaps there can never be real stable incompetents.

Unstable incompetents

Just as it was difficult to think of jobs where emotional stability would be a handicap, so it is difficult to think of jobs where neuroticism is an advantage. The unstable individual is a worrier, prone to much anxiety. A generation ago, they would be described as 'having nerves', as they tend to be fearful and tense.

They are called unstable primarily because they are so moody. They can easily be irritated, changing their outlook very quickly. They are excitable, changeable and fickle, and are therefore difficult to predict. They can be shy, timid, inhibited and defensive one moment and sarcastic, self-centred and loud the next.

Neurotics are pessimists, prone to depression. They see the glass as half-empty and exude an air of gloom. At work they are vulnerable to stress, sensitive to criticism, fearful of change. At work they can be hypochondriacal and often *absent* – because of their vulnerability to stress. Their pessimism can be infectious and they tend to lower morale. Their excitability can mean that they are careless and tense. Their emotions can overwhelm their reason as they can be inclined to make *poor decisions*, especially about others. Their *impulsivity* can also cause problems in the sense that they do not always think issues through because they tend to respond to things on an emotional level.

Unstable individuals know they are neurotic but are unable to do much about their condition. They seem drawn to jobs that are about emotions, such as counselling, the dramatic arts and the visual arts. There are many jobs that mean that a person's neuroticism would render them seriously incompetent. They are characterized by

- Safety and security – neurotics would worry too much and their anxiety may result in obsessionality and personal stress.
- Customer contact – customers look for helpful, alert staff with an optimistic outlook. Neurotics cannot disguise their emotional state and may easily 'bite the head off' an innocent customer.
- Senior management – people want predictable bosses who give them a sense of purpose. They need someone who can boost morale not sap it. Neurotics are unpredictable and pessimistic.
- Criticism – some jobs bring a great deal of feedback both positive and

negative. The neurotic needs constantly to be 'stroked' by positive feed-back but can be hypersensitive and 'destroyed' by negative feedback.

Agreeable incompetents

Agreeable people are nice people. They tend to be trusting of others. They are straight-talkers in the sense that they are open, frank and candid. They are also generous and courteous, perhaps with old-fashioned manners and charm. Most of all they are cooperative – they prefer to try to get along with others.

People who score high on agreeableness tend also to be humble, and unwilling to stand in the spotlight and take credit for things they have done. And they are sympathetic to the plight of others.

How, then, is it possible that such 'good' people are ever incompetent in the work place? The answer, of course, is the nature of business. It is often about bluff and bravado, about cut-and-thrust, about bargaining and threat-ening.

Agreeable people tend to be trusting of others: staff, bosses, competitors and customers. This means that they are, and are seen to be, naïve and gullible. Their straightforwardness means that they are unlikely and unwill-ing to conceal, disguise or dress up information. They tell it 'as it is', which can be very bad for morale. They eschew all forms of personal propaganda. Their altruism gets them into trouble because being selfish often pays, in the long and short run, in business.

Cooperativeness is a virtue except when healthy competition and *dis-agreement raise standards*. And modesty rarely gets noticed. The agreeable person is never the selfish publicist, but business is all about publicity.

The helpful, kind, thoughtful, agreeable person can be very incompetent at work because their natural inclinations are very different from the often 'successful' behaviours in the modern world.

Jobs that agreeable people may find they are incompetent at may involve:

- Bargaining and selling: This is a tough world of bluff and concealment, of manipulation and timing, and of win–lose not win–win.
- Propaganda, PR and advertising: People in these worlds are neither mod-est nor frank. Their job is to manipulate others' beliefs, which is the opposite trait to agreeableness.
- Military-type activities: Agreeable people tend to be sympathetic and humanitarian. They like helping others. In the military you have to be extremely tough on occasion.
- Therapy: The therapist is neither trusting nor straightforward. Their job is to get under the skin of the person, to doubt everything they say and to conceal their insights and intentions at the line.

Disagreeable incompetents

Disagreeable people can do very well in business: They tend to be suspicious, wary and hard-headed. This mistrust may allow them to 'smell out a rat' early on. Rather than being straightforward, they are seen as shrewd, charming, clever, even flirtatious. They get what they want by subterfuge and are often very complicated.

They are far from compliant and can be characterized by stubbornness, impatience, intolerance and hard-heartedness. They are *headstrong* and *outspoken*. And, far from being modest, they are *show-offs*. People see them as cocky and very self-confident.

Most of all they are *tough-minded*. They are not swayed by human feelings if their rational judgement tells them otherwise. They put their interests first, and if they are helped by the interest of their staff and customers, so much the better – but if they are not, then too bad.

In big business it probably pays to be disagreeable. It may pay to be mistrusting, devious, selfish, competitive and self-aggrandizing – while at the same time pretending not to be. But there are jobs where this style can be very disadvantageous. They are characterized by:

- Cooperativeness: Where it is essential to work together, disagreeable types have great difficulty.
- Humanitarianism: Jobs such as aid worker, priest or perhaps social worker involve behaviour patterns deeply antithetical to the disagreeable individual.
- Morale booster: In times of stress at work, perhaps characterized by change (mergers and acquisitions, downsizing), the disagreeable person is likely to reduce rather than increase morale.

Incompetent openness

People who are open to experience are dreamers. They are certainly innovative and may therefore have a rich fantasy life. They are often thought of as idealistic and artistic and original.

People with high scores on this trait can be humorous and mischievous, and as a result rather complicated. They certainly have wide interests and are versatile in the way they approach problems. They are inventive, curious and insightful. Most of all they are well known for being unconventional.

Open people live in a world of ideas, possibilities, daydreams and beauty. If clever as well, they can be intellectually challenging. They can also be brave in the sense that they are happy to question authority and take up a strong moral position quite against the current.

They are of course found in research and development, in marketing and advertising, and in design. They are arts, rather than science, students and have always been know for innovativeness, however, quirky. Of course the downside of this is that they are often seen as impractical, unable to concentrate, too easily bored. They always want to challenge and change, to do things differently.

The result is that the creativity of open people means that they are very poorly suited to certain jobs characterized by:

- Quality control: The idea of simply monitoring products perhaps designed by others is anathema to high openness scores.
- Rule-following administration: Any procedurally driven job is deeply unattractive to the open person.

Incompetent closedness

Those with low openness scores may be described as closed. They pride themselves on being *practical*. In terms of value, they tend to be conservative, conventional and cautious.

They live in the present and are not generally known for being creative or imaginative, and it does not worry them. Unlike open people, who they see as 'arty-farty', they are not particularly attached to aesthetics, being low in an appreciation of art, architecture or literature. Nor are they 'touchy-feely'. Some would say that they have a low emotional intelligence coefficient because they are neither interested in, nor attuned to, their own or others' feelings.

Closed people like procedures and routines. They can often be heard to say 'If it ain't broke don't try to fix it'. They are not interested in novelty and variety, preferring the tried and tested path. They may not be particularly intellectually curious, although this is not necessarily a sign of low intelligence. They simply don't enjoy intellectual 'what-if' games. Furthermore, their questioning rarely extends to basic values, where the closed person tends to follow *tradition*.

It is unfair to suggest that a low openness to experience score cannot be a good thing in the workplace. However, certain jobs characterized by the following dimensions would probably render a closed person incompetent.

- Creativity and innovation: This does not come naturally to the closed individual.
- Design: The closed person is little interested in patterns and aesthetics.
- Therapy: The world of feelings is a bit of a mystery to the closed individual.

Incompetent conscientiousness

There are many synonyms for conscientiousness: the work ethic, achievement striving, dutifulness, prudence. And it is a most desirable trait at work.

Conscientious people are confident, *efficient*, resourceful and thorough. They can be well known for being *well organized*, efficient, precise and methodological. They volunteer for extra work and are dutiful. They are, quite simply, hard-working and industrious. They exhibit constant self-discipline through their industriousness.

Conscientious individuals are also often *ambitious*. They can also be very enterprising and entrepreneurial. Their determination and persistence nearly always pay off by being successful at work.

Conscientious people go the extra mile: they are reliable and trustworthy. They establish change strategies or follow systems and procedures to ensure that all work is done optimally. They *plan* and are future oriented. Indeed, they take pride in their work and the way they do it.

Just as it was difficult to think of jobs where emotional stability was not an asset, so incompetent conscientiousness is difficult to consider. Occasionally, however, there may be issues that lead to incompetent conscientiousness:

- Workaholic: Because of their high standards and ambition, conscientious people might become inefficient workaholics.
- Stress: Their self-discipline leads them to push themselves hard, which could quite easily lead to stress.
- Spontaneity: The conscientious person may appear to be very clever, very cautious, but rarely fun-loving and spontaneousness.

Incompetent slovenliness

Just as incompetent conscientiousness is oxymoronic, so low conscientiousness (slovenliness) is a synonym for incompetence itself.

There are a long list of traits that almost no employer would want of an employee and all characterize the person with low and very low conscientiousness scores. They can be *absent minded and careless* about even very important issues. They are easily distracted. Worse, and very unattractively, they are *quick to chide and slow to bless* – that is, they easily find fault with others but are very defensive of themselves if they are criticized.

These individuals also show signs of *immaturity*: they are *impulsive, impatient, hasty* and *moody*. Their behaviour shows little judgement and forethought. They don't obey rules and can be more devious than scrupulous. They *give up easily* and *procrastinate* and the workplace and style are chaotic. It is difficult to think of a job where lazy, incompetent, inefficient people do well. In this sense *all* jobs render them incompetent.

5.6. Personality and Vocational Guidance

One obvious cause of managerial incompetence is that people have been given poor advice when looking for a job. Or they might have ignored good advice, followed bad advice or simply not sought any advice. We know that personality traits and vocational interests are closely linked and that the latter are very stable over time. As noted earlier, traits are different from ability although they can obviously determine how jobs are done.

Costa et al. (1995) argue that understanding a person's personality traits can help both counsellor and client understand both strengths and weaknesses and vocational decision-making (presumably good decisions for first job, job changes and promotion). They note that scores on neuroticism and conscientiousness are relevant to all jobs because of the way they help adaptation:

> Individuals who are high in neuroticism are prone to distress and dissatisfaction regardless of their life situation; they are likely to be unhappy in whatever job they have. ... A different job is unlikely to solve problems that are rooted in the individual's basic emotional make-up ... in general, individuals high in neuroticism are probably best suited for positions that are low in stressfulness and require little emotional control. (Costa et al., 1955: 130–1)

They also consider the trait of conscientiousness:

> High scores are probably best suited to demanding jobs that require initiative, persistence, and organisation (although the career success such individuals attain may be at the expense of personal growth in other aspects of life). Low scorers on the factor are less ambitious (although they may equally be talented) and need to consider carefully their own level of motivation in choosing occupation. (Costa et al., 1995: 131)

The authors then described the NEO Job Profiler test, which they designed specifically for guidance. It measures people on four of the five dimensions and offers possible vocations along with a label (Table 5.4).

One study looked at executive search recruiters. They turned out to be low on neuroticism and high on extraversion and openness but average on conscientiousness. They were described by Dykeman and Dykeman (1996) as '(a) secure, hardy and generally relaxed even under stressful conditions; (b) extraverted, outgoing, active and high spirited; (c) open to new experiences; and (d) dependable and moderately well-organised' (Dykeman and Dykeman, 1996: 83). They argue that this helps both those giving advice as well as those interested in choosing a career in executive search.

Table 5.4 Job suggestions from the NEO Job Profiler

Traits	Description	Job
1. Extraverted Closed (E+ O−)	Mainstream consumers	Salesperson
2. Extraverted Open (E+ O+)	Creative interactors	Anthropologist
3. Introverted Closed (E− O−)	Homebodies	Bookkeeper
4. Introverted Open (E− O+)	Introspectors	Naturalist
5. Extraverted Disagreeable (E+ A−)	Leaders	Politician
6. Extraverted Agreeable (E+ A+)	Welcomers	School teacher
7. Introverted Disagreeable (E− A−)	Competitors	?
8. Introverted Agreeable (E− A+)	Unassuming	General worker
9. Extraverted Non-conscientious (E+ C−)	Funlovers	PR
10. Extraverted Conscientious (E+ C+)	Go-getters	Marketing
11. Introverted Non-conscientious (E− C−)	Lethargic	Security
12. Introverted Conscientious (E− C+)	Plodders	
13. Open Disagreeable (O+ A−)	Free thinkers	Inventor
14. Open Agreeable (O+ A+)	Progressives	
15. Closed Disagreeable (O− A−)	Resolute believers	Religion
16. Closed Agreeable (O− A+)	Traditionalists	
17. Open Non-conscientious (O+ C−)	Dreamers	Creative artist
18. Open Conscientious (O+ C+)	Good students	Academics
19. Closed Non-conscientious (O− C−)	Reluctant scholars	?
20. Closed Conscientious (O− C+)	By the bookers	Engineer
21. Agreeable Non-conscientious (A+ C−)	Well-intentioned	Charity manager
22. Agreeable Conscientiousness (A+ C+)	Effective altruists	Social worker
23. Disagreeable Non-conscientious (A− C−)	Undistinguished	?
24. Disagreeable Conscientious (A− C+)	Self-promoters	Entrepreneur

(Costa et al., 1995)

5.7. Conclusion

This chapter has suggested that a manager's personality may be powerfully implicated in his or her incompetence and derailment. Successful and unsuccessful managers seem to have fairly typical profiles. Using the widely accepted big five traits, the two different profiles will be discussed as a conclusion, selecting traits in order of importance.

Successful managers are nearly always *emotionally stable*. Derailed managers are frequently emotionally vulnerable. Certainly failure at work may increase neurosis but it is more likely to cause it. One needs to be hardy, resilient, even stoical to succeed at work. This does not mean being emotionally illiterate: far from it. Successful managers have *emotional intelligence*. They understand their own and others' emotions and are able to change their behaviour and that of others appropriately. Successful managers are sensitive; derailed ones are over-sensitive. Successful managers do worry, do get depressed, do become anxious – but only occasionally and appropriately to the circumstances. They also have healthily adaptive coping strategies. Unsuccessful managers worry all the time. Their moodiness, fickleness and prickliness cause real problems at work.

Successful managers are *conscientious*. They work smart and hard. They tend to follow instructions and are orderly. They are diligent and prudent. Unsuccessful managers don't have the work ethic and tend to be clock-watchers. Occasionally excessive conscientiousness is the undoing of a manager. Fanatic workaholism and being very low in conscientiousness are both equally associated with derailment. There is a period in all managers' careers when they simply have to work very hard, be well organized and diligent. There is an optimal amount of conscientiousness required at work. People often do not make it to senior positions if they are not conscientious enough. However, bitterness, a broken psychological contract or some other 'organizational mishap' may lead them to be deliberately clock-watching and ineffective. On the other hand, slavish, obsessional dedication to work is also a recipe for disaster.

Successful managers are *open to new experiences*. They have to anticipate and embrace change. They need to be original and creative but they also have to be practical. Few people make it to senior management with low openness scores. They tend to be too dull, conventional and traditional to lead with imagination. But very high scores can easily derail managers. Very high scorers in this dimension may be dreamers and very impractical. They may be prone to wasting large amounts of time and sums of money on 'white elephants' – namely, projects that go badly wrong. They may err too frequently on the side of aesthetic appeal rather than practical function.

Successful managers need to learn to behave as if they were extraverted even if they are not. They need to be socially confident and interpersonally skilled and relaxed. The higher you go in organizations, the less you do – the more you work through others. Extreme introverts do not enjoy many of the tasks of senior management: running interminable meetings, doing PR appearances, hosting parties. Good managers know it has to be done and do it. Very extraverted managers need 'back up' to temper their natural ways of behaving. Although they may enjoy the social aspects of the job, they may well neglect the serious strategy and number-crunching that is equally important.

Do successful managers need to be agreeable? At times. To do well in business a manager needs to be tough at times: competitive, egocentric, arrogant, devious. Probably what characterizes the successful manager is that he or she can act agreeable with his or her own staff, but disagreeable with competition. Successful managers are, in short, very stable, medium or high in conscientiousness and openness, average in extraversion and medium to low in agreeableness.

CHAPTER SIX
Pathological Incompetence

6.1. Introduction

Psychologists are interested in personality traits, psychiatrists in personality disorders. As noted in the previous chapter, psychologists argue that each individual's particular personality profile may be assessed and mapped into personality space. Whichever system we use, the assumption is that people have a unique profile. Just as all people have stable physical characteristics – height, weight, body mass index, eye colour – that may be measured and recorded, so it is with personality traits.

In this sense it is not possible to have 'no personality'. When people say a person has no personality, they usually mean they are introverted, unassertive or lacking in social skills. They are lacking in presence, charm, assertiveness. To this extent personality is synonymous with another's interest in a person. Lay people also talk about 'a personality', meaning a person of importance, prominence, renown or notoriety. Thus film stars are personalities but your local librarian may have no personality. Lay people use the term as a dimension reflecting their interest in others.

Psychologists interested in personality have made great strides in describing, taxonomizing and explaining the mechanisms and processes in normal personality functioning (see Chapter 5). But psychiatrists also talk about personality functioning. They talk about personality disorders that are typified by early onset (recognizable in children and adolescents), pervasive effects (on all aspects of life) and that have relatively poor prognosis (that is, are difficult to cure).

Over the years psychiatrists have labelled various disorders as eating disorders, sexual and gender identity disorders, anxiety disorders and mood disorders. They have made great strides in clarifying and specifying diagnostic criteria and these can be found in the various editions of the *Diagnostic and Statistical Manual of Mental Disorders* (called DSM for short). The manual has changed over the years and is now in its fourth edition (American Psychiatric Association, 1994).

Psychiatrists and psychologists share some simple assumptions with respect to personality. Both argue for the *stability* of personality. The DSM criteria talk of 'enduring pattern', 'inflexible and pervasive', 'stable and of long duration'. The pattern of behaviour is not a function of drug use or some other medical condition. Furthermore, the personality pattern is not a manifestation or consequence of another mental disorder.

Both groups of professionals argue that personality factors relate to *cognitive, affective and social aspects of functioning*. In other words, the disorder or traits affect how people think, feel and act. It is where a person's behaviour 'deviates, markedly' from the expectations of an individual's culture that the disorder is manifest. The psychiatric manual is very clear that 'odd behaviour' is not simply an expression of habits, customs, or religious or political values professed or shown by a people of particular cultural origin.

The DSM manuals note that personality disorders all have a long history and have an onset no later than early adulthood. Moreover, there are some gender differences: thus the antisocial disorder is more likely to be diagnosed in men whereas the borderline, histrionic and dependent personality is more likely to be found in women.

The manuals are at lengths to point out that some personality disorders look like other disorders – anxiety, mood, psychotic, substance related and so on – but have unique features. The essence of the argument is: 'Personality Disorders must be distinguished from personality traits that do not reach the threshold for a Personality Disorder. Personality traits are diagnosed as a Personality Disorder only when they are inflexible, maladaptive, and persisting and cause significant functional impairment or subjective distress' (American Psychiatric Association, 1994: 633).

The DSM-IV provides a clear summary:

General diagnostic criteria for a Personality Disorder

A. An enduring pattern of inner experience and behavior that deviates markedly from the expectations of the individual's culture. This pattern is manifested in two (or more) of the following areas:

(1) cognition (i.e., ways of perceiving and interpreting self, other people, and events)
(2) affectivity (i.e., the range, intensity, liability, and appropriateness of emotional response)
(3) interpersonal functioning
(4) impulse control

B. The enduring pattern is inflexible and pervasive across a broad range of personal and social situations.

C. The enduring pattern leads to clinically significant distress or impairment in social, occupational, or other important areas of functioning

D. The pattern is stable and of long duration and its onset can be traced back at least to adolescence or early childhood

E. The enduring pattern is not better accounted for as a manifestation or consequence of another mental disorder

F. The enduring pattern is not due to the direct physiological effects of a substance (e.g., a drug of abuse, a medication) or a general medical condition (e.g., head trauma). (1994: 633)

Finally, according to the manual, there are 10 or more defined and distinguishable personality disorders, which will be considered in due course:

Paranoid Personality Disorder is a pattern of distrust and suspiciousness such that others' motives are interpreted as malevolent.

Schizoid Personality Disorder is a pattern of detachment from social relationships and a restricted range of emotional expression.

Schizotypal Personality Disorder is a pattern of acute discomfort in close relationships, cognitive or perceptual distortions, and eccentricities of behaviour.

Antisocial Personality Disorder is a pattern of disregard for, and violation of, the rights of others.

Borderline Personality Disorder is a pattern of instability in interpersonal relationships, self-image, and affects, and marked impulsivity.

Histrionic Personality Disorder is a pattern of excessive emotionality and attention seeking.

Narcissistic Personality Disorder is a pattern of grandiosity, need for admiration, and lack of empathy.

Avoidant Personality Disorder is a pattern of social inhibition, feelings of inadequacy, and hypersensitivity to a negative evaluation.

Dependent Personality Disorder is a pattern of submissive and clinging behaviour related to an excessive need to be taken care of.

Obsessive–Compulsive Personality Disorder is a pattern of preoccupation with orderliness, perfectionism, and control.

Personality Disorder Not Otherwise Specified is a category provided for two situations: 1) the individual's personality pattern meets the general criteria for a Personality Disorder and traits of several different Personality Disorders are present, but the criteria for any specific Personality Disorder are not met; or 2) the individual's personality pattern meets the general criteria for a Personality Disorder, but the individual is considered to have a Personality Disorder that is not included in the classification (e.g., passive–aggressive personality disorder). (1994: 629)

One of the most important ways to differentiate personal style from personality disorder is flexibility. There are lots of difficult people at work but relatively few whose rigid, maladaptive behaviours mean they continually have disruptive, troubled lives. It is their *inflexible, repetitive, poor stress-coping responses* that are marks of disorder.

Personality disorders influence the *sense of self* – the way people think and feel about themselves and how other people see them. The disorders often powerfully influence *interpersonal relations at work*. They reveal themselves in how people 'complete tasks, take and/or give orders, make decisions, plan, handle external and internal demands, take or give criticism, obey rules, take and delegate responsibility, and co-operate with people' (Oldham and Morris, 1991: 24). The antisocial, obsessive–compulsive, passive–aggressive and dependent types are particularly problematic in the workplace.

People with personality disorders have difficulty expressing and understanding emotions. It is the intensity with which they express them and their variability that makes them odd. More importantly, they often have serious problems with self-control.

6.2. Traits and Disorders

There have been numerous attempts to relate the two worlds of traits and disorders (Dyce, 1999). Perhaps the most comprehensive attempt has been by Widiger et al. (2001), who believed that having extreme (high or low) scores on personality traits renders individuals *at risk* for certain disorders. Their analysis is set out in Table 6.1 but will be described more simply thereafter.

Paranoid They score *low on agreeableness* (particularly low trust) and straightforwardness. They also score *high on facets of neuroticism*, particularly angry hostility. They also are cold and antisocial (introverts) and rather closed, rather than being open to experience.

Schizoid They are *strongly introverted*: loners, isolated, withdrawn, with little interest in or ability to initiate and maintain social relationships.

Schizotypal They too are *introverted* but can manifest fairly strong *neuroticism traits*. However, they tend to score high on openness, which reflects their association with creativity. This condition is particularly associated with self-consciousness, vulnerability and a rich fantasy life.

Antisocial They are *low on agreeableness and conscientiousness*, being exploitative, vengeful and antagonistic. They have a mixed profile on neuroticism, being high on hostility but low on self-consciousness.

Borderline They are essentially *unstable*, having high scores in most neuroticism facets, particularly hostility, impulsivity, vulnerability, depression and

Table 6.1 DSM-III-R personality disorders and the five-factor model

Diagnostic criteria	PAR	SZD	SZT	ATS	BDL	HST	NAR	AVD	DEP	OBC	PAG
Neuroticism											
Anxiety	h		h	h/L				H	H		
Hostility	H	L		H	H	H	H			h	H
Depression			h	h	H		H/L	h	H	H	
Self-consciousness		L	H	**L**	**H**	H	H	H	h	h	
Impulsiveness				H	H						
Vulnerability			h		H	H	**H**	H	H	H	
Extraversion											
Warmth	l	L	L	l		H		L/H	**h**	L	
Gregariousness	l	L	L		h	H		L			
Assertiveness					h		**H**	L	L	H	
Activity						H		L			
Excitement seeking		**L**		H		H		L		l	
Positive emotions	l	L			h	H				l	
Openness											
Fantasy			H			H	H				
Aesthetics	l					H					
Feelings	l	L	L			H				L	
Actions	**L**					H		L			
Ideas			H			L					
Values						H				L	
Agreeableness											
Trust	L		L			H					
Straightforwardness	L			L	**L**	L	l				L
Altruism				L		L			H	L	
Compliance	L	h		L	L				H	L	L
Modesty	l			**L**			L		H		
Tendermindedness	l			L			L		**h**		
Conscientiousness											
Competence	h					L	**H**				L
Order										H	
Dutifulness				L						H	L
Achievement striving		l			L		**H**		L	H	
Self-discipline				L		L					L
Deliberation				L						H	

H, L = high, low, respectively, based on DSM-III-R (American Psychiatric Association, 1987) diagnostic criteria; h, l = high, low, respectively, based on associated features provided in DSM-III-R (American Psychiatric Association, 1987); H/hm L, l = high, low, respectively, based on clinical literature. Personality disorders: PAR = paranoid; SZD = schizoid; SZT = schizotypal; ATS = antisocial; BDL = borderline; HST = histrionic; NAR = narcissistic; AVD = avoidant; DEP = dependent; OBC = obsessive–compulsive; PAG = passive–aggressive.

anxiety. They are hot-tempered, often apprehensive and easily rattled. They are characterized by vulnerability to stress, impulsivity, dyscontrol and negative emotionality.

Histrionic There are extreme *extraverts*: convivial, assertive, energetic, flashy and high-spirited. They express emotions with inappropriate exaggeration and display inappropriate affection, intimacy and seductiveness. They may also be low in self-discipline.

Narcissistic They tend to score *low on agreeableness and low on neuroticism*. They are, however, suspicious and manipulative, despite low self-consciousness, hostility and depression. Their consciousness scores can be very low.

Avoidant They are clearly *introverted neurotics*. They are anxious, timid and insecure; easily rattled and panicked; apprehensive and prone to feelings of embarrassment and inferiority. They probably also have low openness scores.

Dependent They tend to score *high on agreeableness and neuroticism*. Their pathological agreeableness makes them self-effacing, docile, submissive and sacrificial. They may describe themselves as being low in competence and dutifulness, which makes them look low in consciousness.

Obsessive–compulsive These perfectionistic, *over-conscientious* people tend to be preoccupied with details and order and are often excessively devoted to productive work. But they can be very fearful of making mistakes. They can also be rather antagonistic: low on compliance and altruism, insisting that others follow orders, and stubborn. They are thus *high on conscientiousness and neuroticism but low on agreeableness*.

Passive–aggressive/Negativistic They tend to be *low on both agreeableness and conscientiousness*. They can be said to be sullen, complaining, stubborn, irritable and disgruntled. They may also be high on certain features of neuroticism such as hostility.

Self-defeating/Depressive These are the *neurotics with low conscientiousness scores*. They feel inadequate, pessimistic and worthless and are, as a result, self-blaming, self-critical and brooding. They fail to finish tasks and choose situations that may lead to failure. They may also have low agreeableness.

Sadistic They score *very low on agreeableness*, but also high on extraversion and often low on conscientiousness. They are characterized by their tendency to harm, humiliate, intimidate and act aggressively to others. They are ruthless, domineering and brutal with few signs of warmth, gregariousness or positive emotions.

Another way of marrying classic personality theory with the psychiatric system is by using the three personality trait factors identified by Eysenck. This would mean that the 10 disorders would be classified thus:

Psychotics: Paranoid, Schizoid, Schizotypal
Extraverts: Antisocial, Borderline, Histrionic, Narcissistic
Neurotics: Avoidant, Dependent, Obsessive–Compulsive.

What all this suggests is that there is considerable, logical overlap between the psychologists' categorization scheme for 'normal' personality traits and the psychiatric criteria for personality disorders.

6.3. Disordered Personalities and Derailed Managers

Over the past decade various psychologists have noted that the personality disorders may easily account for people having serious problems at work (Oldham and Morris, 1991). To make the somewhat archaic language more intelligible, various writers have redefined the types. Hence, Oldham and Morris (1991) have the following 'translations':

Obsessive–compulsive	Conscientious
Narcissistic	Self-confident
Histrionic	Dramatic
Paranoid	Vigilant
Borderline	Mercurial
Dependent	Devoted
Schizoid	Solitary
Passive–aggressive	Leisurely
Avoidant	Sensitive
Schizotypal	Idiosyncratic
Antisocial	Adventurous
Self-defeating	Self-sacrificing
Sadistic	Aggressive

However, perhaps the most insightful and useful approach has been that of Hogan and Hogan (2001), who have developed a self-report questionnaire called the Hogan Development Survey (HDS), which quite specifically measures 11 of the personality disorders but expresses them in accessible language (see above).

Hogan and Hogan (2001) say that this 'view from the dark side' gives an excellent understanding of the causes of management derailment. They argue that it is probably easier to define incompetence than competence, that there are obviously many 'mad' managers in organizations and that helping people to identify potentially bad or derailed managers can help to alleviate a great deal of suffering. They also note from their reading of the literature that derailment is more about having undesirable qualities than not having desirable ones.

Table 6.2 Overlapping themes from HDS and DSM-IV, axis 2 personality disorders

DSM-IV personality disorder	HDS themes		
Borderline	Inappropriate anger; unstable and intense relationships alternating between idealization and devaluation	Excitable	Moody and hard to please; intense but short-lived enthusiasm for people, projects or things
Paranoid	Distrustful and suspicious of others; motives are interpreted as malevolent	Sceptical	Cynical, distrustful and doubting others' true intentions
Avoidant	Social inhibition; feelings of inadequacy and hypersensitivity to criticism or rejection	Cautious	Reluctant to take risks for fear of being rejected or negatively evaluated
Schizoid	Emotional coldness and detachment from social relationships; indifferent to praise and criticism	Reserved	Aloof, detached and uncommunicative; lacking interest in, or awareness of, the feelings of others
Passive–aggressive*	Passive resistance to adequate social and occupational performance; irritated when asked to do something he or she does not want to	Leisurely	Independent; ignoring people's requests and becoming irritated or argumentative if they persist
Narcissistic	Arrogant and haughty behaviors or attitudes; grandiose sense of self-importance and entitlement	Bold	Unusually self-confident; feelings of grandiosity and entitlement; over-valuation of one's capabilities
Antisocial	Disregard for the truth; impulsivity and failure to plan ahead; failure to conform with social norms	Mischievous	Enjoying risk-taking and testing the limits; needing excitement; manipulative, deceitful, cunning and exploitative
Histrionic	Excessive emotionality and attention seeking; self-dramatizing, theatrical and exaggerated emotional expression	Colourful	Expressive, animated, and dramatic; wanting to be noticed and needing to be the centre of attention
Schizotypal	Odd beliefs or magical thinking; behavior or speech that is odd, eccentric or peculiar	Imaginative	Acting and thinking in creative and sometimes odd or unusual ways

Table 6.2 Overlapping themes from HDS and DSM-IV, axis 2 personality disorders

DSM-IV personality disorder	HDS themes		
Obsessive–compulsive	Preoccupations with orderliness, rules, perfectionism and control; over-conscientious and inflexible	Diligent	Meticulous, precise and perfectionistic, inflexible about rules and procedures; critical of others' performance
Dependent	Difficulty making everyday decisions without excessive advice and reassurance; difficulty expressing disagreement out of fear of loss of support or approval	Dutiful	Eager to please and reliant on others for support and guidance; reluctant to take independent action or go against popular opinion

*From DSM-III-R (American Psychiatric Association, 1987).

The research of Hogan and Hogan in the area has led them to seven conclusions:

1. There is substantial (between-study) agreement regarding the dysfunctional dispositions/traits associated with management incompetence and derailment.
2. Many derailed managers have impressive social skills, which is why their disorders are not spotted at selection but only later by their subordinates.
3. Bad managers are a major cause of misbehaviour (theft, absenteeism, turnover) by staff: it is poor treatment that often makes them resentful.
4. It is important to take the observer's view in personality – that is, the descriptions of the personality disorders from those that deal with them.
5. The problem for much research is that it can describe what derailed and derailing managers do rather than why they do it.
6. Although the origin (in terms of learning or biology) is not clear for the personality disorders/derailment factors, their consequences are very apparent. And the most obvious one is, quite simply, the inability to learn from experience.
7. A second crucial consequence of the disorders is that they erode trust.

Paranoid personality disorder is worthy of description in considerable detail if we are really to understand managerial incompetence.

Paranoid (argumentative, vigilant)

It is thought that 0.5–2.5% of the population have this disorder, which must not be confused with the paranoid delusions of schizophrenics or the behaviour of refugees and migrants whose personal history leads to widespread mistrust. Paranoids are *super-vigilant*: nothing escapes their notice. They seem tuned into mixed messages, hidden motives and secret groups. They are particularly sensitive to authority and power and are obsessed with maintaining their own independence and freedom.

Distrust and suspiciousness of others at work is their abiding characteristic. The motives of all sorts of colleagues and the boss are interpreted as malevolent, all the time. The 'enemy' is both without and within.

They suspect, without much evidence, that others are exploiting, harming or deceiving them about almost everything both at work and at home. They are preoccupied with unjustified doubts about the loyalty or trustworthiness of subordinates, customers, bosses, shareholders and so on, on both big and small matters. They are reluctant to confide in others (peers at work) because of the fear that the information will be used against them: kept on file; used to sack them. They may even be wary of using email. They read hidden or threatening meanings into most benign remarks or events, from emails to coffee-room gossip, and they remember them. They are certainly *hypersensitive* to criticism. They persistently bear grudges against all sorts of people going back many years and can remember even the smallest slight. They perceive attacks on their character or reputation that others do not see and are quick to react angrily or to counterattack. They seem *hyper-alert and sensitive*. They have recurrent suspicions, without justification, regarding fidelity of their sexual or business partner and can be pretty obsessed with sex.

Paranoid individuals are slow to commit and trust but once they do so are loyal friends. They are very interested in others' motives and prefer 'watchdog' jobs. They like being champions of the underdog, whistle-blowers on corruption. They are courageous because they are certain about their position. They are on the side of right: idealists striving for a better world. But they can be overly suspicious or fearful of certain people, which can manifest itself in an irrational hatred towards certain races, religions or political groups.

They are not compromisers and they attack attackers. Many of their characteristics make them excellent managers: they are *alert, careful, observant* and *tactical*. But they can have problems with authority and in dealing with those who hold different opinions from their own. However, they are more sensitive to the faults in others than the faults in themselves. The business world, they believe (sometimes correctly) is full of danger, dishonest people and those who are untrustworthy and will let them down. Because they believe that others are out to harm them they can be over-argumentative, bellicose, belligerent, hostile, secretive, stubborn and consumed with mistrust. They are not disclosive, they are suspicious of others and they are experts at projecting blame on to others.

Psychoanalysts believe that the paranoid feel weak and dependent but that they are sensitive to weakness in others and disclaim them for it. They yearn for dependency but fear it. Instead of showing personal doubt, they doubt others. Their self-righteousness, morality and punitiveness can be very attractive to some people.

According to Oldham and Morris (1991) the DSM-III-R describes paranoid personality disorder as:

A. A pervasive and unwarranted tendency, beginning by early adulthood and present in a variety of contexts, to interpret the actions of people as deliberately demeaning or threatening, as indicated by at least four of the following:

(1) expects, without sufficient basis, to be exploited or harmed by others
(2) questions, without justification, the loyalty or trustworthiness of friends or associates
(3) reads hidden, demeaning or threatening meanings into benign remarks or events, e.g., suspects that a neighbour put out trash early to annoy them
(4) bears grudges or is unforgiving of insults or slights
(5) is reluctant to confide in others because of unwarranted fear that the information will be used against him or her
(6) is easily slighted and quick to react with anger or to counterattack
(7) questions, without justification, fidelity of spouse or sexual partner

B. Occurrence not exclusively during the course of Schizophrenia or Delusional Disorder. (1991: 167–8).

The personality disorders website www.personalityresearch.org/pd.html helps to define this through a simple mnemonic, SUSPECT:

S: Spouse fidelity suspected
U: Unforgiving (bears grudges)
S: Suspicious of others
P: Perceives attacks (and reacts quickly)
E: 'Enemy or friend' (suspects associates, friends)
C: Confiding in others feared
T: Threats perceived in benign events.

Hogan and Hogan (2001) call this disorder 'Argumentative'. These types, they argue, expect to be wronged, to be betrayed, to be set up, to be cheated or to be deceived in some way. They see the world as a dangerous place, full of potential enemies, and they enjoy conspiracy theories; they are keenly alert for signs of having been mistreated. When they think they have been unfairly treated they retaliate openly and directly. This may involve physical violence, accusations, retaliation or litigation. Retaliation is designed to send the signal that they are prepared to defend themselves. They are known for their suspiciousness, their argumentativeness and their lack of trust in others. They are hard to deal with on a continuing basis because you never know when they are going to be offended by something (unpredictability), and because they are so focused on their own private agenda that they don't have much time for others (unrewarding).

> At their best they are very insightful about organisational politics and the motives of their counter players, and they can be the source of the good intelligence regarding the real agendas of others, and the real meaning of events. Although they are very insightful about politics, they are often not very good at playing politics. This is because they are true believers, they are deeply committed to their worldview, and they tend to be unwilling to compromise, even on small issues. Nonetheless, with their passionate commitment to a theory about how the world works, they can be visionary and charismatic, and people may be drawn to them .... Because they are unpredictable and not rewarding to deal with, they have trouble maintaining a team over a long period. (Hogan and Hogan, 2001: 48)

Paranoids mishandle stress by retreating, by withdrawing into their ideology and then attacking whatever is threatening them. They are very persistent and tend to accumulate enemies. They are self-centred and ideology centred – all information and experience is filtered through their odd world view and evaluated in terms of the degree to which it fits with or threatens that view, which somehow reflects on them.

To work with paranoids, those who report to them have no alternative but to agree with them, because they will defeat your objections in a way that makes sense to them. Those who report to them won't be able to persuade them that they are wrong, and risk alienating them by challenging them, and once paranoids decide people can't be trusted, the relationship will be over. Those who report to paranoids are either for them or against them.

According to Oldham and Morris (1991), the following six traits and behaviours are clues to the presence of what they call the 'Vigilant' style. A person who reveals a strong vigilant tendency will demonstrate more of these behaviours more intensely than someone with less of this style in his or her personality profile.

1. *Autonomy.* Vigilant-style individuals possess a resilient independence. They keep their own counsel, they require no outside reassurance or advice, they make decisions easily, and they can take care of themselves.
2. *Caution.* They are careful in their dealings with others, preferring to size up a person before entering into a relationship.
3. *Perceptiveness.* They are good listeners, with an ear for subtlety, tone, and multiple levels of communication.
4. *Self-defence.* Individuals with Vigilant style are feisty and do not hesitate to stand up for themselves, especially when they are under attack.
5. *Alertness to criticism.* They take criticism very seriously, without becoming intimidated.

6. *Fidelity*. They place a high premium on fidelity and loyalty. They work hard to earn it, and they never take it for granted. (Oldham and Morris, 1991: 151–2)

They also provide tips on dealing with paranoid types.

1. The Vigilant person in your life may appear very confident, independent, tough, and assertive. You may not realize how much this person needs your respect. Express, show, and otherwise prove it often.

2. The Vigilant person in your life is new on the scene and you would like to get to know him or her better, do not hesitate to pursue this person. Even though he or she may be painfully slow to reciprocate and to begin to trust you, persistence usually pays off. Go the whole distance.

3. Do not misinterpret the Vigilant reserve as indifference .... Accept the emotional reserve, and if the relationship is solid and stable, trust that this person cares deeply for you.

4. Avoid competition and power struggles. The Vigilant person needs to feel in complete control of his or her destiny. Respect that ....

5. Expect defensiveness when you criticise or confront this person .... The best way to confront a Vigilant person is simply to express your feelings without criticizing or finding fault. Try saying that you care and are looking for a way to better your relationship, not to blame anybody ....

6. Take the lead socially. The Vigilant person in your life will appreciate your greater ease in getting to know people and making plans with them.

7. Don't tease. Vigilant people often have a good sense of humor, but not about themselves.

8. If the Vigilant person in your life is unjustifiably jealous or worried about your loyalty, don't be flippant or dismiss these concerns as silly. Don't underestimate the seriousness of such worries to a Vigilant person.

9. Accept that if you slight this person, unintentionally or otherwise, he or she will have a long memory. If the Vigilant person in your life is unforgiving, at least forgive yourself. (Oldham and Morris, 1991: 163–5)

Some jobs suit these people well: security, the military, perhaps insurance. But the hyper-vigilant, argumentative, wary manager can be very difficult to live with.

Schizoid (solitary, reserved)

These are the cold fish of the world of personality disorders: distant, aloof, emotionally flat, often preferring the affection of animals to that of people. These are the solitary loners of the world of personality disorders. They are very self-contained: they do not need others to admire, entertain, guide or amuse them. And yet they report being free of loneliness. They seem completely dispassionate. They are doers and observers, not feelers. They seem stoical in the face of pain and passion. Relationships? They can take them or leave them. They don't really understand emotions.

The personality website www.personalityresearch.org/pd.html uses the mnemonic DISTANT:

D: Detached (or flattened) affect
I: Indifferent to criticism and praise
S: Sexual experiences of little interest
T: Tasks (activities done solitarily)
A: Absence of close friends
N: Neither desires nor enjoys close relations
T: Takes pleasure in few activities

Here the manager seems detached from social relationships. They often have a restricted range of expression of emotions in interpersonal settings. They seem more emotionally flat than necessary. They are thought of as unresponsive, and as low in emotional intelligence (EQ).

They neither desire nor enjoy close relationships at work, including being part of a family. They are never team players and hate the idea of being so. They choose solitary activities, feeling uncomfortable even in informal gatherings. They have little, if any, interest in having sexual contact with others – which is perhaps not a bad thing at work. They take pleasure in few, if any, activities. They seem joyless, passionless and emotionless. They lack close friends or confidants other than first-degree relatives. They are isolates at work but apparently are not unhappy with their friendlessness. They seem indifferent to the praise or criticism of others. Absolutely nothing seems to get them going. They show emotional coldness, detachment or flattened emotionality.

Schizoid people are not team players; nor are they sensitive or diplomatic. They are not aware of office politics. Hence they may be more successful in solitary careers. They are not antisocial but are asocial. They are the 'hollow man': empty, flat, emotionally unmovable. They may have a rich fantasy life but a very poor emotional life.

According to Oldham and Morris (1991), who call schizoids the solitary style, the DSM manual specifies the diagnostic criteria as:

A. A pervasive pattern of indifference to social relationships and a restricted range of emotional experience and expression, beginning by early adulthood and present in a variety of contexts, as indicated by at least four of the following:

    (1) neither desires nor enjoys close relationships, including being part of a family

(2) almost always chooses solitary activities

(3) rarely, if ever, claims or appears to experience strong emotions, such as anger or joy

(4) is indifferent to the praise and criticism of others

(5) has no close friends or confidants (or only one) other than first-degree relatives

(6) displays constricted affects, e.g. is aloof, cold, rarely reciprocates gestures or facial expressions, such as smiles or nods.

B. Occurrence not exclusively during the course of Schizophrenia or a Delusional Disorder. (Oldham and Morris, 1991: 279)

Hogan and Hogan (2001) call these types self-absorbed, self-focused, indifferent to the feelings or opinions of others – especially their staff. They are introverted, misanthropic, imperceptive and lacking in social insight. They appear thick-skinned and indifferent to rejection or criticism. They prefer to work alone, and are more interested in data and things than in people. They tend to work in finance, accounting, programming and information technology, where their progress will depend on their technical skills and not their social insight. They are often uncommunicative and insensitive, which makes them unpredictable and unrewarding, and they have trouble building or maintaining a team.

They can be very tough in the face of political adversity; they have a hard surface, and they can take criticism and rejection where others would tremble. They can also stay focused and on task, and not be distracted by tumult, emotional upheavals and stressful meetings; through it all, they will continue to do their jobs. But because they are indifferent to the needs, moods or feelings of others, they can be rude, tactless, insensitive and gauche. They are therefore very poor managers. They are unperturbed by daily stress and heavy workloads; at the same time, they are insensitive or indifferent to the stress levels of their staff. When the pressure is really on, they retreat to their office, begin handling matters themselves and stop communicating – which leaves others at a loss to know what they want or need. Always extremely self-centred and self-reliant, they do not need emotional support from others, and they don't provide any to others. They primarily don't want to be bothered by other people's problems; they just want to do their work.

To work with the detached, those who report to them should stay task oriented and keep questions and comments related to the job. Schizoids will ignore requests for more and better communications, and will tend to work by themselves. Those who report to the detached should observe what they do so that they do not act that way themselves, and should develop lines of communication to other people in the organization so that you will have a source of advice during times of trouble.

Oldham and Morris (1991) note:

The following five traits and behaviours are clues to the presence of the Solitary style.

1. *Solitude*. Individuals with the Solitary personality style have small need of companionship and are most comfortable alone.
2. *Independence*. They are self-contained and do not require interaction with others in order to enjoy their experiences or to get on in life.
3. *Sangfroid*. Solitary men and women are even-tempered, calm, dispassionate, unsentimental, and unflappable.
4. *Sexual composure*. They are not driven by sexual needs. They enjoy sex but will not suffer in its absence.
5. *Feet on the ground*. They are unswayed by either praise or criticism and can confidently come to terms with their own behavior. (Oldham and Morris, 1991: 264–5)

They have seven tips for dealing with these types:

1. Let this person be .... They may not mix much in the Real World or react deeply to you, but they are very competent and responsible, and their inner worlds can be very interesting.

2. Do not assume that the Solitary person is uncomfortable or unhappy because he or she is alone ....

3. Do not assume that the Solitary person in your life is uncomfortable with you because he or she prefers to spend much time outside your presence or just sitting quietly instead of interacting with you ....

4. Look for signs of caring that are different from the standard I-want-you, I-need-you, I-love-you ....

5. Ensure this person plenty of time to be alone. Anyone with even a small amount of Solitary style requires time to him- or herself to feel sane, well adjusted, and productive ....

6. Take up hobbies or find activities to occupy yourself while the Solitary person is off on his or her own.

7. When you need to work out a problem with a non-emotional Solitary person, appeal to logic instead of emotion. (Oldham and Morris, 1991: 275–6)

Again there may be jobs where detached, solitary ways of behaving may be adaptive. Research and development (R&D) scientists, meteorologists on an uninhabited island or the artistic crafts person may work very well alone. It is when they are promoted to the position of managing teams that the problem arises.

Schizotypal (imaginative, idiosyncratic)

This disorder, which is more common in males than females, has been esti-mated to affect about 3% of the population. In a sense they are mild schizophrenics but they do not show their gross disorganization in thinking and feeling and their severe symptoms. However, they all appear to be pret-ty idiosyncratic and are often creatively talented and curious. They often hold very strange beliefs concerning the occult. They have odd habits, eccentric lifestyles and a rich inner life.

Schizotypal people have a rich inner life and often seek emotional exper-ience. Hence they are drawn to religion and pharmacological techniques that promise 'testing the limits'. They seek rapture and nirvana.

Here the manager is marked by acute discomfort with, and reduced capacity for, close relationships. They show many eccentricities of behav-iour. They may look odd and have a reputation for being 'peculiar'.

They often have very odd ideas about business: how to succeed, who to hire, what controls what. They can have very odd beliefs or magical think-ing that influences behaviour and is inconsistent with business norms – for example, superstitiousness, belief in clairvoyance, telepathy. They get into crystals, feng shui and so on in a big way. They can have odd thinking and speech styles, being very vague or very elaborate. They can seem 'other-worldly' and may be difficult to follow. They can have unusual perceptual experiences – seeing things that are not there, smelling and tasting things differently. Some are very suspicious or paranoid around the home and office. They show inappropriate or constricted affect, and can react oddly emotionally in various contexts – that is, they may become very emotional around some trivial issues but be strangely and unpredictably cold at others.

The personality disorders website www.personalityresearch.org/pd.html suggests a mnemonic ME PECULIAR:

M: Magical thinking or odd beliefs
E: Experiences unusual perceptions

P: Paranoid ideation
E: Eccentric behaviour or appearance
C: Constricted (or inappropriate) affect
U: Unusual (odd) thinking and speech
L: Lacks close friends
I: Ideas of reference
A: Anxiety in social situations
R: Rule out psychotic disorders and pervasive developmental disorder

Many organizations do not tolerate the odd behaviours of these idiosyn-cratic types. They dress oddly and work odd hours. They are not very loyal to their companies and do not enjoy the corporate world. They don't 'connect' with staff, customers and their bosses. Their quirky, quasi-religious beliefs estrange them yet more from the normal world of the other people. They are often loners.

Oldham and Morris (1991) report the DSM criteria thus:

A. A pervasive pattern of deficits in interpersonal relatedness and peculiarities of ideation, appearance, and behavior, beginning by early adulthood and present in a variety of contexts, as indicated by at least five of the following:

  (1) ideas of reference (excluding delusions of reference) (e.g., 'I'm sure those two people over there are talking about me')
  (2) excessive social anxiety, e.g., extreme discomfort in social situations involving unfamiliar people
  (3) odd beliefs or magical thinking, influencing behavior and inconsistent with sub-cultural norms, e.g., superstitiousness, belief in clairvoyance, telepathy, or 'sixth sense', 'others can feel my feelings' (in children and adolescents, bizarre fantasies or preoccupations)
  (4) unusual perceptual experiences, e.g., illusions, sensing the presence of a force or person not actually present (e.g., 'I felt as if my dead mother were in the room with me')
  (5) odd or eccentric behavior or appearance, e.g., unkempt, unusual mannerisms, talks to self
  (6) no close friends or confidants (or only one) other than first-degree relatives
  (7) odd speech (without loosening of associations or incoherence), e.g., speech that is impoverished, digressive, vague, or inappropriately abstract
  (8) inappropriate or constricted affect, e.g., silly, aloof, rarely reciprocates gestures or facial expressions, such as smiles or nods
  (9) suspiciousness or paranoid ideation. (Oldham and Morris, 1991: 259)

Hogan and Hogan (2001) call these types 'Imaginative' and describe them thus: they think about the world in unusual and often quite interesting ways. They may enjoy entertaining others with their unusual perceptions and insights. They are constantly alert to new ways of seeing, thinking and expressing themselves, and unusual forms of self-expression. They often seem bright, colourful, insightful, imaginative, playful and innovative, but also eccentric, odd and flighty.

These people are curiously interesting and may be fun to be around. But they are distractible and unpredictable and as managers they often leave people confused regarding their directions or intentions. They tend to miscommunicate in idiosyncratic and unusual ways. At their best these people are imaginative, creative, interesting and amazingly insightful about the motives of others, but at their worst they can be self-absorbed, single-minded, insensitive to the reactions of others and indifferent to the social and political consequences of their single-minded focus on their own agendas.

Under stress and heavy workloads they can become upset, lose focus, lapse into eccentric behaviour and not communicate clearly. They can be moody and tend to get too excited by success and too despondent over failure. They want attention, approval and applause, which explains the lengths that they are willing to go to in order to attract it.

To work with the imaginative, those who report to them need primarily to be a good audience, to appreciate their humour, creativity and spontaneity, and to understand that they do not handle reversals very well. They will not mind suggestions and recommendations regarding important decisions, and in fact may even appreciate them. Reports should study their problem-solving style, listen to their insights about other people and model their ability to 'think outside the box'.

Oldham and Morris (1991), who call these types idiosyncratic, note:

> The following six traits and behaviours are clues to the presence of the Idiosyncratic style. A person who reveals a strong Idiosyncratic tendency will demonstrate more of these behaviors more intensely than someone with less of this style in his or her personality profile.

> 1. *Inner life*. Idiosyncratic individuals are tuned in to, and sustained by, their own feelings and belief systems, whether or not others accept or understand their particular worldview or approach to life.
> 2. *Own world*. They are self-directed and independent, requiring few close relationships.
> 3. *Own thing*. Oblivious to convention, Idiosyncratic individuals create interesting, unusual, often eccentric lifestyles.
> 4. *Expanded reality*. Open to anything, they are interested in the occult, the extrasensory, and the supernatural.
> 5. *Metaphysics*. They are drawn to abstract and speculative thinking.
> 6. *Outward view*. Though they are inner-directed and follow their own hearts and minds, Idiosyncratic men and women are keen observers of others, particularly sensitive to how other people react to them. (Oldham and Morris, 1991: 242–3)

They also provide five tips for working with these odd-balls:

> 1. The Idiosyncratic person is one-of-a-kind. Accept, tolerate, and treasure this person for his or her uniqueness, not despite it ....

> 2. Do not pressure the Idiosyncratic person to conform to the Real World – and do not be pressured into conforming to his or her world either ....

> 3. To widen your life together and to bring you closer, share the interests of the Idiosyncratic person in your life ....

> 4. Help the Idiosyncratic person to have more time for his or her spiritual or otherwise special interests ....

5. To deal with a very Idiosyncratic person, accept that you are the one who is more attached to conventional reality; take charge of meeting the fundamental responsibilities of life. (1991: 256–7)

The imaginative, idiosyncratic person is unlikely to reach a very high position in organizations, although they may be promoted in advertising or academia. The absent-minded, nutty professor and the creative advertising genius may share many schizotypical behaviours. If they are talented, they may do well, but rarely as managers of others.

Antisocial (adventurous, mischievous)

The term psychopath or sociopath was used to describe antisocial personality types whose behaviour is amoral or asocial, impulsive and lacking in remorse and shame. It is indeed, perhaps for obvious reasons, the most studied of all the personality disorders. Once called 'moral insanity', it is found more commonly among lower socio-economic groups, no doubt because of the 'downward drift' of these types. Since the 1940s it has been shown that the characteristics defining this disorder – self-centredness, irresponsibility, impulsivity and insensitivity to the needs of others – are found in many professions.

These managers show a disregard for, and violation of, the rights of others. They often have a history of being difficult, delinquent or dangerous. They show a failure to conform to social norms with respect to lawful behaviours (repeatedly performing acts that are grounds for arrest, imprisonment and serious detention). This includes lying, stealing and cheating. They are always deceitful, as indicated by repeated lying, use of aliases or conning others for personal profit or pleasure. They are nasty, aggressive, con artists – the sort who often get profiled on business crime programmes. They are massively impulsive and fail to plan ahead. They live only in, and for, the present. They show irritability and aggressiveness, as indicated by repeated physical fights or assaults. They can't seem to keep still – ever. They manifest a terrifying reckless disregard for the physical and psychological safety of self or others – or the business in general. They are famous for being consistently irresponsible. Repeated failure to sustain consistent work behaviour or to honour financial obligations is their hallmark. Most frustrating of all, they show lack of remorse. They are indifferent to or rationalize having hurt, mistreated or stolen from another. They never learn from their mistakes. It can seem as if labelling them as antisocial is a serious understatement.

In his famous book called *The Mask of Insanity*, Cleckley (1941) set out 10 criteria: superficial charm and intelligence; absence of anxiety in stressful situations; insincerity and lack of truthfulness; lack of remorse and shame;

inability to experience love or genuine emotion; unreliability and irresponsibility; impulsivity and disregard for socially acceptable behaviour;
clear-headedness with an absence of delusions or irrational thinking; inability to profit from experience; and lack of insight.

Antisocial, adventurous challengers are not frightened by risk: indeed,
they thrive on it. They love the thrill of adventure and are happy to put others' lives at risk as well as their own. They tend to be self-confident and not
overly concerned with the approval of others. They live for the moment:
they are neither guilty about the past nor worried about the future. They
can be seriously reckless and they tend not to tolerate frustration well. They
resist discipline and ignore rules. They have poor self-control and think little about the consequences of their actions.

Antisocial adventurers do not hide their feeling and they don't experience
stress unless confined or frustrated. They are adolescents all their life: careless, irresponsible, hedonistic, forever sowing wild oats. They need excitement
all the time and are very easily bored. They can be successful entrepreneurs,
journalists, bouncers, lifeguards. They like outwitting the system – opportunis-
tically exploiting who and what they can. They are rolling stones who gather no
moss. They hate routine and administration, which are seen as drudgery.

They make bad bosses and bad partners because they are egocentric,
continuing a relationship as long as it is good for them. They rarely have
long-lasting, meaningful relationships. They have two human ingredients
missing which are pretty crucial: conscience and compassion. Hence they
can be cruel, destructive, malicious and criminal. They are unscrupulous,
and are exploitatively self-interested with little capacity for remorse. They
act before they think and are famous for their impulsivity.

Oldham and Morris (1991) indicate the DSM criteria:

A pattern of irresponsible and antisocial behavior since the age of 15, as
indicated by at least four of the following:

(1) is unable to sustain consistent work behavior, as indicated by any of
the following (including similar behavior in academic settings if the
person is a student):
  (a) significant unemployment for six months or more within five years
      when expected to work and work was available
  (b) repeated absences from work explained by illness in self or family
  (c) abandonment of several jobs without realistic plans for others
(2) fails to conform to social norms with respect to lawful behaviour, as
indicated by repeatedly performing antisocial acts that are grounds
for arrest (whether arrested or not), e.g., destroying property, harass-
ing others, stealing, pursuing an illegal occupation
(3) is irritable and aggressive, as indicated by repeated physical fights or
assaults (not required by one's job or to defend someone or oneself),
including spouse- or child-beating

(4) repeatedly fails to honor financial obligations, as indicated by default-ing on debts or failing to provide child support or support for other dependants on a regular basis

(5) fails to plan ahead, or is impulsive, as indicated by one or both of the following:

   (a) travelling from place to place without a prearranged job or clear goal for the period of travel or clear idea about when the travel will terminate

   (b) lack of a fixed address for a month or more

(6) has no regard for the truth, as indicated by repeated lying, use of aliases, or 'conning' others for personal profit or pleasure

(7) is reckless regarding his or her own or others' personal safety, as indi-cated by driving while 'intoxicated', or recurrent speeding

(8) if a parent or guardian, lacks ability to function as a responsible par-ent, as indicated by one or more of the following:

   (a) malnutrition of child

   (b) child's illness resulting from lack of minimal hygiene

   (c) failure to obtain medical care for a seriously ill child

   (d) child's dependence on neighbors or non-resident relatives for food or shelter

   (e) failure to arrange for a caretaker for young child when parent is away from home

   (f) repeated squandering, on personal items, of money required for household necessities

(9) has never sustained a totally monogamous relationship for more than one year

(10) lacks remorse (feels justified in having hurt, mistreated, or stolen from another). (1991: 236–7)

The personality disorders website www.personalityresearch.org/pd.html suggests the mnemonic CORRUPT:

C: Conformity to law lacking
O: Obligations ignored
R: Reckless disregard for safety of self or others
R: Remorse lacking
U: Underhanded (deceitful, lies, cons others)
P: Planning insufficient (impulsive)
T: Temper (irritable and aggressive)

Hogan and Hogan (2001) call the antisocial person 'Mischievous'. They note that these types expect that others will like them and find them charm-ing; and they expect to be able to extract favours, promises, money and other resources from other people with relative ease. However, they see others as merely to be exploited, and therefore have problems maintaining commitments, and are unconcerned about violating expectations. They are

self-confident to the point of feeling invulnerable, and have an air of daring
and sang-froid that others often find attractive and even irresistible.

They are highly rewarding to deal with, but are unpredictable. They can
be charming, fun, engaging, courageous and seductive; but they are also
impulsive, reckless, faithless, remorseless and exploitative. They also have
problems with telling the truth. Their self-deception, self-confidence and
recklessness lead to lots of conflicts, but they have almost no ability to learn
from experience. According to Hogan and Hogan (2001: 49):

> They tend to be underachievers, relative to their talent and capabilities; this
> is due to their impulsivity, their recklessness, and their inability to learn from
> experience. These people handle stress and heavy work loads with great
> aplomb. They are easily bored, and find stress, danger, and risk to be invig-
> orating – they actively seek it. As a result, many of these people become
> heroes – they intervene in robberies, they rush into burning buildings, they
> take apart live bombs, they volunteer for dangerous assignments, and they
> flourish in times of war and chaos. Conversely, they adapt poorly to the
> requirements of structured bureaucracies.

To work with antisocial types, those who report to them must be prepared to help them follow through with commitments and pay attention to
details, and to encourage them to think through the consequences of their
actions. Those who report to them should not expect a lot of gratitude or
even loyalty, but can learn a lot by watching how they handle people and
how they are able to get what they want through charm and persuasion.

Oldham and Morris (1991) call these types 'Adventurous' and note:

> The following eleven traits and behaviors are clues to the presence of the
> Adventurous style. A person who reveals a strong Adventurous tendency will
> demonstrate more of these behaviors more intensely than someone with less
> of this style in his or her personality profile.
>
> 1. *Nonconformity*. Men and women who have the Adventurous personality
>   style live by their own internal code of values. They are not strongly influ-
>   enced by other people or by the norms of society.
> 2. *Challenge*. To live is to dare. Adventurous types love the thrill of risk and
>   routinely engage in high-risk activities.
> 3. *Mutual independence*. They do not worry too much about others, for they
>   expect each human being to be responsible for him- or herself.
> 4. *Persuasiveness*. They are silver-tongued, gifted in the gentle art of winning
>   friends and influencing people.
> 5. *Sexuality*. Adventurers relish sex. They have a strong sex drive and enjoy
>   numerous, varied experiences with different partners.
> 6. *Wanderlust*. They love to keep moving. They settle down only to have the
>   urge to pick up and go, explore, move out, move on.
> 7. *Free lance*. Adventurous types avoid the nine-to-five world. They prefer to
>   earn an independent, free-lance living, do not worry about finding work,

and live well by their talents, skills, ingenuity, and wits.

8. *Open purse.* They are easy and generous with money, believing that money should be spent and that more will turn up somewhere.

9. *Wild oats.* In their childhood and adolescence, people with the Adventurous personality style were usually high-spirited hell-raisers and mischief makers.

10. *True grit.* They are courageous, physically bold, and tough. They will stand up to anyone who dares to take advantage of them.

11. *No regrets.* Adventurers live in the present. They do not feel guilty about the past or anxious about the future. Life is meant to be experienced now. (1991: 218)

Oldham and Morris also give advice as to how to deal with these types:

1. Have fun. But make sure you know exactly what's going on .... Adventurous types are charming and disarming. This person may flatter, persuade, cajole, or even manipulate you into an affair or an adventure, but just because you share this intimacy doesn't mean the Adventurer loves you or feels any responsibility toward you.

2. No illusions. Accept what this person gives you, and recognize that he or she is not likely to start adapting to your needs. You be the flexible one ....

3. Don't crowd. The Adventurous person needs freedom to do as she or he pleases. Don't try to prevent the Adventurer from taking off ....

4. Be responsible. The Adventurous person may not make decisions about money, children's safety, safe sex, or other things the way you would ....

5. Know your limits. Adventurous types have a great tolerance and capacity for drugs and alcohol, for fear, and for risk ....

6. Expect a lot of yourself, not of the Adventurous person. To maintain a relationship with an Adventurous person requires that you have strong self-esteem and don't need him or her to support you emotionally and help you love yourself ....

7. Stay as sexy as you are .... Toss your inhibitions and be ready and willing to experiment. (1991: 231–3)

In many ways these types are the most common in the business world because, if they are bright and good looking, their pathology may benefit them. They can be found in all sectors but may be most attracted to those jobs that involve persuading others, such as the media, politics and religion.

Borderline (excitable, mercurial)

These are people 'living on the edge'. About 2% of the population have this disorder, which is more common in women than in men. The term border-line originally referred to the border between neuroses and psychoses.

There are often signs of other disorders: mood, depression, histrionic. People such as Marilyn Monroe, Adolf Hitler and Lawrence of Arabia have been diagnosed with this disorder, being impulsive, unpredictable and reckless. Most of all they tend to have problems with their self-image, often 'splitting' their positive and negative views of themselves. They can vacillate between self-idealization and self-abhorrence.

These poor souls show chronic instability of interpersonal relationships, self-image and emotion. They are also marked by impulsivity in their daily behaviour.

Sometimes they show frantic efforts to avoid real or imagined abandonment by managers, their staff and so on. They can become dependent and clinging. They often show a pattern of unstable and intense interpersonal relationships characterized by alternating between extremes of love and hate, worship and detestation. Most have identity disturbance: markedly and persistently unstable self-image or sense of self. They are not really sure who they are and their assumed identity can easily change. They are impulsive with money, sex, booze, driving and so on, and in every sense of the word are accident prone. They might spend lavishly the one day and miserly the next. At the extremes they can show recurrent suicidal behaviour or threats. Most noticeable is their marked change of mood (for example, intense episodic dysphoria, irritability or anxiety, usually lasting a few hours and only rarely more than a few days). They seem to be on an emotional rollercoaster, with ups and downs even in the same day. They often talk about chronic feelings of inner emptiness. Unfortunately for those who report to them and their managers, they have inappropriate, intense anger or difficulty controlling anger (for example, frequent displays of temper, constant anger, recurrent physical fights).

These mercurial types are on the rollercoaster of life. They are intense and demanding. Their emotional world is geological: full of volcanic explosions and movement of tectonic plates. They can blow hot and cold very quickly. They are driven by emotions and find emotional significance in everything. Hence they are very moody. People can drop from idols to 'bad objects' in the space of days. But because they cannot control their emotional states they are frequently in torment.

They act on impulse and can have a real self-indulgent side. They can change their lifestyle quite easily and do not have a strong sense of self. In this sense they can be a little unsure of their identity.

At work they can be passionately involved with others. They can really admire their bosses when praised but this can just be a phase. They insist on being treated well and have a keen sense of entitlement. They can easily see themselves as more important than others do. As managers they get very involved with their staff and expect total dedication. When their unrealistic expectations are not met they can get very moody and churlish.

Their sense of who they are, what they believe and what is the meaning of their life is ever-changing. They do not like mixed feelings, ambiguity or solitariness. They prefer to see the world in terms of good and bad. They can have great difficulty concentrating.

Some experts believe that the term personality disorganization is best suited to this disorder because they seem midway between the functional and dysfunctional.

Oldham and Morris (1991: 302) summarize the diagnostic criteria thus:

A pervasive pattern of instability of mood, interpersonal relationships, and self-image, beginning by early adulthood and present in a variety of contexts, as indicated by at least five of the following:

(1) a pattern of unstable and intense interpersonal relationships characterized by alternating between extremes of over-idealization and devaluation

(2) impulsiveness in at least two areas that are potentially self-damaging, e.g., spending, sex, substance use, shoplifting, reckless driving, binge eating

(3) affective instability: marked shifts from baseline mood to depression, irritability, or anxiety, usually lasting a few hours and only rarely more than a few days

(4) inappropriate intense anger or lack of control of anger, e.g., frequent displays of temper, constant anger, recurrent physical fights

(5) recurrent suicidal threats, gestures, or behavior, or self-mutilating behavior

(6) marked and persistent identity disturbance manifested by uncertainty about at least two of the following: self-image, sexual orientation, long-term goals or career choice, type of friends desired, preferred values

(7) chronic feelings of emptiness or boredom

(8) frantic efforts to avoid real or imagined abandonment.

The website on personality disorders www.personalityresearch.org/pd.html suggests the following way to remember this disorder:

A: Abandonment
M: Mood instability (marked reactivity of mood)

S: Suicidal (or self-mutilating) behaviour
U: Unstable and intense relationships
I: Impulsivity (in two potentially self-damaging areas)
C: Control of anger
I: Identity disturbance
D: Dissociative (or paranoid) symptoms that are transient and stress related
E: Emptiness (chronic feelings of).

Hogan and Hogan (2001) call these types 'Excitable' because they expect to be disappointed in relationships; they anticipate being rejected, ignored, criticized or treated unfairly. They are on guard for signs that others have treated or will treat them badly. They erupt in emotional displays that may involve yelling, throwing things and slamming doors. Because they are so alert for signs of mistreatment, they find them everywhere, even when others can't see them. They are neither predictable nor rewarding to deal with. As a result they have a lot of trouble building and maintaining a team – the fundamental task of leadership.

They can be sensitive to the plight of others; they have some capacity for empathy; because they know that life is not always fair, they can genuinely feels others' pain. They sometimes tend to be enthusiastic about, and to work very hard on, new projects. But, they are seriously high maintenance – they require a lot of handholding and reassurance, and they are seriously hard to please.

They do not handle stress or heavy workloads very well, and they tend to explode rather easily. Also they are hard people to talk to and to maintain a relationship with. Consequently they change jobs frequently and they have a large number of failed relationships. They are so easily disappointed in working relationships that their first instinct is to withdraw and leave. They are self-centred – all information and experience are evaluated in terms of what they mean for them personally – and they take the reaction of others personally. They personalize everything, but they do so privately; what others see are the emotional outbursts and the tendency to withdraw. To work with excitable managers, those who report to them must be prepared to provide them with a lot of reassurance, keep them well informed so as to minimize surprises, and give them a lot of preview so they know what is coming. Think of trying to soothe a fretful child.

In lay language Oldham and Morris (1991) suggest that these types, which they call Mercurial, have six characteristics.

1. *Romantic attachment*. Mercurial individuals must always be deeply involved in a romantic relationship with one person.
2. *Intensity*. They experience a passionate, focused attachment in all their relationships. Nothing that goes on between them and other people is trivial. Nothing is taken lightly.
3. *Heart*. They show what they feel. They are emotionally active and reactive. Mercurial types put their hearts into everything.
4. *Unconstraint*. They are uninhibited, spontaneous, fun-loving, and undaunted by risk.
5. *Activity*. Energy marks the Mercurial style. These individuals are lively, creative, busy, and engaging. They show initiative and can stir others to creativity.
6. *Open mind*. They are imaginative and curious, willing to experience the experiment with other cultures, roles, and value systems and to follow new paths. (1991: 282–3)

Oldham and Morris (1991) also provide six tips on dealing with the Borderline personality:

1. Step up on your pedestal. The Mercurial person wants and needs to idealize and overvalue you .... It is inevitable that you will fall from grace by being human and fallible, which will deeply disappoint the Mercurial person.

2. Step down from your pedestal. You may need to remind the Mercurial person – and yourself – rather regularly that although you appreciate his or her feelings and expectations, you are after all a mere mortal who at times is selfish, uninteresting, weak, and even unkind. Ask for acceptance and understanding of all aspects of you ....

3. Don't be surprised or thrown by the Mercurial person's changeable moods, and try not to overreact to them. Realize that little things set off Mercurial people ....

4. Mercurial individuals often expect you to understand what they are reacting to and are hurt when you don't figure it out. Save time and trouble: ask for an explanation.

5. Mercurial individuals can be impulsive and excessive and may let the necessary business of life slide. You be the responsible one if you're good at that ....

6. Show your warmth, love, devotion, and dedication frequently. Hearing how much you love them and how special they are to you is important to Mercurial people. (1991: 297–8)

The borderline manager is unlikely to be very senior but if they are bright and have frequently left jobs they may be appointed to leadership roles that they are very unsuited to fulfil. They certainly are relatively easy to spot but really unpleasant to work for.

Histrionic (colourful, dramatic)

The term is derived from the Latin to mean actor, but the original term was 'hysterical', from the Latin root to mean uterus. This disorder is found more frequently in women. They are attracted to 'limelight' jobs and strive for attention and praise, but setbacks can lead easily to serious inner doubts and depression.

Histrionics are certainly emotionally literate: they are open with all their emotions. But these emotions can change very quickly.

The website on personality disorders www.personalityresearch.org/pd.html suggests PRAISE ME as a way to identify the histrionic personality disorder:

P: Provocative (or sexually seductive) behaviour
R: Relationships (considered more intimate than they are)
A: Attention (uncomfortable when not the centre of attention)
I: Influenced easily
S: Style of speech (impressionistic, lacks detail)
E: Emotions (rapidly shifting and shallow)

M: Made up (physical appearance used to draw attention to self)
E: Emotions exaggerated (theatrical).

These managers have excessive emotionality and attention seeking. They are the 'drama-queens' of the business world.

Most are uncomfortable in situations in which they are not the centre of attention and try always to be so. They delight in making a drama out of a crisis. Their interaction with others is often characterized by inappropriate, sexually seductive or provocative behaviour. Needless to say this causes more of a reaction in women than men. They display rapidly shifting and shallow expression of emotions. They are difficult to read. Most use physical appearance (clothes) to draw attention to self and this may include body piercing or tattooing. They certainly get a reputation in the office for their 'unique apparel'. Many have a style of speech that is excessively impressionistic and lacking in detail. Always they show self-dramatization, theatricality and exaggerated expression of emotion – usually negative. Even the dullest topic is imbued with drama. They are easily influenced by others or circumstances – and therefore both unpredictable and persuadable. Many consider relationships to be more intimate than they actually are. Being rather dramatic, they feel humdrum working relationships more intensely than others.

Histrionics do not make good managers. They get impatient with and anxious about details and routine administrative functions. They prefer gossip to analysis and tend not to be good at detail. They are highly sociable and have intense relationships. They live to win friends and influence people and can do so by being very generous with compliments, flattery and appreciation. They hate being bored: life with them is never staid and dull. They don't like being alone.

Interestingly, the definition of themselves comes from the outside: they see themselves as others say they see them. They therefore lack a consistent sense of who they are. They need constant reassurance and positive feedback from others. And because their heart rules their head they can be impulsive, impetuous and impatient. They live not in the real world but in a storybook world.

At work they can be persuasive and insightful. They enjoy the world of advertising, PR, sales and marketing but need strong back-up for things such as plans, budgets and details. At work they are volatile and are known for being moody. They can be effusive with both praise and blame. But everything is an emotional drama and emotionally they can be both child-like and childish. They don't do stable relationships. At work they need to be the star, the centre of attention or else they can feel powerless or desperately unworthy. They are not introspective. And it is important not to overreact to their overreactions.

Hogan and Hogan (2001) call these types colorful and seem persuaded that others will find them interesting, engaging and worth paying attention to. They are good at calling attention to themselves – they know how to make dramatic entrances and exits, they carry themselves with flair, and self-consciously pay attention to their clothes and to the way that others react to them.

Histrionics are marked by their stage presence or persona, their self-conscious and distinctive aura – they perform extremely well in interviews, in assessment centres and in other public settings:

> They are great fun to watch, but they are also quite impulsive and unpredictable; everything that makes them good at sales (and selling themselves) makes them poor managers – they are noisy, distractible, over-committed, and love to be the centre of attention. They are not necessarily extraverted, they are just good at calling attention to themselves. At their best, they are bright, colorful, entertaining, fun, flirtatious, and the life of the party. At their worst, they don't listen, they don't plan, they self-nominate and self-promote, and they ignore negative feedback. (Hogan and Hogan, 2001: 49)

Histrionics deal with stress and heavy workloads by becoming very busy, enjoying high-pressure situations when they can then be the star. Breathless with excitement, they confuse activity with productivity and evaluate themselves in terms of how many meetings they attend rather than how much they actually get done. A key feature of these people that others may not appreciate is how much they need and feed off approval, and how hard they are willing to work for it. And this explains why they persist in trying to be a star after their lustre has faded. To work with them, those who report to them have to be prepared to put up with missed appointments, bad organization, rapid change of direction and indecisiveness. This will never change, although they can be planned for. Yet by watching reports you can learn how to read social clues, learn how to present your views effectively, forcefully and dramatically, and learn how to flatter and quite simply dazzle other people.

Oldham and Morris (1991) noted seven characteristics of this type, which they call 'Dramatic':

> A person who reveals a strong Dramatic tendency will demonstrate more of these behaviors more intensely than someone who has less of this style.

1. *Feelings*. Dramatic men and women live in an emotional world. They are sensation orientated, emotionally demonstrative, and physically affectionate. They react emotionally to events and can shift quickly from mood to mood.

2. *Color*. They experience life vividly and expansively. They have rich imaginations, they tell entertaining stories, and they are drawn to romance and melodrama.

3. *Spontaneity*. Dramatic individuals are lively and fun. Their joie de vivre leads them to act on impulse to take advantage of the moment.

4. *Attention*. Dramatic people like to be seen and noticed. They are often the centre of attention, and they rise to the occasion when all eyes are on them.

5. *Applause*. Compliments and praise are like food and water to persons with Dramatic style: they need them to go on.

6. *Appearance*. They pay a lot of attention to grooming, and they enjoy clothes, style and fashion.

7. *Sexual attraction*. In appearance and behaviour, Dramatic individuals enjoy their sexuality. They are seductive, engaging, charming tempters and temptresses. (1991: 126–7)

Oldham and Morris also offer six tips on dealing with Dramatic people:

1. You are attracted to the Dramatic person's spontaneity, passion, sensuality, and ability to have a good time .... Allow the Dramatic person his or her emotional freedom, and enjoy the range of experience that will result.

2. Appreciate, praise, flatter, and give feedback. The Dramatic person needs you to react openly and verbally, especially about your positive feelings, at all times. Don't hold back; there's no such thing as too much of a good thing with this personality style. But be sure to be honest ....

3. Be romantic .... Even if the Dramatic person in your life is a friend, relative, or parent, these sentimental attentions will delight and thrill him or her.

4. Be realistic about this person's relative inability or reluctance to handle certain responsibilities, including money. Handle the finances or the financial planning yourself, if need be. Better, supervise or double check essential details ....

5. Don't hold grudges. Dramatic persons don't hold things in, and the Dramatic person in your life may be emotionally tempestuous .... Try to let go of your own anger or annoyance. Don't take the Dramatic person's emotional reactions personally and don't be frightened by the drama.

6. Avoid jealousy .... Dramatic individuals like to charm other people. Try feeling flattered and turned on by the warm attentions of others to your mate and have a good time at the party. (1991: 139–40)

There are drama-queens in all sectors, although they are likely to be found in the more human resource-oriented world. They can do very well in

PR, marketing and training, particularly if they are talented. But they certainly remain hard work for those who report to them.

Narcissistic (arrogant, self-confident)

It may surprise some to learn that this disorder apparently occurs in only 1% of the population. There are a lot of them in business striving for adulation and power. There is of course a fine line between healthy self-esteem and serious self-defeating narcissism. The latter is characterized by insatiable craving for adoration, feeling a special entitlement and right to be insensitive to others, but at the same time being either enraged or crushed by criticism – it is the feeling that one deserves special treatment but then being extremely upset if you are treated like the ordinary other person.

The website www.personalityresearch.org/pd.html suggests that the word SPECIAL is a helpful way to diagnose the narcissistic personality disorder:

S: Special (believes he or she is special and unique)
P: Preoccupied with fantasies (of unlimited success, power, brilliance, beauty, or ideal love)
E: Entitlement
C: Conceited (grandiose sense of self-importance)
I: Interpersonal exploitation
A: Arrogant (haughty)
L: Lacks empathy.

This manager is marked by grandiosity (in fantasy or behaviour), need for admiration and lack of empathy. Self-centred, selfish, egotistical: they are everywhere in business – alas.

They have a grandiose sense of self-importance (for example, exaggerated achievements and talents, expects to be recognized as superior without commensurate achievements). Most are preoccupied with fantasies of unlimited success, power, brilliance and money. They believe that they are 'special' and unique and can only be understood by, or should associate with, other special or high-status people (or institutions). They may try to 'buy' themselves into exclusive circles. Always they require excessive admiration and respect from everyone at work. Bizarrely, often they have sense of entitlement – that is, unreasonable expectations of especially favourable treatment or automatic compliance with their manifest needs. Worse, they take advantage of others to achieve their own ends, which makes them terrible managers. They lack empathy. All are unwilling to recognize or identify with the feelings and needs of others. They have desperately low EQ. Curiously they are often envious of others and believe that others are envious of them. They show arrogant, haughty behaviours or attitudes all the time and everywhere at work (and home). At times this can be pretty amusing but is mostly simply frustrating.

Narcissists are super-self-confident: they express considerable self-certainty. They are 'self-people' – self-asserting, self-possessed, self-aggrandizing, self-preoccupied, self-loving – and ultimately self-destructive. They really believe in themselves: they were born lucky. At work they are out-going, high energy, competitive and very 'political'. They can make good leaders as long as they are not criticized, or made to share glory. They seem to have an insatiable need to be admired, love and be needed. They are often a model of ambitious, driven, high-self-esteem, self-disciplined, socially successful people. The world is their stage.

But narcissism is a disorder of self-esteem: it's a cover-up. They self-destruct because their self-aggrandizement blinds their personal and business judgement and perception. At work they exploit others to get ahead yet they demand special treatment. But their reaction to any sort of criticism is extreme: shame, rage, tantrums. They aim to destroy that criticism, however well intentioned and useful. They are poor empathizers and thus have low emotional intelligence. They can be consumed with envy and disdain of others, and are prone to depression, manipulative, demanding and self-centred; even therapists don't like them. Oldham and Morris (1991: 93–4) summarize the psychiatric diagnostic criteria thus:

A pervasive pattern of grandiosity (in fantasy or behaviour), lack of empathy, and hypersensitivity to the evaluation of others, beginning by early adulthood and present in a variety of contexts, as indicated by at least five of the following:

(1) reacts to criticism with feelings of rage, shame or humiliation (even if not expressed)
(2) is interpersonally exploitative: takes advantage of others to achieve his or her own ends
(3) has a grandiose sense of self-importance, e.g., exaggerates achievements and talents, expects to be noticed as 'special' without appropriate achievement
(4) believes that his or her problems are unique and can be understood only by other special people
(5) is preoccupied with fantasies of unlimited success, power, brilliance, beauty, or ideal love
(6) has a sense of entitlement: unreasonable expectation of especially favorable treatment, e.g., assumes that he or she does not have to wait in line when others must do so
(7) requires constant attention and admiration, e.g., keeps fishing for compliments
(8) lack of empathy; inability to recognize and experience how others feel, e.g., annoyance and surprise when a friend who is seriously ill cancels a date
(9) is preoccupied with feelings of envy.

Hogan and Hogan (2001) call these types 'Arrogant': 'the lord of the high chair'. A two year old, sitting in its high chair demanding food, and attention, and squealing in fury when his or her needs are not met. Narcissists expect to be liked, admired, respected, attended to, praised, complimented and indulged. Their most important and obvious characteristic is a sense of entitlement, excessive self-esteem and quite often an expectation of success that often leads to real success. They expect to be successful at everything they undertake, they believe that people are so interested in them that books will be written about them, and when their needs and expectations are frustrated, they explode with 'narcissistic rage'.

What is most distinctive about the narcissists is their self-assurance, which often gives them charisma. Hogan and Hogan (1999) note that they are the first to speak in a group, and they hold forth with great confidence, even when they are wrong. They so completely expect to succeed, and take more credit for success than is warranted or fair, that they refuse to acknowledge failure, errors or mistakes. When things go right, it is because of their efforts; when things go wrong, it is someone else's fault. This is a classic attribution error. This leads to some problems with truth telling because they always rationalize, and reinterpret their failures and mistakes, usually by blaming them on others.

Narcissists can be energetic, charismatic, leader like, and willing to take the initiative to get projects moving. They can be successful in management, sales and entrepreneurship. However, they are arrogant, vain, overbearing, demanding, self-deceived and pompous. They are so colourful and engaging that they often attract followers.

Narcissists handle stress and heavy workloads with ease; they are also quite persistent under pressure and they refuse to acknowledge failure. As a result of their inability to acknowledge failure or even mistakes and the way they resist coaching and ignore negative feedback, they are unable to learn from experience.

Oldham and Morris (1991: 80) note nine characteristics of these types they call 'Self-Confident':

1. *Self-regard.* Self-Confident individuals believe in themselves and in their abilities. They have no doubt that they are unique and special and that there is a reason for their being on this planet.
2. *The red carpet.* They expect others to treat them well at all times.
3. *Self-propulsion.* Self-Confident people are open about their ambitions and achievements. They energetically and effectively sell themselves, their goals, their projects, and their ideas.
4. *Politics.* They are able to take advantage of the strengths and abilities of other people in order to achieve their goals, and they are shrewd in their dealings with others.

5. *Competition*. They are able competitors, they love getting to the top, and they enjoy staying there.

6. *Dreams*. Self-Confident individuals are able to visualize themselves as the hero, the star, the best in their role, or the most accomplished in their field.

7. *Self-awareness*. These individuals have a keen awareness of their thoughts and feelings and their overall inner state of being.

8. *Poise*. People with the Self-Confident personality style accept compliments, praise, and admiration gracefully and with self-possession.

9. *Sensitivity to criticism*. The Self-Confident style confers an emotional vulnerability to the negative feelings and assessments of others, which are deeply felt, although they may be handled with this style's customary grace.

More importantly, they note four tips for working with narcissists:

1. Be absolutely loyal. Don't criticize or compete with them. Don't expect to share the limelight or to take credit. Be content to aspire to the number-two position.

2. Don't expect your Self-Confident boss to provide direction. Likely he or she will expect you to know what to do, so be sure you are clear about the objectives before you undertake any task. Don't hesitate to ask.

3. You may be an important member of the boss's team, but don't expect your Self-Confident boss to be attentive to you as an individual. Don't take it personally.

4. Self-Confident bosses expect your interest in them, however. They are susceptible to flattery, so if you're working on a raise or a promotion or are trying to sell your point of view, a bit of buttering up may smooth the way. (Oldham and Morris, 1991: 85)

The business world often calls for and rewards arrogant, self-confident, self-important people. They seek out power and abuse it. They thrive in selling jobs and those where they have to do media work. But, as anyone who works with and for them knows, they can destabilize and destroy working groups by their deeply inconsiderate behaviour.

Avoidant (cautious, sensitive)

This disorder is equally common in men and women and is believed to affect 0.5–1% of the population. People with this disorder seem to be social phobics in that they are socially isolated and withdrawn. Feelings of possible rejection drive them to situations where they are likely to be shunned. They seek acceptance, approval and affection.

The website www.personalityresearch.org/pd.html suggests that CRINGES is a good way to remember the key characteristics of this disorder:

C: Certainty (of being liked required before willing to get involved with others)

R: Rejection (or criticism) preoccupies one's thoughts in social situations

I: Intimate relationships (restraint in intimate relationships due to fear of being shamed)

N: New interpersonal relationships (is inhibited in)

G: Gets around occupational activity (involving significant interpersonal contact)

E: Embarrassment (potential) prevents new activity or taking personal risks

S: Self viewed as unappealing, inept or inferior.

These poor souls show social inhibition, feelings of inadequacy and hypersensitivity to negative evaluation. They are supersensitive, delicate flowers.

They avoid occupational activities that involve significant interpersonal contact, because of fears of criticism, disapproval or rejection. Any chance of negative feedback is to be avoided. They are unwilling to get involved with people unless they are certain of being liked, which is pretty difficult at work – indeed, anywhere. They show restraint in intimate relationships because of the fear of being shamed or ridiculed. They are cold fish. They seem always preoccupied with being criticized or rejected in work situations. They are inhibited in new interpersonal situations because of feelings of inadequacy. They see themselves as socially inept, personally unappealing or inferior to others. It can be puzzling to wonder how they ever became managers in the first place. Certainly people with low self-esteem rarely make it to the top in business.

These rather sensitive types seek safety: in people and environments they know and trust. But they can easily become anxious, guarded and worried. Beneath a polite and cool façade they can feel very uneasy. They cope with their anxiety by being prepared for everything. They like life, their friends and work to be safe, secure and predictable. They do not like the new: strangers, unfamiliar people or ways of working. They prefer what they know and they try to make work a home away from home. They can be effective, reliable and steady, and show little need for variety and challenge. They like routine and are pleased to help their seniors. But they are not political in organizations and can take refuge in their professionalism. They do well in technical fields that require routine, repetition and habit.

But the avoidants are so afraid of rejection that they live impoverished social lives. The paradox is that they avoid close relationships that could bring them exactly what they want: acceptance and approval. Because they feel isolated, unwanted and incompetent, they are sure others will reject them and often they are rejected because of their cold, detached behaviour. They are supersensitive to negative feedback and want unconditional love. Yet they believe you cannot really be loveable unless you are without imperfections. They are often very self-conscious and can feel strong self-contempt and anger towards others. Allergic to social anxiety, they routinize themselves in a safe world.

Oldham and Morris (1991: 188–89) summarize the diagnostic criteria thus:

> A pervasive pattern of social discomfort, fear of negative evaluation, and timidity, beginning by early adulthood and present in a variety of contexts, as indicated by at least four of the following:
>
> (1) is easily hurt by criticism or disapproval
> (2) has no close friends or confidants (or only one) other than first-degree relatives
> (3) is unwilling to get involved with people unless certain of being liked
> (4) avoids social or occupational activities that involve significant interpersonal contact, e.g., refuses a promotion that will increase social demands
> (5) is reticent in social situations because of a fear of saying something inappropriate or foolish, or of being unable to answer a question
> (6) fears being embarrassed by blushing, crying, or showing signs of anxiety in front of other people
> (7) exaggerates the potential difficulties, physical dangers, or risks involved in doing something ordinary but outside his or her usual routine, e.g., may cancel social plans because she anticipates being exhausted by the effort of getting there.

Hogan and Hogan (2001) call this type 'Cautious' and stress their fear of being criticized, shamed, blamed, humiliated or somehow disgraced: 'They do not handle failure, rejection, or criticism well; as a result, they are constantly on guard against the possibilities of making errors, mistakes, or blunders, that might cause them to be publicly embarrassed. Because they are so alert to possible criticism, they see hazards and threats everywhere, even when others cannot see them. They respond to the possibility of being criticized by hand wringing, perseverance, freezing, becoming very cautious and taking no action at all. When they are threatened, they will also forbid their staff from taking any initiative. These people are unpopular managers because they are so cautious, indecisive, and controlling.'

Avoidant types can be prudent, careful and meticulous about evaluating risk. They rarely make rash or ill-advised moves, and they can provide sound, prudential advice about intended future courses of action. However, they avoid innovation and resist change, even when it is apparent that something needs to be done. They seem particularly threatened by the new, the different, and the strange, and they vastly prefer to react rather than take the initiative. If their working world is stable they can thrive: if not their behaviour may be maladaptive.

Under stress, avoidants begin to adhere to established procedures, and will rely on the tried and true rather than on any new technology or other procedures. They may try to control their staff, in the fear that someone on the staff will make a mistake and embarrass them, especially with their seniors. They do exactly what their seniors tell them and they enforce standard rules and procedures on their staff and others over whom they have any power. They hate to be criticized; what others will see is cautiousness, rigidity, adherence to standardized procedures, and resistance to innovation and change.

To work with the cautious type, those who report to them need to keep them well informed about activities that concern them – where negative outcomes could reflect on them, and to consult them about intended future actions. When rapid action is needed, or when some form of innovation needs to be implemented, it is best to avoid it or put in writing the fact that you recommended action or innovation, and then be prepared for nothing to happen.

The following five traits and behaviours are clues to the presence of what Oldham and Morris (1991: 174) call the 'Sensitive' style:

A person who reveals a strong Sensitive tendency will demonstrate more of these behaviors more intensely than someone with less of this style in his or her personality profile:

1. *Familiarity*. Individuals with the Sensitive personality style prefer the known to the unknown. They are uncomfortable with, even inspired by, habit, repetition, and routine.
2. *Family*. They stick close to the family and/or a few close friends. They do not require a wide network of friends and acquaintances, and they appreciate the comforts of home.
3. *Concern*. Sensitive individuals care deeply about what other people think of them.
4. *Circumspection*. They behave with deliberate discretion in their dealings with others. They do not make hasty judgments or jump in before they know what is appropriate.
5. *Polite reserve*. Socially they take care to maintain a courteous, self-restrained demeanour.

They provide seven tips for dealing with these types:

1. Count your blessings. Treasure the closeness and loyalty that your Sensitive person offers you ....

2. Accept the Sensitive person complete with shortcomings. If your Sensitive mate becomes stiff or withdrawn among strangers or is otherwise not him or herself in company, so what?

3. Avoid emotional torture. Don't insist that a Sensitive person do things he or she shuns just to please you. Sensitive individuals want you to be happy

with them, but there are some things they just can't stand doing ....

4. Compromise .... Sensitive people want to please the important people in their lives, so your willingness to compromise may encourage them to take a few steps farther out than they would ordinarily go.

5. Help. Act as a guide to the unfamiliar. Go to social events with this person and accompany him or her on jaunts into unfamiliar territory. But don't overdo it ....

6. Recognise the signs .... Reassure the Sensitive person that everyone is going to like him or her – what's not to like?

7. Talk about it. If the Sensitive person's anxieties are cramping your style, don't keep it to yourself. Don't attack your loved one for having these difficulties. Rather, express the problems openly and directly. Say you are interested in finding a solution that accommodates both of you. (Oldham and Morris, 1991: 184–5)

Frankly, few cautious, sensitive, avoidant personality-disordered types make it to the top. Those that do soon find they can't hack it, so leave.

Dependent (devoted)

People with this disorder are more heavily reliant on other people for support or guidance than most. Like young children they can be clinging, submissive and subservient in all relationships, fearing separation. Dependents are carers – most are happy helping others be happy. Others give meaning to their lives. They worry about others and need others. They find contentment in attachment and define themselves by others. They are not good at giving (or receiving) criticism and negative feedback. At work they are cooperative, supportive, caring and encouraging. They do brilliantly in jobs such as nursing, social work and voluntary organizations.

The website www.personalityresearch.org/pd.html believes the mnemonic RELIANCE is a good way to diagnose the dependent personality disorder:

R: Reassurance required for decisions
E: Expressing disagreement difficult (due to fear of loss of support or approval)
L: Life responsibilities (needs to have these assumed by others)
I: Initiating projects difficult (due to lack of self-confidence)
A: Alone (feels helpless and discomfort when alone)
N: Nurturance (goes to excessive lengths to obtain nurturance and support)
C: Companionship (another relationship) sought urgently when close relationship ends
E: Exaggerated fears of being left to care for self.

These managers have a pervasive and excessive need to be taken care of by others. This leads to submissive and clinging behaviour and fears of separation.

These managers suffer analysis paralysis. They cannot make decisions on their own without continual advice and reassurance from others. Others need to assume responsibility for most major areas of the dependent's life. Inevitably they are good at delegating. But they seem always to need help and reassurance. Most have difficulty expressing disagreement with others because of fear of loss of support or approval. They publicly agree while privately disagreeing. This of course makes them difficult to read. They all have difficulty initiating projects or doing things on their own (because of a lack of self-confidence in judgement or abilities rather than a lack of motivation or energy). So they resist change, particularly where it leads to their being isolated or threatened. Some go to excessive lengths to obtain nurturance and support from others, often humiliating themselves in the process. All feel uncomfortable or helpless when alone because of exaggerated fears of being unable to care for themselves at work (and home).

Dependent people do not make good managers because they are too quick to be apologetic, submissive and self-deprecating. They attach themselves to others who may all too easily take advantage of them. Kind, gentle, generous and full of humility, they do not believe in themselves. They have very low self-confidence in all aspects of life and acquire self-esteem through their attachments to others. Despite their smiling exterior they often feel depression and dejection. Furthermore, they can doom the relationships they value so much because they are too clinging and eager to please.

Oldham and Morris (1991: 122–3) noted the nine psychiatric diagnostic criteria:

A pervasive pattern of dependent and submissive behavior, beginning by early adulthood and present in a variety of contexts, as indicated by at least five of the following:

(1) is unable to make everyday decisions without an excessive amount of advice or reassurance from others
(2) allows others to make most of his or her important decisions, e.g., where to live, what job to take
(3) agrees with people even when he or she believes they are wrong, because of fear of being rejected
(4) has difficulty initiating projects or doing things on his or her own
(5) volunteers to do things that are unpleasant or demeaning in order to get other people to like him or her
(6) feels uncomfortable or helpless when alone, or goes to great lengths to avoid being alone
(7) feels devastated or helpless when close relationships end
(8) is frequently preoccupied with being abandoned
(9) is easily hurt by criticism or disapproval.

Hogan and Hogan (2001) note that dependent personalities are deeply concerned about being accepted, being liked and getting along, especially with authority figures. They are hyper-alert for signs of disapproval, and for opportunities to ingratiate themselves, to be of service, to demonstrate their fealty and loyalty to the organization. When they think they have given offence, they redouble their efforts to be model citizens. People notice their good nature, their politeness, their cordiality and their indecisiveness. As managers, they will do anything their boss requires, which means that they are reluctant to stick up for their staff or challenge authority, and this inevitably erodes their legitimacy as leaders.

They are polite, conforming and eager to please. They rarely make enemies and they tend to rise in organizations. But they have problems making decisions, taking initiative or taking stands on tough issues. Thus their sections tend to drift, and they can have trouble maintaining a team.

They respond to stress by freezing and becoming passive, and by hoping that someone else will take the initiative, step up, make a decision, assign responsibility and get things moving. They are too reliant on the initiative of others and can become a bottleneck for productivity and a source of delay and lost time.

They are deeply concerned with pleasing authority, which, in turn, is pleasing to authority, but they provide little leadership for those who must work for them. To work with them those who report to them must be prepared for indecisiveness, inaction and lack of leadership. They must also be prepared to take the initiative when processes get stalled, but accept the fact that they will not be supported should their initiative fail or backfire. Hogan and Hogan (2001) believe that, to work with these people, you must be prepared to flatter them, to agree with them, to be exploited, to allow them to take credit for your accomplishments, and to allow them to blame you for their failures: 'Along the way, however, you will profit from observing their pluck, stamina and ability to manipulate others to their ends.'

Oldham and Morris (1991: 104) noted seven typical characteristics of what they call the 'Devoted' style:

1. *Commitment.* Individuals with the Devoted personality style are thoroughly dedicated to the relationships in their lives. They place the highest value on sustained relationships, they respect the institution of marriage as well as unofficial avowals of commitment, and they work hard to keep their relationships together.
2. *Togetherness.* They prefer the company of one or more people to being alone.
3. *Teamwork.* People with this personality style would rather follow than lead. They are cooperative and respectful of authority and institutions. They easily rely on others and take direction well.

4. *Deference*. When making decisions, they are happy to seek out others' opinions and to follow their advice.
5. *Harmony*. Devoted individuals are careful to promote good feelings between themselves and the important people in their lives. To promote harmony, they tend to be polite, agreeable, and tactful.
6. *Consideration*. They are thoughtful of others and good at pleasing them. Devoted people will endure personal discomfort to do a good turn for the key people in their lives.
7. *Self-Correction*. In response to criticism, they will try hard to change their behaviour.

They also offer four tips on dealing with these types:

1. The Devoted person likes to help and to please. Don't fight it, and don't feel guilty for accepting it. Enjoy.

2. Don't take the attentions of this person for granted. The Devoted person may be so good at anticipating your desires and putting you first that you may not recognize that he or she has unfulfilled, unexpressed needs and longings. Devoted types often seem more confident and assertive than they actually are ....

3. Keep in mind that criticizing this individual, or blowing your top, will likely lead to Devoted self-doubt and self-blame, not particularly constructive reactions. When you need to resolve a conflict with a Devoted person, or deal with unpleasant personal business, contribute as much reassurance as you can ....

4. Take the stated opinions of this person with a grain of salt. The more Devoted a person is, the more that person will express an opinion that he or she thinks you want to hear .... (1991: 113–14)

This personality disorder is nearly always associated with being a number two rather than a number one in any relationship. But even so they may have a staff that they inevitably do not manage well.

Passive–aggressive (leisurely)

This personality type is very concerned about 'doing their own thing'. They demand the 'right to be me'. They have a right to do their thing in their way and no one has the right to deprive them of it. They believe that nobody has the right to own them at work and in private relationships. They like the companionship of others but need strong defences against being ill-used. They are particularly sensitive to fairness.

They do not find the workplace of great importance. They can be good managers and workers. But they do not work overtime, take it home or worry much about it. They certainly will not do any more than their contract specifies. They do not work to please the boss or feel better about themselves. They are often heard saying 'It's not my job' and they tend to be suspicious of workplace authority. If their boss asks them to work harder, faster or more accurately, they feel unfairly treated, even abused. They are supersensitive to their rights, fairness and exploitation avoidance. They seem leisurely; they believe success is not everything. They tend not to be above middle-management levels because they are not ambitious or thrusting enough. For them the game is not worth the candle.

Passive–aggressive types are not usually stressed. They sulk, procrastinate and forget when asked to do things they think are not fair. They are called passive–aggressive because they are rarely openly defiant; yet they are often angry. They snipe rather than confront. And they are often furious. Then can be needy but resentful about those moods. They are in essence oppositional: not assertive. They often have downward job mobility.

According to Oldham and Morris (1991: 212–13), the DSM-III-R describes 'Passive-Aggressive' personality disorder as:

A pervasive pattern of passive resistance to demands for adequate social and occupational performance, beginning by early adulthood and present in a variety of contexts, as indicated by at least five of the following:

(1) procrastinates, i.e., puts off things that need to be done so that deadlines are not met
(2) becomes sulky, irritable, or argumentative when asked to do something he or she does not want to do
(3) seems to work deliberately slowly or to do a bad job on tasks that he or she really does not want to do
(4) protests, without justification, that others make unreasonable demands on him or her
(5) avoids obligations by claiming to have 'forgotten'
(6) believes that he or she is doing a much better job than others think he or she is doing
(7) resents useful suggestions from others concerning how he or she could be more productive
(8) obstructs the efforts of others by failing to do his or her share of the work
(9) unreasonably criticizes or scorns people in positions of authority.

Hogan and Hogan (2001) call these people 'Leisurely'. They argue that these types march to the sound of their own drum, they are confident about their skills and abilities, cynical about the talents and intentions of others – especially superiors – and they insist on working at their own pace. They tend to get angry and slow down even more when asked to speed up. They tend to feel mistreated, unappreciated and put upon and, when they sense that they have been cheated, they retaliate, but always under conditions of high deniability. They are curiously quite skilled at hiding their annoyance and pretending to be cooperative, and their peevishness and foot dragging are often very hard to detect.

They are often late for meetings, they procrastinate, they work at about 80% of their capacity, and they are very stubborn and hard to coach. They will rarely directly confront others. Their prickly sensitivity, subtle cooperativeness, stubbornness and deep absorption make them both unpredictable and unrewarding to deal with. As a result, they have trouble building and maintaining a team.

Passive–aggressives handle stress and heavy workloads by slowing down, by simply ignoring requests for greater output, and by finding ways to get out of work. Because they seem overtly cooperative and agreeable, it takes a long time to realize how unproductive and refractory they actually can be. They are self-centred, they focus on their own agendas, and they believe deeply in their own superior natural talent and their right to leisure. They believe that they have nothing to prove to themselves, are quite indifferent to feedback from others, and therefore become annoyed and resentful when criticized or asked for extra effort.

People need to be aware that they are not nearly as cooperative as they seem, and that they are only pretending to agree with you about work and performance issues. Also you need to get them to commit to performance goals in public, in front of witnesses, so that a community of people can hold them accountable. Social pressure won't change their views of the world, but it will serve to make their performance deficits less easily deniable.

Oldham and Morris (1991: 194–5) claim that the following five traits and behaviours are clues to the presence of what they too call the 'Leisurely' style. A person who reveals a strong leisurely tendency will demonstrate more of these behaviours more intensely than someone with less of this style in his or her personality profile.

1. *Inalienable rights.* Leisurely men and women believe in their right to enjoy themselves on their own terms in their own time. They value and protect their comfort, their free time, and their individual pursuit of happiness.
2. *Enough is enough.* They agree to play by the rules. They deliver what is expected of them and no more. They expect others to recognize and respect that limit.
3. *The right to resist.* Leisurely individuals cannot be exploited. They can comfortably resist acceding to demands that they deem unreasonable or above and beyond the call of duty.
4. *Mañana.* Leisurely men and women are relaxed about time. Unlike Type-A individuals, they are not obsessed by time urgency or the demands of the clock. To these individuals, haste makes waste and unnecessary anxiety. They are easygoing and optimistic that whatever needs to get done will get done, eventually.

5. *I'm okay*. They are not overawed by authority. They accept themselves and their approach to life. They are content with their place in the universe.

They offer eight tips on dealing with the leisurely passive–aggressive type:

1. Accept the Leisurely person as he or she is. Don't approach a relationship with such a person with the expectation of changing him or her to suit your needs. Rather, ask yourself what it is in this person that you like and are attracted to ....

2 If you are having difficulty with a Leisurely person, ask yourself whether the problems arise because you two have different value systems. Perhaps you come from a push-hard, get-ahead, make-a-success-of-yourself tradition, while the Leisurely person sees more value in doing his or her own thing. Instead of judging one system as better than the other, ask yourself whether your two value systems can coexist or merge ....

3. Be realistic. Life with a Leisurely person may demand more sacrifices from you than from him or her. Can you make these without bitterness or resentment?

4. Make life easier for yourself. People with the Leisurely personality style don't automatically tune in to what's important to you. Instead of waiting for this person to figure it out, let him or her know your basic, essential expectations ....

5. Leisurely types can be stubborn about protecting their rights to do or to be as they please. Offer to assist in projects that need doing and/or make a deal.

6. When the Leisurely person in your life starts stalling, refusing, or forgetting, ask, 'Are you angry about something?' People with this personality style have a hard time expressing their anger directly.

7. Try to share in the Leisurely person's pleasures. Observe his or her habits and routines and join in.

8. Take good care of him or her. Leisurely people are suckers for pampering and loving attention. (1991: 208–9)

There are many senior managers with this rather unattractive profile. Their 'pathology' may have served them well even if the burden of it has been 'picked up' by their long-suffering staff.

Obsessive–compulsive (diligent, conscientious)

This disorder is more common in men and about 1% of the population exhibit the symptoms. They are often known for their zealous perfectionism, for their attention to detail, for their rigidity and for their formality. They are also often the workaholics – those who really 'live' the work ethic.

They are competent, organized, thorough, loyal. They enjoy, even in their holidays and leisure time, intense, detailed, goal-oriented activity.

The website www.personalityresearch.org/pd.html suggests that LAW FIRMS is a way to remember the essential features of the obsessive–compulsive type:

L: Loses point of activity (due to preoccupation with detail)
A: Ability to complete tasks (compromised by perfectionism)
W: Worthless objects (unable to discard)

F: Friendships (and leisure activities) excluded (due to a preoccupation with work)
I: Inflexible, scrupulous, over-conscientious (on ethics, values, or morality, not accounted for by religion or culture)
R: Reluctant to delegate (unless others submit to exact guidelines)
M: Miserly (toward self and others)
S: Stubbornness (and rigidity).

These managers show a preoccupation with orderliness, perfectionism, and mental and interpersonal control, at the expense of flexibility, openness and efficiency. They make for the most anal of bureaucrats. Always they are preoccupied with details, rules, lists, order, organization or schedules, to the extent that the major point of the business activity is lost and forgotten. All show perfectionism that interferes with task completion (for example, they are unable to complete a project because their own overly strict standards are not met). And of course they demand it in others, however unproductive it makes them. These managers are often workaholics, often excluding leisure activities and friendships. They are seriously driven workaholics. They have a well-deserved reputation for being over-conscientious, scrupulous and inflexible about matters of morality, ethics or values.

Amazingly, they are unable to discard worn-out or worthless objects, even when they have no sentimental value. They hoard rubbish at home and in the workplace. They are reluctant to delegate tasks or to work with others unless they submit to exactly his or her way of doing things. They do not let go and pay the price. They are misers towards both self and others; money is viewed as something to be hoarded for future catastrophes. Because they never fully spend their budget, they never get it increased. In short, they show rigidity and stubbornness – and are very unpleasant to work for.

Conscientious obsessive–compulsives rise through the ranks through hard work. But at certain levels they start to derail because they have problems making quick decisions, setting priorities and delegating. They tend to want to check the details again and again. They function best as right-hand-men or -women to leaders with strong conceptual skills and visions. They are very self-disciplined and put work first. They are often not very emotionally literate and can be fanatical and fundamentalist about moral, political and religious issues. They can find it difficult to relax and difficult to throw things away. Their relationships are marked by conventionality and coolness. They are faithful and responsible but unromantic and unemotional. They can be seen as mean and over-cautious.

The obsessive–compulsive manager *must* have everything done *perfectly*. They get wrapped up in details and lose their sense of directions and priorities. They can be tyrannical bosses who are super-attentive to time, orderliness and cleanliness. They are driven by 'oughts' and 'shoulds' and expect others to be likewise. They make rules for themselves and others but don't see themselves as rigid, perfectionistic and controlling. They are the overbearing, fault-finders of the business world. They are driven to achieve respect and approval and control their, and others', dangerous impulses, desires and feelings.

Oldham and Morris (1991: 71–2) describe the psychiatric criteria:

(1) perfectionism that interferes with task completion, e.g., inability to complete a project because own overly strict standards are not met

(2) preoccupation with details, rules, lists, order, organization, or schedules to the extent that the major point of the activity is lost

(3) unreasonable insistence that others submit to exactly his or her way of doing things, or unreasonable reluctance to allow others to do things because of the conviction that they will not do them correctly

(4) excessive devotion to work and productivity to the exclusion of leisure activities and friendships (not accounted for by obvious economic necessity)

(5) indecisiveness: decision making is avoided, postponed, or protracted, e.g., the person cannot get assignments done on time because of ruminating about priorities (do not include if indecisiveness is due to excessive need for advice or reassurance from others)

(6) over-conscientiousness, scrupulousness, and inflexibility about matters of morality, ethics, or values (not accounted for by cultural or religious identification)

(7) restricted expression of affection

(8) lack of generosity in giving time, money, or gifts when no personal gain is likely to result

(9) inability to discard worn-out or worthless objects even when they have no sentimental value.

Hogan and Hogan (2001) called these types 'Diligent' because they are concerned with doing a good job, being a good citizen and pleasing authority. They note that the diligent type is hard working, careful, planful, meticulous and that they have very high standards of performance for themselves and other people. They live by these rules and expect others to do so too, and they become irritable and erratic when others do not follow their rules. What is most distinctive is their conservatism, their detail orientation and their risk aversion, but they are also thought of as reliable, dependable and predictable. They are often desirable organizational citizens who can always be relied on to maintain standards, to do their work competently and professionally, and to treat their colleagues with respect.

Hogan and Hogan note that they are good role models who uphold the highest standards of professionalism in performance and comportment. They are popular with their bosses because they are so completely reliable, but not necessarily with those who report to them. However, they are fussy, particularly nit-picking, micro-managers who deprive their subordinates of any choice or control over their work. Their sin is micro-management. This alienates their staff, who soon refuse to take any initiative and simply wait to be told what to do and how to do it. Diligent, conscientious obsessive–compulsives also cause stress for themselves; their obsessive concern for quality and high performance makes it difficult for them to delegate. It also makes it difficult for them to prioritize their tasks. They also have problems with vision and the big picture. Consequently, they have a kind of ambivalent status as managers and can function in some environments at certain levels.

Diligent obsessionals tend to become stressed by heavy workloads. They respond to increased workloads by working longer and harder (not smarter) and they fall further and further behind, and they find this intolerable. They often become a bottleneck to productivity – because everything must pass through them, be checked and revised by them, be approved by them, and they won't let anything go that isn't completed according to their standards. They closely supervise their staff. You can help by making suggestions regarding prioritizing work, and by putting tasks into context by reflecting on the big picture. In everyday language, Oldham and Morris (1991: 57) describe nine characteristics of these types:

1. *Hard work.* The conscientious person is dedicated to work, works very hard, and is capable of intense, single-minded effort.
2. *The right thing.* To be Conscientious is to be a person of conscience. These are men and women of strong moral principles and values. Opinions and beliefs on any subject are rarely held lightly. Conscientious individuals want to do the right thing.
3. *The right way.* Everything must be done 'right', and the Conscientious person has a clear understanding of what that means, from the correct way to balance the cheque book, to the best strategy to achieve the boss's objectives, to how to fit every single dirty dish into the dishwasher.
4. *Perfectionism.* The Conscientious person likes projects to be complete to the final detail, without even minor flaws.
5. *Love of detail.* Conscientious men and women take seriously all the steps of any project. No detail is too small for Conscientious consideration.
6. *Order.* Conscientious people like the appearance of orderliness and tidiness. They are good organizers, cataloguers and list makers, and they appreciate schedules and routines.

7. *Pragmatism.* Conscientious types approach the world and other people from a practical, no-nonsense point of view. They roll up their sleeves and get to work without much emotional expenditure.

8. *Prudence.* Thrifty, careful, and cautious in all areas of their lives, Conscientious individuals do not give in to reckless abandon or wild excess.

9. *Accumulation.* A 'pack rat', the Conscientious person saves and collect things (storing them in orderly bundles), reluctant to discard anything that has, formerly had, or someday may have value for him or her.

They also offer tips for dealing with these types:

1. Be humorously tolerant. Let the Conscientious person have his or her habits ....

2. Stay flexible ....

3. Don't wait for the Conscientious person to change. Bring your strengths to the relationship and use them ....

4. Don't expect compliments or easy expressions of affection; these are not a barometer of how a Conscientious person feels about you ....

5. Avoid arguments and power struggles at all costs. Conscientious people must win – it's their nature. Conscientious men and women are consummate arguers and may nit-pick and split hairs until you walk out or give in ....

6. Appreciate and enjoy the security and stability that the Conscientious person brings to the relationship. Be reassured that he or she takes care of your life so well. (1991: 67–8)

The diligent, conscientious type can do very well in business. Certain jobs demand obsessive–compulsive checking, such as health and safety and quality control. But like all the other disorders it is too much of this trait that leads to serious problems for both the individual and their staff.

Self-defeating (self-sacrificing)

These are the self-sacrificing altruists of the personality-disordered world. They achieve meaning in life and satisfaction through serving others and sacrificing for them. They may feel undeserving of attention and pleasure and unworthy of love; therefore they have to earn it. They work long and hard for others and give their all in relationships. But they do not want thanks or attention and feel discomfort with positive compliments or praise. They seem guilty but they can be seriously neglected and under-recognized, which does cause pain and confusion. They tend not to have their own needs met. They see life as tough, unfair and uncompromising, and their job is to help those less fortunate than themselves. They are good under stress but can get resentful if they are consistently ignored.

To a large extent the self-defeating personality is ideal at work. Hard-working, respectful and adaptable, they are, however, very concerned about the value and meaning of the work. They make reliable, loyal, undemanding, non-assertive workers. However, they rarely realize their potential: they turn down promotion for others.

Self-defeatists rarely end up as managers. But their dedication and loyalty may mean they end up in middle-management positions. But inevitably they have problems with delegation and discipline and take on too much themselves. They may feel, quite rightly, that their staff are ungrateful and under-perform. Some, a minority, may demand that their subordinates adopt similar self-sacrificial behaviour to themselves.

Because they have problems with success they may suffer from the impostor's syndrome and consciously or unconsciously self-destruct. And, of course, they are immensely vulnerable to exploitation by others. Their generosity makes them masochists, which was the term previously used for this disorder.

Oldham and Morris (1991: 331) note the eight diagnostic criteria as:

A pervasive pattern of self-defeating behavior, beginning by early adulthood and present in a variety of contexts. The person may often avoid or undermine pleasurable experiences, be drawn to situations or relationships in which he or she will suffer, and prevent others from helping him or her, as indicated by at least *five* of the following:

(1) chooses people and situations that lead to disappointment, failure, or mistreatment even when better options are clearly available
(2) rejects or renders ineffective the attempts of others to help him or her
(3) following positive personal events (e.g., new achievement), responds with depression, guilt, or a behavior that produces pain (e.g., an accident)
(4) incites angry or rejecting responses from others and then feels hurt, defeated, or humiliated (e.g., makes fun of spouse in public, provoking an angry retort, then feels devastated)
(5) rejects opportunities for pleasure, or is reluctant to acknowledge enjoying himself or herself (despite having adequate social skills and the capacity for pleasure)
(6) fails to accomplish tasks crucial to his or her personal objectives despite demonstrated ability to do so, e.g., helps fellow students write papers, but is unable to write his or her own
(7) is uninterested in or rejects people who consistently treat him or her well, e.g., is unattracted to caring sexual partners
(8) engages in excessive self-sacrifice that is unsolicited by the intended recipients of the sacrifice.

Oldham and Morris (1991: 308–9) specify seven characteristics in every-day language of the 'Self-Sacrificing' type:

> The following seven traits and behaviors are clues to the presence of the Self-Sacrificing personality style. A person who reveals a strong Self-Sacrificing tendency will demonstrate more of these behaviors more intensely than someone with less of this style in his or her personality profile.

1. *Generosity*. Individuals with the Self-Sacrificing personality style will give you the shirts off their back if you need them. They do not wait to be asked.
2. *Service*. Their 'prime directive' is to be helpful to others. Out of deference to others, they are non-competitive and unambitious, comfortable coming second, even last.
3. *Consideration*. Self-Sacrificing people are always considerate in their dealings with others. They are ethical, honest, and trustworthy.
4. *Acceptance*. They are non-judgmental, tolerant of others' foibles, and never harshly reproving. They'll stick with you through thick and thin.
5. *Humility*. They are neither boastful nor proud, and they're uncomfortable being fussed over. Self-Sacrificing men and women do not like being the centre of attention; they are uneasy in the limelight.
6. *Endurance*. They are long-suffering. They prefer to shoulder their own burdens in life. They have much patience and a high tolerance for discomfort.
7. *Artlessness*. Self-Sacrificing individuals are rather naive and innocent. They are unaware of the often deep impact they make on other people's lives, and they tend never to suspect deviousness or underhanded motives in the people to whom they give so much of themselves.

They also offer seven tips in dealing with them:

1. Remember to recognize and acknowledge this person's efforts no matter how frequently he or she insists 'it's nothing.' Your Self-Sacrificer may be embarrassed by compliments but inwardly needs to know that you notice and appreciate.

2. Try to find a comfortable give-and-take formula. Self-Sacrificing people must keep giving, helping, and doing, but they could use a little help from you in being able to relax and enjoy themselves ....

3. Learn how to translate 'Self-Sacrificing language.' 'Heavens, don't thank me' may mean, 'I don't feel right taking the credit, but thanks for the compliment.'

4. Try not to reject what this person has to give, and don't be embarrassed by the constant attention. Self-Sacrificers think of you first. They love it. So relax and enjoy being well looked after ....

5. Be careful not to take advantage. Some extreme Self-Sacrificers may give away too much or go too far out of their way to please you. If the Self-Sacrificer won't draw the line, you do it. But when you refuse a favour, always explain why.

6. Insist on being more helpful. This will help you to establish balance in your relationship and make it difficult to take advantage of this person's willingness to do everything.

7. Talk about it. Try to convey to the Self-Sacrificing person that the way he or she can do something really nice for you is to share your leisure time with them. Unless you provide this feedback, this person may be truly unaware that you want something other than what he or she is giving to you. (1991: 319–20)

The self-defeating person is frankly unlikely to make it to senior management positions – ever.

Sadistic (aggressive)

Sadistic personality-disordered individuals are aggressive. They are strong, forceful, courageous, pugilistic and confident. They want to be leader, 'top dog'. They have a need to dominate and organize others. Hence they are autocratic and dictatorial, and can be immoral. They give orders, make rules, run the show.

At work they are ambitious and purposeful. They have the drive for power. They thrive in the win–lose, dog-eat-dog, rough-and-tumble of the business world. They are not squeamish or sentimental and can be very tough. They thrive when they have clear goals and directions. And the end justifies the mean: which is where the problem can begin.

They can make brilliant managers: goal oriented, organized, disciplined. But they focus on results not feelings. They demand total loyalty and hard work and have little patience with errors, inefficiency, waste or failure of any type. They also do not like being bored. The most serious source of stress for them is losing power. They need to know how to manipulate power.

They have strong emotions but have strong control over them. They tend to be more crafty and shrewd than physically aggressive, but they do bully, hurt and humiliate others who are subordinate to, and dependent on, them. They are disciplinarians who can easily inflict pain. Hence they can be very malevolent.

According to Oldham and Morris (1991: 345), the diagnostic criteria are:

A pervasive pattern of cruel, demeaning, and aggressive behavior, beginning by early adulthood, as indicated by the repeated occurrence of at least four of the following:

(1) has used physical cruelty or violence for the purpose of establishing dominance in a relationship (not merely to achieve some non-interpersonal goal, such as striking someone in order to rob him or her)

(2) humiliates or demeans people in the presence of others

(3) has treated or disciplined someone under his or her control unusually harshly, e.g., a child, student, prisoner, or patient

(4) is amused by, or takes pleasure in, the psychological or physical suffering of others (including animals)

(5) has lied for the purpose of harming or inflicting pain on others (not merely to achieve some other goal)

(6) gets other people to do what he or she wants by frightening them (through intimidation or even terror)

(7) restricts the autonomy of people with whom he or she has a close relationship, e.g., will not let spouse leave the house unaccompanied or permit teenage daughter to attend social functions

(8) is fascinated by violence, weapons, martial arts, injury, or torture.

Oldham and Morris (1991: 336–7) specify six criteria of the 'Aggressive' style, as they call this type:

> The following six traits and behaviors are clues to the presence of the Aggressive style. A person who reveals a strong Aggressive tendency will demonstrate more of these behaviours more intensely than someone with less of this style in his or her personality profile.

> 1. *Command.* Aggressive individuals take charge. They are comfortable with power, authority, and responsibility.
> 2. *Hierarchy.* They operate best within a traditional power structure where everyone knows his or her place and the lines of authority are clear.
> 3. *Tight ship.* They are highly disciplined and impose rules of order that they expect others in their charge to follow.
> 4. *Expedience.* Aggressive men and women are highly goal-directed. They take a practical, pragmatic approach to accomplishing their objectives. They do what is necessary to get the job done.
> 5. *Guts.* They are neither squeamish nor fainthearted. They can function well and bravely in difficult and dangerous situations without being distracted by fear or horror.
> 6. *The rough-and-tumble.* Aggressive people like action and adventure. They are physically assertive and often participate in or enjoy playing competitive sports, especially contact sports.

They also record some ways of dealing with these types:

> 1. Know yourself. In a personal relationship, this individual can be very easy to deal with if you understand and accept that he or she must be the boss. Even if you are a very strong person yourself, although you might come close you will never be equal in power if you pair up with an Aggressive type ....

> 2. Beware of competing with an Aggressive person. Never try to undermine this person's authority or to unseat him or her – unless you don't care about maintaining your relationship. If you expect to gain this person's respect by being more powerful than he or she is, think again. Aggressive

people like to have strong, worthy, loyal individuals around them, in positions lower in the hierarchy ....

3. Know the precise parameters of your job and/or your role so that you do not overstep the boundaries that the Aggressive person may have set. In military terms, you need to know your orders and then to carry them out, no more, no less.

4. Be strong and maintain your self-esteem. Just because you are in the presence of power doesn't mean you must fawn or fall back into a weak position. It is all too easy for an Aggressive person to push people around and overwhelm them ....

5. To resolve conflicts that crop up in your personal life with an Aggressive person, do not go after the win. Do not, in other words, insist that he or she do it your way or admit guilt or error. The Aggressive individual cannot tolerate losing, so don't seek all-or-nothing, I'm right-you're-wrong solutions. Work toward compromises in which the Aggressive person can still maintain his or her top-dog self-esteem ....

6. Appeal to reason, not to feelings. Aggressive people often give little weight to how a person feels. If you want to make your point, paint a very reasonable case; with a show of emotion, you'll be up against a brick wall. Point out how your plan or approach directly benefits the Aggressive person ....

7. If the Aggressive person is your parent, look for ways to cope creatively with his or her possibly harsh rules and regulation ....

8. Accept that the Aggressive person has a temper and avoid pushing the predictable buttons that will ignite it. Look for other ways to solve your problems. To deal with this person's anger, don't fight back and don't blow off your steam in his or her face. Back off and let the anger wind down. (1991: 349–51)

The bullying, aggressive sadists have often punched, clawed and scratched their way to the top. They are very difficult to work with and soon derail established working groups.

6.4. Conclusion

Academics interested in personality disorders have disagreements and debates over three issues: classification, the origin of the disorders and the treatment for them.

The issue of classification is that there may be, quite simply, too much *overlap* among the diagnoses really to justify so many categories. Thus, although some personality disorders have quite unique and distinctive features, they seem to share common traits. The *line* between normal, rational, healthy behaviour and abnormal, self-defeating behaviour is often a fine one. It is where behaviours (suspiciousness in the paranoid; exaggerating importance in the narcissistic) are pervasive, inflexible and maladaptive, causing chronic and acute personal distress, that they probably should be diagnosed as a fully blown personality disorder. There are also suggestions and indeed evidence of *sex bias* – women are more likely to be diagnosed as borderline or histrionic and men as schizoid.

Most importantly, perhaps, diagnosticians should not *confuse labels with explanations*. Such labelling also causes attribution errors by ignoring social, cultural and environmental factors that may play a part. Thus a history of abuse, neglect and prejudice may lead to the maladaptive behaviour.

But what of the theories of the origin of the illness? The *Freudians* look to early childhood for explanations. Thus they argue that narcissists are actually trying to cover up deep feelings of anxiety. Much depends on how parents socialize their children and give them a sense of who they are, particularly how to develop a consistent self-identity separate from parents. *Learning theorists* are also happy to see the origins of disorders in childhood and cite examples of parental reward and punishment schedules. Thus, rigidly controlling parents or those who are over-attentive to particular behaviours (that is, appearance) can be the origin of those disorders. Inconsistent, unpredictable or neglecting parents may have a lot to answer for. Early childhood emotional deprivation is often cited as a cause.

Those psychologists who are more interested in nature than nurture tend to emphasize rather different features. For instance, from twin and adoptive studies there is evidence of *genetic* factors playing a part, although these are more common in some areas than in others. Others point to physiological evidence (for example, heart rate) of very (abnormally) low anxiety in threatening situations. No fear of punishment renders threats and laws ineffective and may, in part, account for the antisocial personality. People with antisocial personalities have been shown to show little anxiety in anticipation of impending pain of all types.

Others see some of the disorders (for example, antisocial) as a craving for excitement and stimulation. That is, to feel uncomfortable and function well some people have to create a sense of danger and variety to prevent boredom. There are also controversial views about differences in brain function, such as in the cerebral cortex or limbic system, which may be implicated in certain of the disorders.

Naturally sociologists have stressed socio-cultural factors. One argument goes that people from large and poor families bought up in areas of crime, drug addiction and unemployment receive inconsistent and neglectful nurturing, which has been implicated in the origins of these problems. Furthermore, they are exposed to many devious and deviant role models. The idea, of course, is that the disorder is a result of, and reaction to, the social environment.

No approach does very well in accounting for the origin of all the disorders. Psychoanalysts believe that they can in part explain the borderline and narcissistic disorders, whereas those with a more physiological bent believe they are good at explaining the aetiology of the antisocial personality.

What about treatment? As noted earlier, personality-disordered people are more likely to be referred to treatment by others than they are to seek it themselves. What do they find? Interestingly, many therapists do not like dealing with patients who can be demanding, manipulative and fickle. Some even believe that people with certain disorders are really beyond the reach of therapy.

Some therapies attempt to teach acceptable interpersonal behaviours; others actively confront a person's defences. Some try to work on a person's beliefs about themselves, trying to correct distortions that suggest they are either all good or all bad. Personality-disordered patients need social and problem-solving skills, which can be taught. Incarcerated patients (in prisons, residential homes) may be put on a token economy schedule such that they get rewarded (in tokens) for good behaviour (only), which can be exchanged for all sorts of privileges. Interestingly, drug therapies are very seldom used for this disorder.

CHAPTER SEVEN

Teams and Team Managers

7.1. Introduction

Most of us work with other people, and most of us have to help, support and reward one another at work. No one can whistle a symphony; it takes the effort of an orchestra to play it. Whether we call them groups, sections, squads or teams, most of us realize that our productivity and satisfaction depend on them. This obvious point is now the latest management obsession. And it is the primary job of managers to get the best out of their teams.

Supporters of the team concept argue that, because management is the art of getting things done through people, you need to let your people know what your goals are – what you want to accomplish, why you want to accomplish those goals, how your people will benefit from accomplishing them and the role each person will play in the process. This is another way of saying that the members of the management team must be able to identify themselves individually with the company's, and therefore each other's, overall goals. No chief executive or top management group ever reached their goals by themselves. Unless the entire management team is on board, the company will never get where it wants to go.

What has caused this explosion in restating the obvious about teams? The answer partly comes from the American obsession with the Japanese, whom the Pearl Harbor generation still perceive as dangerous and highly disciplined killers. The post-war Japanese economic miracle has puzzled the Americans. What is the secret of Japanese success? Answer – teamwork. Of course the stagnation of the Japanese economy for almost the past decade has meant less fascination with the Japanese but not with teamwork. How managers form, maturate and guide work groups and teams remains a very popular question for senior managers – and team members.

The Japanese come from a collectivistic culture and are disposed to do things in groups or teams. We in the Anglo-Saxon world come from an individualistic culture, which selects on, rewards and values individual effort.

No matter how much teamwork achieves in our culture, the results tend to get identified with a single name. Managers, therefore, are sent to various mildly humiliating training courses (many in the great outdoors) to teach them teamwork because it is not natural to them. The Japanese do not feel obligated to attend individualism courses to learn how to 'become their own person' or 'do things their own way'. They are natural collectivistic team players.

The individualism in our culture runs deep. We are, however, loyal to some groups: these are usually groups we have been forced to join, or with whom we have endured hardship and difficulty. Family, school classmates and fellow military conscripts often retain our loyalty. But, because we do not have jobs for life and because it is easier to get promoted by moving between organizations, we rarely stay long enough in a team really to be part of it.

But how seriously do companies really take the idea of team solutions to organizational problems? They do talk it up, go on endless (and expensive) courses, and even partly restructure sections into 'new teams'. Yet very few reward the team rather than the individual for good performance. Most performance management systems (the euphemism for how pay is determined) are explicitly geared to individual performance. Teamwork, in the sense of contribution to the team, may be a criterion that is rated, but it is usually only one of many. Moreover, we rarely hire people with a team in mind or indeed hire whole teams.

Michael Winner got it right when he said: 'Team effort is a lot of people doing what I say.' The teamwork philosophy of cooperation, interdependence and group loyalty is counter-cultural. Our business heroes are for the most part egocentric, rugged individuals, not team players. Teamwork may be a really good idea, but it is not a magic bullet.

None the less, it is self-evidently true that all significant human achievement is the result of some sort of team effort. Even great artists, novelists, musicians, playwrights and scientific researchers – ostensibly solitary workers – are members of extended communities, and rely on, and are influenced by, the work of their colleagues, predecessors and competitors. This fact suggests that it should be important to understand the dynamics of team performance. A review of the empirical research literature on teams suggests four conclusions. First, psychologists have made little progress in the *empirical* understanding of group or team phenomena; the literature on team performance tends to be heavy on anecdotes and personal experience and light on real data. Second, although the major reason for studying teams would be to determine how to make them more effective, the topic of effectiveness rarely comes up in this literature. Third, we still lack a persuasive or comprehensive taxonomy of teams; having a taxonomy of teams available would substantially enhance our ability to do research on teams, and would generally facilitate conversations about team phenomena.

And, finally, the concept of personality is largely absent from the team literature primarily because team research is the historical province of sociology – and sociologists do not believe in personality. None the less, teams are staffed with people; thus the characteristics of people must surely be relevant to understanding team performance, and personality psychology concerns the nature of human nature. This chapter concerns how personality influences effective team performance. The chapter consists of three sections: the first concerns people, the second concerns teams and the third concerns people in teams – more precisely, how and why personality affects team performance.

For Hogan (2000) there are five features of effective team performance:

1. The talent of the team for the task: The ability and personality of the team members. Things being equal (which of course they rarely are), the more talented team wins.
2. The more motivated the team is to do well, the better the performance. And it is primarily the role of the leader to motivate the team. It is the central function and responsibility of leadership.
3. Teams need a clear, realistic strategy for how to deal with their business competitors. All team leaders need to be task-oriented strategists, which is an analytical skill.
4. Self-evidently, team leaders need to understand the importance and meaning of the role of leadership.
5. Team leaders need to put in place monitoring or management systems. Essentially this means setting goals and giving support to others but making sure that team members get feedback on their performance.

Competent managers need to recruit and bind the team together, according to Hogan. This takes social skill and integrity. They also need to give a team a credible rationale for their membership. They need to give an attractive, purposeful and meaningful vision.

7.2. Team Roles and Team Effectiveness

There is very little psychological research on, as opposed to speculation about, what makes an effective team. An exception is the work of Meredith Belbin, whose book on teams has become a sort of handbook to many British and European managers. Belbin argues that when people work in teams they tend to adopt certain roles. He defines eight such roles, and the successful performance of a team requires these roles be filled.

For well over a decade Belbin (1981) attempted to understand why some business teams (that is, groups playing a week-long MBA-type 'business game') were successful and others were not. He contended that five principles define an effective team: (1) each member contributes to achieving objectives by performing a functional role (professional/technical knowledge) and a team role. (2) An optimal balance in both functional and team roles is needed, depending on the team's goals and tasks. (3) Team effectiveness depends on the extent to which members correctly recognize and adjust to the relative strengths in the team (available expertise and team roles). (4) Personality and mental abilities fit members for some team roles and limit their ability to play others. (5) A team can deploy its technical resources to best advantage only when it has the range and balance of team roles to ensure sufficient teamwork. His research led him to conclude that people adopt particular roles in teams. The 'theory' is rich on description and taxonomization.

Over the last decade a number of studies have examined the Belbin instrument on which the theory is based (Table 7.1).

Excellent teams tend to have the following characteristics, which can be described in terms of the team members' roles in the team:

- The team leader should have attributes similar to the 'chairman'-type profile, described above. He or she should be a patient but commanding figure who generates trust and who knows how to use the spread of abilities in the team effectively.
- Excellent teams often include a person who generates creative and original solutions to problems (a plant).
- There should be a spread of mental abilities. If everyone in the team is *very* bright, then the team will spend most of its time arguing and won't agree on any effective solutions to problems.

Teams that excel have a wide spread of abilities, which include, in particular, one completer (to finish the work) and one company worker (to organize the team). A winning team often contains people with a wider spread of team roles than the other successful groups. To quote Belbin (1981: 132–3): 'A team can deploy its technical resources to best advantage only when it has the requisite range of team roles to ensure efficient teamwork'.

Another mark of excellent teams is that the team members often occupy the team roles to which they are most suited; they best perform a role that fits their personal characteristics and abilities. In less successful teams, people may be given a role just because they have done it before, and no account is taken of how well they performed in that role last time.

An excellent team can sense its own faults and do something about them by *compensating* for its team role weaknesses. One way in which it can compensate is by allocating appropriate members of the team to cover missing roles. The greater the spread of abilities in the team, the easier it is to do this. An excellent team is also sensitive to competition for particular roles,

Table 7.1 A description of Belbin's team role types

Type	Symbol	Typical features	Positive qualities	Allowable weakness	Observed contributions
1. Team leaders a. Chairman	CH	Calm, self-confident, controlled	A capacity for treating and welcoming potential contributors on their merits without prejudice – a strong sense of objectives	No more than ordinary in terms of intellect, creative abilities	1. Clarifying the goals, objectives 2. Selecting the problems on which decisions have to be made, and establishing their priorities 3. Helping establish roles, responsibilities and work boundaries within the group 4. Summing up the feelings and achievements of the group, and articulating group verdicts
b. Shaper	S	Highly strung, outgoing, dynamic	Drive and a readiness to challenge inertia, ineffectiveness, complacency	Proneness to provocation, irritation and impatience	1. Shaping roles, boundaries, responsibilities, tasks and objectives 2. Seeking to find pattern in group discussion 3. Pushing the group towards agreement on policy and action towards making decisions
2. Creative thinkers a. Plant	PL	Individualistic, serious minded, unorthodox	Genius, imagination, intellect, knowledge	Up in the clouds, inclined to disregard practical details or protocol	1. Advancing proposals 2. Making criticisms that lead to counter-suggestions 3. Offering new insights on lines of action already agreed
b. Monitor evaluator	ME	Sober, unemotional	Judgement, discretion, hardheadedness	Lack inspiration or the ability to motivate others	1. Analysing problems or situations 2. Interpreting complex written material and clarifying obscurities 3. Assessing the judgements and contributions of others.

3. Negotiators a. **Resource investigator**	RI	Extraverted, enthusiastic, curious, communicative	A capacity for contacting people and exploring anything new. An ability to respond to a challenge	Liable to lose interest once the initial fascination has passed	1. Introducing ideas and development of external origin 2. Contacting other individuals or groups of own volition 3. Engaging in negation-type activities
b. **Team worker**	TW	Socially oriented, rather mild	An ability to respond to people and to situations and to promote team spirit	Indecisiveness at moments of crisis	1. Giving personal support and help to others 2. Building on to or seconding a member's ideas and suggestions 3. Drawing the reticent into discussion 4. Taking steps to avert or overcome disruption of the team
4. Company workers a. **Company workers**	CW	Conservative, dutiful, predictable	Organizing ability, practical common sense, hard-working, self-discipline	Lack of flexibility, unresponsiveness to unproven ideas	1. Transforming talk and ideas into practical steps 2. Considering what is feasible 3. Trimming suggestions to make them fit into agreed plans and established systems
b. **Completer finisher**	CF	Painstaking, orderly, conscientious, anxious	A capacity for follow-through, perfectionism	A tendency to worry about small things. A reluctance to 'let go'	1. Emphasizing the need for task completion, meeting targets and schedules and generally promoting a sense of urgency 2. Looking for and spotting errors, omissions and oversights 3. Galvanizing others into activity

because, when such a situation exists, there may be a 'personality clash'. Two team members may work against each other and may have a damaging effect on the team's overall performance. Being aware of this possibility, the team can work out how the role could be shared or, alternatively, how to allocate one person to another role.

Belbin's (1981) self-perception inventory (BSPI) first appeared in his popular book *Management Teams*. It outlines the 'theory' that suggests eight quite distinct team-role types. Although he provides norms based on a very limited number of people (78 in all), he offers little evidence of the psychometric properties of the test. Thus, we know little of the test's reliability (test–retest, split-half, internal), validity (concurrent, content, predictive, construct) or its dimensionability. The BSPI questionnaire is unusual and problematic for several reasons (Furnham, 1999). First, it is an ipsative (forced-choice) test, where subjects are required to read seven hypothetical situations, and then rate several behaviour statements relating to each situation and 'distribute a total of ten points among the sentences which you think most accurately describe your behaviour'. Psychologists are highly critical of ipsative tests in general, particularly when used in occupational settings.

A second problem with the BSPI concerns the way in which the questions are asked. Questionnaires are arranged such that, for each of the seven sections, subjects are required to specify their typical behaviour. Thus, for instance, one reads: 'When involved in a project with other people ...' or: 'I gain satisfaction in a job because ...'. These situations are vague, inconsistent and do nothing to let the subject know about crucial aspects of the nature of the group or team that they are involved with. This could easily lead to poor reliability.

A third problem concerns the fact that the measure is entirely atheoretical. As Belbin explains in his book, he gathered team data on standard psychometrically validated measures such as the 16PF and the EPI, but then developed his typology by observational and inductive means rather than through a larger theory of team performance. The problem with this approach lies in the fact that it ignores previously well-documented and theoretically important traits, such as neuroticism.

Broucek and Randall (1996: 404) noted, after their studies showed little support for Belbin's theory: 'it is understandable that little support has been given to team role theory in the academic literature. Nevertheless Belbin's work has attracted considerable support among trainers and consultants. Perhaps this is because the group roles themselves have more than intuitive appeal.' Academics are both puzzled and annoyed to find that consultants and clients seem uninterested in evaluating the theories and measures that they often use to make enormously important decisions.

Even more perplexing is the fact that, once measures have been shown to be seriously wanting, this information has little or no effect on the popular use and retention of the measure.

Herriot and Pemberton (1995) have offered important criticisms of 'team theories', which they call myths. They outline two myths:

- All friends together: A team cannot function effectively and complete its tasks until interpersonal relations within the team are optimal.
- Seven stages of a team: Teams have to go through a sequence of group development stages in a particular order to be successful.

Their argument is thus: work tasks determine interpersonal processes, not the other way around. The organizational context sets the tasks that teams have to tackle and this also impacts on work processes. Roles, which are almost epiphenomenal, are simply the different parts that people play in helping to move the process. Different processes require different roles. The work context determines the tasks that need to be done. The tasks determine the processes that must occur. The processes determine the roles.

The problem lies in distinguishing 'real teams' from experimental teams. Real teams have a well-known set of characteristics: shared leadership roles, collective work products, discussion, decisions and so on. Experimental teams such as those set up to 'play' business games and those used for studies are different. It may be that they tend to focus on their individual roles and personalities precisely because they are 'unreal', whereas real groups get on with their tasks. In other words, Belbin's emphasis on roles is misplaced and primarily a methodological artefact.

Belbin's work has both helped and hindered our understanding of efficient and incompetent teams. His focus on individual differences and fit has been helpful. But to discuss the issue of team effectiveness in terms of team roles is misleading. Researchers have argued that you can calculate team role scores from standard personality inventions (that is, the 16 Personality Profile). It seems therefore unwise to invent a whole new nomenclature of teams rather than rely on the extensive literature on personality theory.

Very few personality theorists think in team or group terms and very few group/team researchers think much in personality terms. Hogan (2000) believes that the reason for this lies in the fact that so much personality theory and research has been influenced by clinical rather than organizational psychology. People are social animals: they choose to, indeed need to, live and work in groups that inevitably develop a status of hierarchy. Thus, he notes the problems for group members in simultaneously achieving acceptance and status in groups.

With both humour and accuracy Roderick (1997a) reinterpreted the Belbin types in terms of the darker side (Table 7.2).

Table 7.2 Reinterpretation of the Belbin type by Roderick (1997a)

Belbin team type	Dark side team type
Chairman	Demotivator
Company Worker	Corridor Lurker
Team Worker	Extreme Shirker
Resource Investigator	Remorse Instigator
Completer Finisher	Completely Sinister
Shaper	Draper
Plant	Vegetable
Monitor Evaluator	Massacre Exacerbator

He provides both shorthand and extensive description of these team role types. The brief outline goes thus:

- *Demotivator*: Binds team together by being the focus for mutual hatred. Uses gloom as a weapon to the point that people would view the prospect of a serious depressive illness as a light at the end of the tunnel.

- *Draper*: Nattily dressed psychopath. Driven to earn so much money that the mere sight of the labels on their clothing will cause a C&A suit to spontaneously combust.

- *Vegetable*: If ignorance is bliss, the Vegetable inhabits a permanent Nirvana.

- *Massacre Exacerbator*: Anyone who turns something merely disastrous into a threat to civilisation as we know it. In organisational terms, anyone who tries to introduce Performance Related Pay.

- *Corridor Lurker*: The organizationally 'homeless'. Nobody wants them living next door. As welcome and as subtle as a fart in an elevator, their only role is to give Vegetables someone to look down on and everyone else someone to bitch about.

- *Extreme Shirker*: Anyone with the term 'co-ordination', 'global', 'strategic' or 'policy' in their job titles. When you actually get to the point that you have collected all of these tags and become a 'Global co-ordinator of strategic policy', you don't have to get out of bed at all.

- *Remorse Instigator*: They use feedback in the same way that an amateur acupuncturist uses needles – i.e., with great enthusiasm, maximum pain and no measurable benefit. Strangely enough, people are daft enough to sit still for amateur feedback!

- *Completely Sinister*: With all the charm and warmth of a Labour Government Whip, CSs who have learned how to 'fake good' on the major psychiatric tests become your CEO; those who can't are guarding your company car park as you read this. They are all simply marking time while they wait to report back to their home planet. (Roderick, 1998: 18)

Roderick (1997a: 19) has also provided more detailed descriptions of these types, for instance:

The Remorse Instigator: The classic RI is someone that people are sorry they ever met. Their chief talent is a capacity to engender guilt in others, and on a good day a gifted Remorse Instigator can make you feel guilty about feeling guilty. Uncannily accurate in identifying and then highlighting for the benefit of the team your most profound weaknesses and insecurities, their ability to simultaneously patronize, sympathize and criticize makes them highly effective Bank Managers and Doctors' Receptionists. Masters of giving feedback that undermines confidence without risking any performance improvement, they are to motivation what Nero was to municipal fire safety. RIs in senior positions are very effective change agents: companies change their address in order to avoid meeting them (even by accident), and they are the potent force behind the rise of teleworking ....

The Completely Sinister: A political animal, the Completely Sinister has more than the usual complement of Y-chromosomes. To a CS, diplomacy is the art of saying 'nice doggy' while looking for a big stone. The auditioners who refused Charles Manson a role as one of the original 'Monkees' knew a Completely Sinister when they saw one. The most reliable means of identification is a handshake, since an imperfect acclimatization to Earth's atmosphere gives them hands that are hot and clammy. But be warned, they remedy this by extensive attendance on neurolinguistic programming workshops where they are taught complete mastery of warm air hand-dryers. Totally at home on Business Process Re-engineering Consultancies, the Completely Sinister can be confused with the Draper in terms of appearance, the difference is the bulge under the left armpit. People take an instant dislike to them because it saves time.

In his final article on types, Roderick (1998: 19) considers examples of mixed types:

RI/Draper: At their best when they have been drowned at birth, the RI/Draper blends a talent for engendering a death wish in all to whom they speak with aspirational qualities that lead them to see assisted suicide as a legitimate tool for personal career management. A 'normal' RI at least has the excuse that they find the concept of Original Sin pretty motivating; factor in the Draper's vaulting-ambition and you have someone who uses their capacity to create feelings of guilt and inadequacy – particularly about dress sense – as a potent weapon for advancement. The Draper merely sneers at your sartorial ineptitude; the RI/Draper gets you to confess it, tearfully, in front of large groups of colleagues and superiors.

Mediocre RI/Drapers become the sort of infant school headmistresses who make you stand up in front of the whole class when you have wet yourself. The most talented RI/Drapers usually pot for a strictly commercial route to success and seek fame as American TV evangelists, heading up nonconformist sects such as The Church of the Immaculately Pressed Trousers.

Closer to home, aspiring RI/Drapers need look no further than their nearest estate agent to find a role model. Here, the combination of Rolex watch, Vuitton briefcase and deep scorn at your palpable inability to afford the country villa that they are showing you, tells you whom you are dealing with. As soon as you hear them say: 'I'm afraid we are in Ride On Mower territory here, Sir' make the sign of the cross and run away.

Just to be safe, always go to the toilet before meeting anyone who you think might be an RI/Draper. (Or is this just a personal hang up?)

Roderick (1997a) even provides a spoof quiz for his dark side team role types:

What is your dominant 'Dark Side' team type?
This questionnaire has been carefully designed using a chain-link validation model keyed to an ipsatively modified factorially rotated critical incident data bank.

In meetings I usually...

1. Take the opportunity to point out how far behind target we are.
2. Compliment a co-worker on their interesting choice of tie.

My work is important to me because...

3. My co-workers respect my ability for detail and accuracy.
4. I can make courageous decisions with someone else's money.

Each day at work is a chance to...

5. Meet and influence new people.
6. Facilitate preliminary investigations.

When I get to my place of work...

7. I ring directory enquiries to find out where they have moved.
8. I take care to wash my hands several times.

On meeting my boss I usually...

9. Point out the dangerous positioning of the fourth-floor photocopier.
10. Sneer inwardly at their choice of footwear.

Business Process Re-engineering is...

11. All about re-engineering the processes of the business.
12. A chance to better control the Earthlings (oops!).

The company appraisal system...

13. Takes no account of dress sense.
14. Will be finished any day now.

The sinking of the Titanic was...

15. A chance to learn from partial success.
16. Your fault! Come on now, what did you do to prevent it, eh?

Scoring key

Demotivator 1, 9
Draper 2, 13
Vegetable 3, 11
Massacre Exacerbator 4, 15
Corridor Lurker 5, 10
Extreme Shirker 6, 14
Remorse Instigator 7, 16
Completely Sinister 8, 12

7.3. TIG

The difficulty with being a manager or team leader is that you have a number of different tasks to complete simultaneously. You have to divide your time and attention between processes that require different skills. They can be remembered in terms of the anagram TIG (or GIT), which stands for task, individual, group.

All jobs are task related even when doing the emotional labour of service-type jobs. Nearly all managers have specific goals, especially with respect to monetary targets (profits, revenues, costs). They also have productivity, administrative, security and innovative tasks as well as simply maintaining (even enhancing) the effectiveness of the team. They need to be political, strategic and tactical. They need to plan and to understand task requirements. It is often the semi-intellectual and technical part of the job: understanding and carrying out specific tasks.

Managers also need to understand the individuals in the team: their strengths and weaknesses (now called developmental opportunities). Managers need to know when individuals are under stress and what to do about it. They need most of all to understand themselves and what their preferences and predictions do to others. They need the language of personality theorists and the understanding of mature researchers. Teams are made up of individuals whose uniqueness is important.

Third, and as relevant as being good at the task and understanding individuals, managers need to understand how groups or teams work. People work in teams for various reasons: to increase synergy, to have specialization of labour and to ensure the accuracy of work outcomes. But, as all managers know, the whole is greater than the sum of the parts. Group or team morale is a product of how the group is managed; the ritual normative behaviour of the group; the internal 'chemistry' between members as well as how the group relates to other supportive and oppositional groups. The success and failure of the group can be both a cause and a consequence of group or team morale. Indeed there is much (anecdotal) evidence of virtuous and vicious spirals in teamwork.

Groups who succeed at their allotted task get various rewards, which improves morale, which leads to better work, which leads to more success. Groups who fail (albeit only comparatively) get lethargic, depressed and squabble. They take their 'eye off the ball' and become self-obsessed. This leads to further failure.

There used to be a distinction between tasks and socio-emotional leadership styles. The former preferred the analytical work, the latter the supportive work. The former often failed because they ignored the needs of individuals and the team; the latter failed because they were insufficiently task oriented.

All managers have their abilities and preferences. The task oriented need to find ways to do the individual and group best; the socio-emotional need help with task analysis. Incompetent managers play to their preferences (which may or may not be strengths) and ignore or downplay their other essential duties. It is a recipe for disaster.

But worse, incompetent managers use groups for their own gratification or to compensate for one particular weakness that they have.

Team as audience

There are incompetent managers who prefer to use their team as a compulsively admiring audience. They choose and reward members not for their ability to complete the task, nor for their loyalty, but rather for their own personal gratification.

Incompetent managers enjoy team meeting and brainstorming sessions not as ways to communicate goals or find solutions to important problems but rather to ensure that they have captive audiences. Subordinate reporting staff feel obliged often to humour a narcissistic manager. They laugh at dull and familiar jokes; they 'fully and enthusiastically' endorse dim and half-thought-out plans; they encourage their team leaders to stand longer in the limelight.

The narcissistic team leader naturally chooses and 'loses' those who report to him or her in terms of their audience material. They are distinguishable from their peers by the number of meetings they have, by the conferences they attend (and try to talk at) and by their grandiosity. They may even have 'amateur-dramatic' hobbies to top up their options to appear on stage.

They are of course self-obsessed and are often not cognizant of or willing or able to bind their team members together. The morale of the team is their morale.

Inevitably, capable team members leave these team leaders. They see quite quickly what is going on and want nothing to do with it. Those who stay seem happy to fake their appreciation and curse when the occasion calls for it but even they leave when the team begins noticeably to fail and their jobs are on the line. Marketing and sales managers seem perhaps most prone to this 'leadership' style.

Team as support network

Clinical psychologists know the power of self-help groups. Support groups of fellow sufferers/victims can be extremely important in helping individuals to accept their condition. Alcoholics Anonymous is an example of such a group, occasionally frequented by all sorts of managers.

Some managers treat their staff in their teams as self-help groups for their personal problems. They may even astutely and/or unconsciously be aware of the fact that they seem to be seeking out as team members those with a similar pathology profile. The anxious seek out the anxiety ridden; the depressed seek out gloomy pessimists; the hypochondriacal seek those with various and varied ailments.

The incompetent team leader sees the job more as a counselling exercise. They may use the group/team for either of two asymmetrical functions: to give or receive counselling or therapy. There are those who enjoy nothing more than practising their amateur psychology and psychoanalysis on their team members, who can feel obliged to disclose and confess certain problems. They may enjoy both one-to-one appraisal-type sessions or group meetings as opportunities for emotion talk. The task, it seems, is often irrelevant.

Sometimes the incompetent team leader sees the team as a forum for him or her to discuss exclusively their problems. They may be frighteningly frank in an effort to get others to reciprocate some emotional issue. Some feel it is the role of the team to support them – and to a lesser extent each other.

Supportive teams are good teams. The manager needs to set clear goals and support their staff in achieving them. They also need to encourage an atmosphere of support whereby members of the team help each other. But the support needs to be functional, not dysfunctional. It needs to be task oriented as well as socio-emotional. It needs to be directed at everybody and not just the (needy) manager.

Team as responsibility diffusion device

Some managers accept the old dictum that the 'buck stops here', meaning that passing the buck stops at the top. Managers have frequently to make

difficult decisions that have serious consequences. There are selection decisions and redundancy decisions; there are inevitably important financial
decisions; and there are inevitably strategic and even tactical decisions.
These decisions have important consequences in the long and short run,
and they are a significant source of stress to many managers.

Incompetent mangers like to diffuse responsibility. They use their team
not specifically to ensure that decisions are better (more accurate, faster)
but that others are equally responsible. The worst trait associated with this
particular form of incompetence is making team decisions and taking exclusive responsibility for success but collective responsibility for failure.

Some people know that their meetings have nothing to do with communication and take place simply to agree to the ideas of the manager who
offers them an opportunity to speak and vote, although they already know
the 'correct' or desirable response. The meeting 'rubber-stamps' the
motions placed in front of them. Some managers are particularly subtle in
the way that they indicate their preferred answers. Others are so incompetent that they genuinely have no idea and need the group for its ideas as well
as its approval.

The more important the decision, the more likely these managers are to
use (and abuse) their team. Some managers do this when unpopular decisions have to be made. Others do it when the consequences are particularly
important. They are often eager to pretend that their democratic committee style of decision-making is a virtue rather than a vice.

The incompetent manager defuses responsibility particularly when he or
she is concerned about the outcome. When decision outcomes are more
certain they are happy to dispense with all that nonsense of helping a committee make the decision.

Team as idea givers

Despite hopes and hype to the contrary, there is little evidence that creativity can be taught. One can learn a few tricks but the level of creativity is tied
to both personality and ability. In their heart of hearts most managers know
how creative they are. They also know pretty well how intelligent they are.
So what does the somewhat uncreative manager of below-average intelligence do? They get their ideas and analysis from others.

Incompetent managers sometimes need their team: they can't function
without them. They might delegate where they should not and become
highly reliant on individuals who are able to do that which they cannot. The
question, of course, is, who the manager should be.

Those incompetent managers who seem reliant on their team for ideas
have often been over-promoted or badly appointed.

7.4. Understanding Teams

Although it has been disputed, there is a popular concept that groups go through stages in their development. As Furnham (1999) notes, this concept suffers all the problems of all stage-wise theories, such as not clarifying *how long* each stage lasts, what determines the *change* from one to another; whether the sequence is always linear, whether one can skip a stage, and so on.

However, it is important to understand what competent and incompetent managers do at various stages.

Forming

In the forming stage, team members supposedly focus their efforts on defining goals and developing procedures for performing their task. Group development in this stage involves getting acquainted, and understanding leadership and other members' roles. In this stage, individual members might:

- keep feelings to themselves until they know the situation
- act more securely than they actually feel about how the team functions
- experience confusion and uncertainty about what is expected of them
- be reserved and polite, at least superficially, and certainly not hostile to others
- try to size up the personal benefits relative to the personal costs of being involved in the team.

At this stage they are concerned with 'sniffing' out and around other team members to see if they are going to stay in the group and how they are going to get involved. Competent managers help team members get to know each other and to be clear about their roles and goals. It is an ideal time to set standards and to provide an example of what behaviours are expected, desired, pre- and proscribed.

Storming

Conflicts often emerge over task behaviours, relative priorities of goals, who is to be responsible for what, and the task-related guidance and direction of the leader. Competition over the leadership role and conflict over goals are supposedly dominant themes at this stage. Some members may withdraw or try to isolate themselves from the emotional tension generated. Suppressing conflict may create bitterness and resentment, which will last long after members attempt to express their differences and emotions. Withdrawal by key members can cause the team to fail more quickly at this stage. Some teams genuinely have little to 'storm' about, but others suppress this stage, which can cause problems at a later date. This is controversial stuff. Certainly some incompetent managers are conflict aware, fearing any sort of disagreement or challenge to their position; others may induce conflict that is not there, believing that it is healthy. Knowing who and how to deal with challenges to one's position is a key feature of management competence.

Norming

Task-oriented behaviours in the norming stage usually evolve into the sharing of information, acceptance of different opinions, and positive attempts to reach mutually agreeable (or compromise) decisions on the team's goals. The team sets the rules by which it will operate, and emotions often focus on empathy, concern and the positive expressions of feelings, leading to a group cohesion. Cooperation within the team is a dominant theme while a sense of shared responsibility develops. However, it is both noticeable and surprising that different teams under similar circumstances find very different solutions to their psychological processes and, hence, develop spectacularly different behavioural norms. The job of a manager is to help develop healthy behavioural norms about time-keeping, cooperation, productivity and absenteeism. It is also their job to change normative behaviour when it is patently unhealthy for the team.

Performing

During the performing stage, the team supposedly shows how effectively and efficiently it can perform its task. This is the stage characterized by interdependence and problem-solving. The roles of individual members are usually accepted and understood. The members understand when they should work independently and when they should help each other. Teams differ after the performing stage: some continue to learn and develop from their experiences, and new inputs improve their efficiency and effectiveness. Other groups – especially those that developed norms not fully supportive of efficiency and effectiveness – may perform only at the level needed for their survival. A minimally adequate level of performance may be caused by excessive self-oriented behaviours by group members, the development of norms that inhibit task effectiveness and efficiency, poor group leadership or other facts. It is often as hard to establish team performance as it is to maintain it. It involves courage, energy, tact and insight to keep up the success of a high-performing team.

Adjourning

The adjourning stage involves the termination of task behaviours and dis-engagement from relations-oriented behaviours. Some groups, such as a project team created to investigate and report on a specific problem within six months, have a well-defined point of adjournment. This stage has also been called the mourning stage, as it is not unusual for groups that have dis-integrated to leave members feeling sad and nostalgic. There is the problem not only of teams breaking up but of dealing with destabilization when team members leave and get replaced by very different people.

To create functional and effective working teams, it may be useful to consid-er how people behave naturally. Thus, Hackman (1989) suggests that there need to be four stages in creating work teams. This adjourning or mourning stage should be considered by people setting up formal, task-oriented, workgroups:

1. 'Pre-work', considering the group's goals, the authority it might need; indeed, more importantly, even whether it needs to exist at all.
2. Create performance conditions, specifically the equipment, material and personnel.
3. Form and build the team by making clear who is, and is not, in the group, agreeing on expected behaviour, tasks, roles and so on.
4. Providing continuing assistance by eliminating group problems, replen-ishing material and replacing people who leave.

Stages 1 to 3 can be done in the planning stage. The chemistry of indi-vidual personalities is a powerful force in any group. Groups develop and change over time. The cycle described may repeat itself when new members arrive or old ones leave. Because of these developmental changes, few groups are totally stable and easily predictable.

7.5. Incompetence and Group Think

Groups that are bullied or chosen for their 'yes-men' qualities often fall victim to group think. Group Think (Janis, 1972) is the term given to the pressure that highly cohesive groups exert on their members for uniform and acceptable decisions, which actually reduces their capacity to make effective decisions.

The concept of group think was proposed as an attempt to explain inef-fective decisions made by US government officials, which led to such fiascos as the Bay of Pigs invasion in Cuba, the successful Japanese attack on Pearl Harbor and the Vietnam War. Analyses of these cases have revealed that, every time, the president's advisers actually discouraged the making of more effective decisions. Members of very cohesive groups have more faith in their group's decisions than in any different idea they may have personally. As a result, they may suspend their own critical thinking in favour of conforming to the group. When group members become tremendously loyal to each other, they may ignore information from other sources if it challenges the group's decisions. The result of this process is that the group's decisions may be completely uninformed, irrational or even immoral (Table 7.3).

Table 7.3 The warning signals of group think

Symptoms	Description
Illusion of invulnerability	Ignoring obvious danger signals, being overly optimistic and taking extreme risks
Collective rationalization	Discrediting or ignoring warning signals that run contrary to group thinking
Unquestioned morality	Believing that the group's position is ethical and moral and that all others are inherently evil
Excessive negative stereotyping	Viewing the opposing side as being too negative to warrant serious consideration
Strong conformity pressure	Discouraging the expression of dissenting opinions under the threat of expulsion for disloyalty
Self-censorship of dissenting ideas	Withholding dissenting ideas and counter-arguments, keeping them to oneself
Illusion of unanimity	Sharing the false belief that everyone in the group agrees with its judgements
Self-appointed mind guards	Protecting the group from negative, threatening information

Some of the potential consequences of group think include:

- Few alternatives are considered when solving problems; preferred accepted solutions are implemented.
- Outside experts are seldom used; indeed, outsiders are distrusted.
- Re-examination of a rejected alternative is unlikely.
- Facts that do not support the group are ignored or their accuracy challenged.
- Risks are ignored or glossed over; indeed, risk is seldom assessed.

Wise managers can take steps to reduce the likelihood of group think. Most of these steps can also reduce the effects of group think once it occurs. Reducing group think, however, is much more difficult than preventing it in the first place, because groups engaging in group think seldom realize that they are doing so. To prevent or reduce the effects of group think, competent managers can:

- encourage each member of the group to evaluate ideas openly and critically
- ask influential members to adopt an initial external (even critical) stance on solutions
- discuss plans with disinterested outsiders to obtain reactions
- use expert advisers to challenge group views
- assign a devil's advocate role to one or more members to challenge ideas
- explore alternative scenarios for possible external reactions
- use subgroups (select committees) to develop alternative solutions
- meet to reconsider decisions prior to implementation.

Indeed, an incompetent team manager is one who not only does not do these things (the sin of omission) but who does the opposite (sin of commission). Given that group think is potentially dangerous, organizations often choose to implement decisions that avoid it:

- *Promote open inquiry*: Group think arises in response to group members' reluctance to 'rock the boat' and challenge the leader. Good leaders encourage group members to be sceptical of all solutions and to avoid reaching premature agreements; bad ones demand loyalty. It helps to play the role of the 'devil's advocate' – to find fault intentionally with a proposed solution – so that all its shortcomings are considered. The idea is that decisions that were successful in the past may not be successful in the future.
- *Use subgroups*: Split the group, because the decisions made by one group may be the result of group think; basing decisions on the recommendations of two or more groups trying to solve the same problem is a useful check. If the split groups disagree, a spirited discussion of their differences is likely to raise important issues. This is not divide and conquer but an attempt to find a better answer. In such a strategy there is always a risk that it causes friction and reduces cohesion, but the ultimate benefit for decision-making probably makes it worth while.
- *Admit shortcomings*: When group think occurs, group members feel very confident that they are doing the right thing, which discourages people from considering contrary information. However, if group members acknowledge some of the flaws and limitations of their decisions, they may be more open to corrective influences. Thus, asking others to point out their misgivings and hesitations about a group's decision may avoid the illusion of perfection that contributes to group think. Groups must be encouraged to believe that doubt, not certainty, is always acceptable. But this is often impossible for incompetent team managers, particularly those at extreme ends of the self-esteem scale.

- *Hold 'second-chance' meetings*: Before implementing any decision it may be a good idea to hold a second-chance meeting in which group members are asked to express any doubts and to propose any new ideas that they may have. As people get tired of working on problems, they may hastily reach agreement on a solution. A second-chance meeting can be useful to see whether the solution still seems as good after 'sleeping on it'.

Not all groups are susceptible to group think. But to promote successful group decision-making, Zander (1982) suggests the practical manager follow various points. Those that seem more sensible are detailed below, but note once again how little this is done by incompetent managers:

- State the problem clearly, indicating its significance and what is expected of the group when faced with solving it.
- Break a complex problem into several parts, and make decisions affecting each part.
- Focus discussion on the key issues and, when all avenues are explored, put a stop to analysis, and call for a vote, if necessary, when the time is right.
- Assist members in coping with other people's ideas, and then ask them to substantiate the correctness of their own ideas.
- Before making a final decision, encourage members to consider any adverse repercussions likely to flow from a given solution.
- Be suspicious of unanimous decisions, particularly those arrived at quickly, and avoid them.
- Make sure that those who are charged with the implementation of a group's decision understand exactly what they are expected to do.
- Avoid wide differences in status among members, or alternatively help members recognize these differences and explore ways of reducing their inhibitions with respect to 'status' in the group.
- Prepare procedures in advance to deal with urgent or crisis decisions.
- Protect the group from damaging effects of external criticism, but at the same time let the group benefit from critical ideas or observations of a constructive nature that are likely to improve the quality of its deliberations.
- Encourage members to evaluate the skills residing in the group and to find ways of improving them.

Ideally, groups improve the quality of decision-making but under the direction of incompetent managers they often make things worse.

7.6. Conclusion

Incompetent managers under-rate the prevalence and importance of teamwork. They are poor at selecting, motivating and directing teams. And they tend to use teams to support their own pathology rather than support their team members to fulfil their goal.

The task a team should be doing often dictates how the team works. People who lead teams need to be, in part, strategists. They need to work out who is best at tasks, how to do tasks the most efficient way and they need to keep an eye on competitors. It is an analytical task, often based on a mixture of professional training and intelligence. Competent managers are not afraid of innovation and are always on the lookout for better ways of performing tasks.

A good team leader is also in some sense a psychologist. They need to understand the strengths, preferences and weaknesses (developmental opportunities) of the people in the team. Leaders often have a big impact on team culture, morale and maturation.

Teams rarely 'work automatically': it takes insight, nurturing, vigilance and courage to manage teams well. Think of how the military teaches leadership skills. Incompetent managers lack either the insight for what to do or the ability or courage to do it. They do not understand their role or impact and may 'use' the team more for therapy than goal achievement. They are always more aware of their own needs than the needs of either the task or the team members. This can quickly demoralize or disorient a good team.

Managers work with and through teams. Some seem to have a natural understanding of the dynamics of teams. Others seem to have no insight at all, which often can't be fixed by training or education.

PART III
CURING THE PROBLEM

CHAPTER EIGHT

Possible Cures of Management Incompetence

8.1. Introduction

Managerial incompetence has many consequences because there are many stakeholders in the world inhabited by the bad manager. The *individual* manager is the first obvious stakeholder. Incompetence can, quite rightly and justly, lead to dismissal, which will affect income, health and reputation. If the manager is insightful enough to perceive his or her own incompetence, that may lead to reduced self-confidence and the beginning of a downward spiralling career pattern. If the manager is deluded (or in denial) about his or her incompetencies, the consequences for those around him or her, and him- or herself in due course, can be worse. However, accurate self-perception may lead the incompetent manager to attempt to seek help, and that choice may have a happy outcome.

The second stakeholder is the *manager's work group*. The morale, productivity and well-being of a group of talented, conscientious workers can be undermined by an incompetent manager. Morale is a delicate flower that needs constant and careful nurturing. Furthermore, productivity does not occur by chance and can speedily slip; the speed with which a successful group can turn into the opposite is surprising. Most people have witnessed a competent manager being replaced with the hopeless, hapless, helpless kind and then watched all indices of group effectiveness evaporate.

Many people witness this when a restaurant or bar changes hands. A quality eating establishment which begins to be badly run will deteriorate; the quality of the cooking and service plummets and a fine reputation built up over years of hard work can evaporate, not to be easily recovered. It takes a great deal of time for a good manager to undo the damage of a bad one.

Worse, perhaps, is the fact that, for young people, their manager provides a crucial role model. If all they see is managerial incompetence, young people who are subsequently thrust unprepared into managerial or supervising roles will tend to do likewise. Hence we find self-perpetuating cultures of incompetence. Naturally these are most frequently found in state-run, subsidized, non-profit organizations. Private, profit-dependent companies with such cultures would soon collapse.

The third stakeholder in the incompetent manager's world is his or her *family*. Sometimes managerial incompetence spills over into the family world. We drive as we live, so most managers' behaviour at work resembles their behaviour at home. In the jargon of psychology, there is more evidence of spill-over than compensation. In other words, it is more common to find similar, rather than different, behaviours in the work and home. The lazy manager is a slob around the house; the irascible manager has temper tantrums at home; the pusillanimous manager at work tends not to stand up for (or to) his family at home. The family is also affected by the inevitable consequences of incompetence – sacking, redundancy, erratic and poor income levels. The spouse and children of the incompetent manager often shoulder a heavy burden over a long period. They have to bear the shame, the uncertainty and the many failures of the person who is often the only bread-winner.

The fourth stakeholder is the manager's *company as a whole*. Customers shun management incompetence. Being forced to deal with slow, insensitive, egocentric, lazy, obsessive people soon leads customers to seek out alternatives. Most people have experienced the surprise of the sudden and dramatic decline when a small business changes hands. Good staff and loyal customers are quick to leave a ship captained by an incompetent manager. Bad decisions, poor motivational skills, capriciousness and laziness can lead businesses to the precipice of disaster.

The fifth stakeholder is the *shareholder*. Some shareholders are utterly dependent for their livelihood on the interest from their investments. Badly run companies are likely to lead to a decline, even collapse, in the share price. Hence the interest and often powerless obsession of shareholders in the appointment and promotion of senior managers who they hope are the very opposite of the helpless, hopeless, hapless manager.

Finally, the *society as a whole* is a stakeholder in management incompetence. This is most notably the case in smaller countries or in bigger companies; towns and regions can be devastated by the failure of companies that employ many hundreds of people. It is inappropriate to suggest that all, even most, plant and company closures are exclusively the fault of management incompetence. Economic and technological forces are often equally to blame – but not always, as business studies are quick to show.

The point is that managerial (like military) incompetence has innumerable consequences. Business failure as a result of incompetence does far more than provide case studies for MBA students or pathos for the financial pages of newspapers. Failures, often caused by incompetence, seriously affect many lives and livelihoods. It is therefore worth investigating both to understand and to help prevent.

8.2. Diagnosis and Cure

Diagnosis not only precedes cure, it predicts it. Inappropriate diagnosis can easily lead to prescribing ineffective, even dangerous 'cures' that exacerbate the problem rather than relieving it. 'The operation was a total success but the patient died' is a bad joke.

Managers fail for a variety of reasons – some of which really have little or nothing to do with them as individuals. Some are given impossible jobs with no chance of success. Others are seriously let down by senior managers, suppliers and colleagues – although it could be argued that they really should have had the insight to spot the problem beforehand. But they do also fail for a number of quite specific reasons. We will consider several of these, and we will spend more time on diagnosis than cure, partly because it is both harder and more important. However, we should note three things: first, it is both likely and common to have multiple symptoms. That is, a manager could have multiple complaints – indeed this is fairly likely because one deficit could easily lead to another. This makes diagnosis difficult because one has to try to disentangle the factors.

Second, the symptoms may not be consistent. They may show up in certain circumstances but not in others. Like a subterranean river that pops above ground erratically in the form of pools, short streams, occasional falls and then disappears underground again, the symptoms may be difficult to trace. So it is with symptoms that seem to come and go. It does not mean that the patient is cured; rather, it alerts one to the particular circumstances that provoke the issue.

And third, managerial incompetence may not fall neatly into labelled categories. Just as psychiatric manuals are frequently updated and changed to include, exclude, re-label and re-categorize, so manuals of incompetence must do likewise. Furthermore, the manual provided here is meant to be non-specialist and user-friendly. Inevitably, then, not all incompetence issues will fall (neatly) into the categories provided. But we believe that enough will to make the manual useful.

8.3. Ability, Intellect and Capacity

There are many synonyms for ability. These include aptitude, capacity, general mental ability, intelligence and talent. In these politically correct and litigation-loving times you have to tread carefully in this area, particularly if you are at all interested in measuring it.

It has been known for a long time that, with certain provisos, ability test scores are perhaps the best predictor of success at work. As Cook (1998: 300) noted, 'Ability tests have excellent validity, can be used for all sorts of jobs, are readily transportable, are cheap and easy to use, but fall foul of the law in the USA'. After an up-to-date review of the validity and use of tests in the workplace, Cook (1998: 135) noted:

> Validity generalisation analysis has proved again what psychologists always knew: tests of mental ability predict work performance very well. For a vast range of jobs, the more able worker is the better worker. The predictive validity of mental ability tests for virtually all work doesn't really need any further demonstration.

In a meta-analysis based on 85 years of research regarding the use of psychological measures to predict on-the-job performance, Schmidt and Hunter (1998) report that three different combinations of selection measures predicted job performance at correlation levels of +0.63 to 0.65: general intelligence (or general mental ability, GMA) paired with a work sample, an integrity test or a structured interview. What is striking about their analyses is the high predictive value of intelligence alone (+0.51), which can be enhanced by using one of the additional procedures. They conclude: 'Because of its special status, GMA can be considered the primary personnel measure for hiring decisions, and one can consider the remaining personnel measures as supplements to GMA measures' (Schmidt and Hunter, 1998: 267). Although Schmidt and Hunter do not directly address the issue of managerial selection, the overall importance of intelligence to success makes it difficult to argue that its importance is reduced at the most senior levels of organizations.

What, exactly, is intelligence? In 1921, 14 experts were asked this question (Thorndike et al., 1921) and listed the following:

- The ability to carry out abstract thinking.
- The ability to adjust to one's environment.
- The ability to adapt to new situations of life.
- The capacity to acquire knowledge.
- The capacity to learn or profit from experience.
- Good responses from the point of view of psychological truth or fact.

Although the experts still cannot agree on an exact definition of intelligence, themes common to many of their definitions are that intelligence is (1) the ability to learn from experience and (2) the ability to adapt to the environment.

Should we describe intelligence with just one number or metric, such as the IQ, or with many numbers, representing different kinds of intelligence? This question has been argued by two groups of psychologists, which Sternberg (1990) describes as the *lumpers* and the *splitters*. The lumpers see intelligence as global, so that one number should suffice to describe it. If the lumpers are correct, then a person who is well endowed intellectually should perform equally well in a wide variety of areas.

The splitters see intelligence as made up of a number of specific mental faculties. According to this idea, a person might be intelligent in some areas and not so intelligent in others. The argument between the lumpers and the splitters is, therefore, about the *basic structure* of intelligence.

Later psychologists proposed structures that more clearly favour the splitters' idea of numerous specific factors. For example, Thurstone (1938) analysed the results of a number of different intelligence tests using the technique called factor analysis. He concluded that intelligence can be described in terms of the following seven *primary mental abilities*:

1. *numerical ability*, measured by arithmetic problems;
2. *reasoning ability*, measured by analogies (LAWYER is to CLIENT as DOCTOR is to ?) or series completion (2, 4, 7, 11, ?);
3. *verbal fluency*, measured by how fast people can produce words (What are 50 words that start with the letter s?);
4. *verbal comprehension*, measured by vocabulary tests and tests of reading comprehension;
5. *spatial visualization*, measured by tests requiring mental manipulation of pictorial representations (How many sides does this solid figure have?);
6. *perceptual ability*, measured by testing for rapid recognition of symbols (Cross out the letter s every time it appears in this sentence);
7. *memory*, measured by testing for recall of words, sentences or picture–word pairs.

But what do we know about intelligence? The publication of a recent, highly controversial book on intelligence (*The Bell Curve*, Herrnstein and Murray, 1994) and the subsequent passionate, but not necessarily well-informed, debate led more than 50 of the world's experts on intelligence to write to the *Wall Street Journal* on 15 December 1994. Their 25-point summary is an excellent and clear statement on what psychologists think about intelligence. Points 9–13 are of particular noteworthiness:

9. IQ is strongly related, probably more so than any other single measurable human trait, to many important educational, occupational, economic and social outcomes. Its relation to the welfare and performance of individuals is very strong in some areas in life (education, military training), moderate but robust in others (social competence), and modest but consistent in others (law abidingness). Whatever IQ tests measure, it is of great practical and social importance.
10. A high IQ is an advantage in life because virtually all activities require some reasoning and decision-making. Conversely, the low IQ is often a disadvantage, especially in disorganized environments. Of course, a high IQ no more guarantees success than a low IQ guarantees failure in life. There are many exceptions, but the odds for success in our society greatly favour individuals with higher IQs.

11. The practical advantage of having a higher IQ increase as life settings become more complex (novel, ambiguous, changing, unpredictable or multifaceted). For example, a high IQ is generally necessary to perform well in highly complex or fluid jobs (the professions, management); it is a considerable advantage in moderately complex jobs (crafts, clerical and police work); but it provides less advantage in settings that require only routine decision-making or simple problem-solving (unskilled work).

12. Differences in intelligence certainly are not the only factor affecting performance in education, training and highly complex jobs (no one claims they are), but intelligence is often the most important. When individuals have already been selected for high (or low) intelligence and so do not differ as much in IQ, as in graduate school (or special education), other influences on performance loom larger in comparison.

13. Certain personality traits, special talents, aptitudes, physical capabilities, experience and the like are important (sometimes essential) for successful performance in many jobs, but they have narrower (or unknown) applicability or 'transferability' across tasks and settings compared with general intelligence. Some scholars choose to refer to these other human traits as other 'intelligences'.

Types of intelligence

Another well-known and more recent attempt at 'splitting' came from Gardner (1999) who distinguished between seven types of intelligence, although more likely he has increased this number to an unlikely easy metric of 10. The celebrated seven are:

1. *Verbal* or linguistic intelligence: The ability to use words
2. Logical or *mathematical* intelligence: The ability to reason logically, solve number problems
3. *Spatial* intelligence: The ability to find your way around the environment, and form mental images
4. *Musical* intelligence: The ability to perceive and create pitch and rhythm patterns
5. *Body-kinetic* intelligence: The ability to carry out motor movement – for example, being a surgeon or a dancer
6. *Interpersonal* intelligence: The ability to understand other people
7. *Intrapersonal* intelligence: The ability to understand yourself and develop a sense of your own diversity.

Others have talked about practical or social intelligence. Indeed, the concept of emotional intelligence may be so popular because most lay people believe that there is more to occupational success than intellectual capacity.

The splitters have identified further levels of intelligence. Raymond Cattell, a British psychologist, first proposed the distinction between 'fluid' and 'crystallized' intelligence. The analogy is to water: water, being fluid, can take any shape, whereas ice crystals remain rigid. Fluid intelligence is defined as our 'on-the-spot reasoning ability, a skill not basically dependent on our experience'. It includes the power to process information, to deal with unfamiliar problems and to acquire new types of knowledge.

Fluid intelligence appears to be linked to biology; it is most active at about 20 when the central nervous system is at its peak of its function. There is some evidence that it declines with age. Crystallized intelligence can be defined as the extent to which a person has absorbed the content of culture: it is the store of knowledge or information that a given society has accumulated. This kind of intelligence continues to develop as long as the person is active, and it remains stable with the passage of time. That is why a schoolchild is quicker than an old-age pensioner at solving unfamiliar problems, but even the most average elderly person will outperform children at solving problems that relate to his or her former occupation.

Managers who try to solve an unfamiliar problem by using their experience – or crystallized intelligence – often find themselves unable to move forward. Part of the problem is the way they are taught: although many business schools now offer creative thinking courses, teaching is still heavily dependent on case histories, which are a form of crystallized intelligence. Yet managers are constantly told that the future will be radically different and that they must change their way of thinking.

Most modern intelligence tests include questions about both types of intelligence, although there seems to be a clear bias towards fluid intelligence. These two types of intelligence are highly correlated, but conceptually different. What you have learned (crystallized intelligence) is determined by how well you learn (fluid intelligence). Inevitably, factors such as personality play a part: introverts like to read, study and learn whereas equally bright extraverts like to socialize and experiment.

Because introverts like to read, they often do better at tests of crystallized intelligence. Motivation is also an important factor. Hard work results in better scores in tests of crystallized ability: even short vocabulary tests give very reliable scores. For this reason popular quizzes concentrate on crystallized intelligence.

The value of crystallized intelligence may fall as technology increasingly drives business. Crystallized intelligence is a repository of knowledge; if that knowledge can be stored cheaply, accurately and efficiently in computers and accessed by bright young people with a high level of fluid intelligence, years of experience quickly lose their value.

Equally, sceptics could argue that computers can help solve problems requiring a fluid intelligence approach, thus rendering the other skills less valuable. But in the business world this seems to be the case less and less. As the phenomenal success of internet start-ups has shown, it is the managers with fluid intelligence, personality and motivation who are most likely to reap the rewards of success.

There will always be a place for those with a high degree of crystallized intelligence. Professions in the law and medicine, and experts such as masters of wine, antiques specialists and classical musicians, all require long hours of study and practice. But in the cut and thrust of a fast-moving business, crystallized intelligence seems useful only in solving those problems where a perspective is needed on how things were done in the past.

Tomorrow belongs to quick-witted, agile and fluid thinkers, not the crusty old stalactites and stalagmites of the past. The future, it seems, is fluid. Managers have to be bright enough for their job.

Emotional intelligence

Most of the researchers who study intelligence argue that it remains relatively fixed. You can learn to do a little better on IQ tests, perhaps increasing your score by 4–8 points, but we are unable to teach intelligence. Intelligence tests measure peak performance, whereas personality tests measure typical performance. A talented and gifted athlete can be trained to perform even more effectively, but one needs the latent talent (endurance, coordination) in the first place. The same is true of intelligence testing.

But people do not like to acknowledge the apparent fatalism of this message. They also do not like to admit that IQ is the best predictor of occupational success. This may account for the high enthusiasm generated by the concept of emotional intelligence (EQ).

The theory was popularized by Daniel Goleman (1998) in his book *Emotional Intelligence* and involves viewing the manner in which you experience and express emotion as a domain intelligence. Goleman's book centred around the 'Emotional Competence Framework', based on *personal* competencies and *social* incompetencies: *personal competence* being competencies that determine how we manage ourselves and social competence being competencies that determine how we handle relationships.

The term 'emotional intelligence' was first used by Salovey and Mayer (1990) and is defined as three categories of ability:

1. Expression of emotion and appraisal (in self and others) divided into verbal/non-verbal and empathy
2. Regulation of emotion in self and others
3. Use of emotion in problem-solving – flexible planning, creative thinking, redirected attention and motivation.

What is EQ? Your grandfather called it charm, your father called it

Table 8.1 The subfactors of emotional intelligence

Personal competence

Self-awareness *Knowing one's internal states, preferences, resources and intuitions*
- Emotional awareness – recognizing emotions and their effects
- Accurate self-assessment – knowing own strengths and limits
- Self-confidence – strong sense of self-worth and capabilities

Self-regulation *Managing one's internal states, impulses and resources*
- Self-control – keeping disruptive emotions and impulses in check
- Trustworthiness – maintaining standards of honesty and integrity
- Conscientiousness – taking responsibility for personal performance
- Adaptability – flexibility in handling change
- Innovation – being comfortable with novel ideas, approaches and new information

Motivation *Emotional tendencies that guide or facilitate reaching goals*
- Achievement drive – striving to improve or meet a standard of excellence
- Commitment – aligning with the goals of the group or organization
- Optimism – persistence in pursuing goals despite obstacles or setback

Social competence

Empathy *Awareness of others' feelings, needs and concerns*
- Understanding others – sensing others' feelings and perspectives and taking an active interest in their concerns
- Developing others – sensing others' development needs and bolstering their abilities
- Service orientation – anticipating, recognizing and meeting customer needs
- Leveraging diversity – cultivating opportunities through different kinds of people
- Political awareness – reading a group's emotional currents and power relationships

Social skills *Adeptness at inducing desirable responses in others*
- Influence – wielding effective tactics for persuasion
- Communication – listening openly and sending convincing messages
- Conflict management – negotiating and resolving disagreements
- Leadership – inspiring and guiding individuals and groups
- Change catalyst – initiating or managing change
- Building bonds – nurturing instrumental relationships
- Collaboration and cooperation – working with others towards shared goals
- Team capabilities – creating group synergy in pursuing collective goals

self-confidence, you called it interpersonal skills, but your children have to call it *EQ*. For Goleman, EQ involves the following subfactors:

The central messages of Goleman's (1998) work are that, at work, relationship building is more important than technical skills. Intuitions are feelings about facts. EQ is emotional labour – the commercialization of human feelings. Jobs are about feelings, emotional labour – understanding, responding and helping staff, peers, clients and customers.

It is no accident that motive and emotion share the same Latin root meaning 'to move'. Great work starts with great feeling. Failed/derailed managers tend to be rigid, have poor relationships, poor self-control and poor social skills, and are weak at building bonds. The 'Peter Principle' shows that people are appointed/promoted on their IQ not their EQ – but the higher you go in an organization, the more you need EQ. EQ pays – higher-level jobs require more EQ. The 'computer nerd/techie' chooses technology to avoid emotions and the fickleness of people.

To acquire many technical skills you need dedication and hence rejection of everyday social intercourse – people trade off opportunities to learn different skills when young. Technical training is easy when compared with teaching EQ skills.

However, there are three serious criticisms to be made of this EQ literature. First, there is little evidence to support the primary claims. Anecdotes are not evidence; although EQ enthusiasts may be right in the long run, at present the jury is still out. Second, EQ really has little to do with IQ – yet there remains no good clear definition or measure of EQ. This makes the whole issue of the relationship between the two immensely problematic. Third, and perhaps most importantly, there is no evidence that the 'facets' of EQ (self-regulation, motivation) can be changed by teaching or training. Consider each facet and then ask the questions: Can it be measured? Can it be learned? How can it be trained? What are the business consequences of each? The whole issue of EQ looks rather different if we study the appropriate psychological literature. And Goleman is right in his view that it is difficult (perhaps impossible) to learn EQ. So perhaps the message is not as positive as one was initially led to believe.

Ability and incompetence

How is it possible that a manager could be in a job he or she is not really able to do? That is, if the real cause of incompetence is insufficient ability (unable to analyse data quickly, to write convincing reports, to respond in good time to change, to learn new skills), how did this situation arise and what lessons are there to be learned? There are a number of non-exclusive possible explanations:

- *A poor selection decision*: The use of mental ability testing for selection has been dropped because of lawsuits and political activists. Faced with repeated evidence of race and sex differences in cognitive test scores, various groups have successfully dissuaded many employers from using them for selection. As a consequence, traditional selection devices such as the interview or reference checks have been used to estimate ability. Obviously these are not ideal methods and it is difficult to imagine how one would validly measure ability without using some sort of verbal IQ test to measure vocabulary or speed of reaction. Hence charm and a silver tongue may cover up insufficient ability. Without data on ability – preferably test data – it is difficult to assess. School and university grades can be a reasonable indicator but only at extremes. Thus, managers with modest to insufficient ability are appointed to positions and offices requiring, quite frankly, more ability than they have.

- *Poor promotion decisions*: If an organization bases its promotional decisions on seniority and service, and not on reasonably measured performance criteria, it is very common for people to be promoted to positions above their ability level. Indeed the Peter Principle is based entirely on this idea: that people get promoted until they are really incompetent to do the job they are in and promotion ends there. However, as this 'law' implies and observation attests, most senior managers in any organization are incompetent – otherwise they would be at the next level.
- *The job has changed*: It may be that a person was perfectly competent at the job for which he or she was carefully selected and trained. However, developments in technology or the marketplace may change the job out of all recognition. The new job requires different skills, a different temperament and a radically different mindset. This may be no fault of the job incumbent unless he or she anticipated these changes and failed to acquire the skills.

The cure

The bad news is this: intelligence is both fixed and pretty important; most aspects/facets/types of IQ are closely related; training and teaching will not change them much. So what are the options if a manager's incompetence arises because he or she does not have the ability to do the job – if the demands of the job exceed the individual's capacity? Most solutions demand courage and honesty – a factor often lacking in most companies. The following are the most obvious:

- *Outplacement*: This is often a politically correct form of saying firing. But it may be done well for the benefit of both the manager and the company. Most managers with insufficient ability know it and are often both stressed and unhappy. If the company offers outplacement assessment and guidance, as well as an appropriate settlement offer, it may be the best solution for both parties.
- *Sideways moves*: Most organizations have a 'dumping ground' for the incompetent. It may be personnel, stores, special projects or some other place where senior managers believe the incompetent can do no real damage. This is not a good solution because all it really does is pass along the problem to someone else. It is often not good for either the company or the manager and it serves to debase the work of the dumping ground area.
- *Demote the manager* (restructure the department): Organizations have fre-

quent restructuring. This provides an ideal opportunity to reduce the managerial responsibilities of any particular incompetent manager. This is in fact a very common and quite satisfactory solution well known to senior staff – so much so that it is often the primary motivation for restructuring.

The idea is simple: people are productive only at their appropriate level of capacity. Not everyone has the intelligence for specific and specialized job-related tasks. Intelligence also predicts ability and willingness to learn. So a set of virtuous and vicious cycles often occurs. The bright manager adapts to job changes and picks up new job skills relatively easily. The dim manager does not and becomes less effective in the role. The secret is to know what level of intelligence is desirable. Very bright people in intellectually less stimulating jobs can, through boredom, be far from productive. They can be underemployed, which, as we saw in Chapter 2, can lead to its own type of incompetence.

8.4. Learning and Training

One obvious and frequent reason why managers fail is that they never learned any of the prerequisite skills of management. As we observed in Chapter 1, many managers are promoted or simply appointed to the role with little or no preparation. Thereafter, Darwinian forces often come into play.

Talent (ability and motivation) alone is not enough to ensure competent, if not excellent, management. What is also required is appropriate learning experiences. McCall (1998: xii) argues that 'leadership ability can be learned, that creating a context that supports the development of talent can become a source of competitive advantage, and that the development of leaders is itself a leadership responsibility'. He rejects the assumption that a shortlist of generic qualities can describe all effective leaders, that those qualities are stable over the course of a person's career, and that through survival of the fittest the best survive, requiring only minor polish and refinement. McCall stresses that continual growth, transition and transformation are as much associated with success as 'natural ability'. He believes that 'leaders are both born and made, but mostly made' (1998: 51), that organizations need to strengthen and polish what already exists and also to bring potential into being. He also distinguished between two models:

- *The Darwinian Model*, which attempts to identify less/more successful executive traits, search for the latter, then give people tests/experience to polish these skills. On-the-job challenges reveal actual talent.
- *The Agricultural Model* attempts to identify strategic challenges that are likely to occur, to search for people who can learn from the experiences, and then help them to succeed.

In a sense McCall argues from *survival* of the fittest to the *development* of the fittest, from being a corporate Darwinist to being a managerial developer. A number of experimental criteria are believed to be good for development. These include job transitions (taking on unfamiliar responsibilities), implementing change strategies, taking on higher levels of responsibility and being influential in non-authority relationships. Developmental opportunities arise from being given *new assignments* (project, task force), dealing with *hardships/setbacks* (business failure), *other people* (who are role models) and 'other events'. Clearly, people who take on continuous modest challenges with occasional changes of function will learn the most. International assignments and training can all justify this process. Some organizations also choose to create and fund company schools and universities. Whether deliberate or serendipitous, organizations can provide powerful experiences that become opportunities to learn.

The Darwinian and developmental approaches are not opposites: organizations need to select talented people in order to assess, and then realize, their potential. Managers need to focus on the range of developmental experiences that their talented people should have in order to develop their abilities rather than find people who currently have the desired qualities. Leadership can be seen as a journey of personal development, and derailment can be seen as the result of talented people not learning from experience or, of course, not having the necessary experience.

Ultimately the question remains about how organizations can provide the learning experiences that their potential leaders need. Most companies insist that managers are accountable for results and not development and hence ignore the development aspects of job assignments. Job rotation focuses on exposure rather than task. Managers need incentives, resources and support in order to change.

What one needs, according to McCall, is a model for developing talent; he is proposing an explicit, systematic and comprehensive effort to take the developmental model seriously.

McCall's (1998) research suggests that the capacity to learn is the most important element of continued development. Successful managers *draw attention to their talent*, which results in better opportunities to develop it. They have a *sense of adventure* to take on challenges and to *create a context* for their own learning. And they are also able to learn from experience, respond to feedback and bounce back after setbacks. In this sense one can pick people with potential by looking at certain characteristics that predict that their potential will be realized.

There are powerful reasons for management training, and arguments as to why management training is not a luxury but a necessity for organizations in the new millennium. The increased global competition, as well as rapid changes in technology and the workforce, demand ever more subtle and higher-level (but trainable) skills. There are inevitably greater demands on management time and the need for well-informed and accurate plans and decisions.

Few people begin a job fully trained. Changes in technology, promotion to higher-level management levels, job rotation and enrichment all mean that managers need to learn new skills, acquire new information and understand different processes. As a consequence, all organizations have to educate and train staff to raise their level of performance. This may be achieved by providing new and relevant knowledge and information, by teaching new skills, or by changing attitudes, values and motives.

The purpose of training is to enhance skill and knowledge. Good training can, and should, provide a focus for aligning the capabilities of the workforce with the company strategy. It can also ensure that workforce skill levels are up to, or even better than, national or industry levels. Good training can be a powerful individual motivator and a good catalyst for change.

Workers seem to be better educated than ever before. Most believe that more education and better qualifications mean better prospects. Consequently, more people spend more time in higher education before starting work and may sponsor their own part-time education while at work.

Whole business sections and divisions receive training, as well as individuals. Topics vary enormously from creativity to computer literacy to team-building and time management. Training is popular partly because it seems like a reward for good performance, although occasionally it can be punishment for incompetence. Many senior managers believe that training helps sustain a flexible and adaptive workforce. It is seen as a powerful management tool to support planned and desired development. Incompetent managers on the other hand often devalue training, or deliver it badly.

Training courses come in many shapes and sizes. Most jobs require *technical knowledge* training, which may be done on the job, via simulated teaching or through traditional classroom instruction. There is now more emphasis on what one may call training in *human relations* or management skills, although this often amounts to EQ training. All sorts of training may occur based on such procedures as in-baskets (learning how to deal with the letters, memoranda, telephone calls, faxes and emails supposedly accumulated in the in-tray of a hypothetical executive), role playing (not acting, but playing the role of a particular executive), management games (complex, often computer-based scenarios usually representing conflict or opportunity situations), sensitivity training (a process- rather than content-oriented programme that attempts to raise awareness) and team training (where the focus is often team integration and interdependence). Training is used to improve various capabilities, basic learning, intellectual skills, cognitive strategies, motor skills and even attitudes.

Organizations provide training, education and development. *Training* is usually thought of as skills based. Skills are specific and usually easy to measure. *Education* refers to 'in-house' or outside courses such as MBAs, which some companies subsidize for specific groups (often fast-trackers or those whose services they wish to retain). *Development*, on the other hand, is usually based on the individual and represents a long-term investment dedicated to trying to get the best out of a particular individual.

Management at all levels *and* those reporting to them are the targets of training. Training seems to be more and more important in the framework of career planning and business innovations. Training is often one response to competition.

What is training?

Psychologists have developed various theories to explain how, when and why people learn (Furnham, 1999). Many of these theories are based on specific principles:

Goal-setting: People learn best when they have clear goals that are difficult enough to challenge them rather than discourage them.

Reinforcement: People learn best when given prompt, continuous and positive reward for having learned new skills.

Feedback: Learning is virtually impossible without clear and accurate feedback results.

Modelling: People can learn efficiently and effectively by copying others who have the required skills.

Distributed practice: Most people prefer to learn complex tasks at various 'sittings', rather than on one occasion.

Whole rather than part: For many complex tasks people prefer and do better with part learning (each part separately) rather than whole training (the complete entity).

Transfer of learning: The more similar the place, tools and conditions of learning to the circumstances under which the learnt behaviour is to be exercised, the better the transfer of learning.

Many people talk of *learning curves*, which are characterized by a rapid increase in knowledge or skill in the earlier learning period and a tapering off towards the end of the process. The reality of these curves has been recognized for nearly 100 years, although their shape depends on what is being taught and how. The principles of learning have been investigated by applied psychologists for 100 years (Blum and Naylor, 1968), and many subtle distinctions have been made. Consider, for example, knowledge of results or feedback, which is important both for its information and for its reinforcing characteristics. Various types of feedback have been analysed:

- *Extrinsic versus intrinsic*: A pilot receives intrinsic feedback about the path of the plane from bodily cues, but extrinsic feedback from the flight-deck instruments.
- *Primary versus secondary*: A competitive archer receives primary feedback from seeing the arrow in (or not in) the target board, but secondary feedback from the facial expression of the instructor.
- *Augmented versus summary*: Augmented feedback is immediate and concurrent with behaviour; summary occurs at a later point: it is both delayed and global.
- *Specific versus general*: This is self-evident.

Interestingly, results suggest that learning is facilitated by increased precision in feedback *up to a point*: too much feedback overloads and can cause a decrease in performance. Learning takes place in many ways in an organization: through association, rewards and punishments, and by observation.

Observational learning

Observational learning occurs when one person acquires new information or behaviours *vicariously* (but sometimes purposefully) by observing what happens to others. But in order for this sort of learning to occur, the learner must pay careful *attention* to the model. Learning will be most effective when management models get the attention of others. Workers must also *remember* the model's actions. The person learning to do the job must be able to develop some verbal description or mental image of the model's actions in order to remember them. If the learner can imagine himself or herself behaving just as the model did – a process known as *symbolic rehearsal* – then learning will be facilitated. In addition, there must be some *behavioural reproduction* (practice) of the model's behaviour. Unless workers are capable of doing just what the model has done, they will not be able to learn observationally from the model. The ability to reproduce many observed behaviours may be initially limited, but can improve with practice. Finally, workers must be *motivated* to learn from the model.

In observational learning, the learning process is controlled by the learners themselves. On the job, observational learning occurs both formally and informally. Observational learning is a key part of many formal job instruction training programmes. Given a chance to observe experts doing their jobs, followed by the opportunity to practise the desired skills, and given feedback on their performance, workers tend to be effectively trained. Observational learning also occurs in an informal and casual manner. Workers who observe the norms and traditions of their organizations, and who subsequently incorporate them into their own behaviour, have also learned through observation. Observational learning is responsible, in part, for the ways new employees are socialized into their organizations (that is, how they 'learn the ropes') and how they come to appreciate their organization's traditions and ways of doing things (that is, its culture).

Learning by observation is frequent, important and often neglected. It is how most managers learn, and how incompetence is perpetuated. If the only models that young people have are incompetent ones, it is not very surprising that they themselves become incompetent. On the other hand, it is possible to achieve a great deal, relatively cheaply, by modelling competence.

The transfer of training

Training needs can be considered at the *organizational* level, the *individual* skills level or through a careful *task* analysis, which looks at individual units of behaviour that are broken down into specific operations in a hierarchical fashion. Task analysis is usually best done for skilled physical tasks, rather than cognitive tasks.

Once training needs have been established, training methods should be considered. Although certain trainers favour certain methods, not because of their proven efficacy but rather out of personal preference, it is difficult to find clear evidence supporting the use of one training technique over others. Popular techniques include case studies, role playing, business games, job rotation, shadowing and 'understudy assignments', as well as on-the-job training. Some organizations believe that the best way to learn is through traditional apprenticeship models, others believe that intensive early instruction is best, and some simulations are a very cost-effective way of learning.

- *Participation*: For training to be effective, trainees must be actively involved, performing the desired skills. People learn more quickly – and tend to retain their learned skills – when they actively participate in learning. The principle of participation applies to learning cognitive skills, just as it does to learning motor skills.
- *Repetition*: The fact that learning is facilitated by repeating the desired behaviours is well established. Practice is more effective when spread out over time than when it is all done at the same time. When practice periods are too long, learning can suffer from fatigue, whereas learning a little at a time allows the material to sink in. The question of exactly how long one should practise and how long one should rest depends on many factors, such as the nature of the task and the ability of the person performing it.

For training to be most effective, what is learned during training must be applied to the job. In fact, the more closely a training programme matches the demands of the job, the more effective the training will be (Baldwin and Ford, 1988). By using sophisticated computer-based techniques to simulate real flight conditions, airline pilot trainees can learn what it is like to manipulate their craft safely, without actually risking their lives and expensive equipment. Naturally, training that is any less elaborate in the degree to which it simulates the actual work environment is less effective (for example, a home computer flight-simulation game).

The success of transfer from the training to the work setting depends on various things. For instance, successful transfer is a function of:

- *Time*: The amount of positive transfer decreases as a function of time.
- *Task similarity*: Having to learn a new response to an 'old' stimulus leads to negative transfer.
- *Amount of initial learning*: The more (and better) the learning on the initial task, the better the transfer.
- *Task difficulty*: There is a greater transfer from a difficult task to an easier task than vice versa.
- *Knowledge of results*: Feedback affects performance but not learning.

Transfer of learning (or training) is the process by which the effects of training learned in one situation transfer to others. If transfer never occurred, there would be little justification for formal education; every element of knowledge, skills and capacity would have to be taught separately. This would effectively damn many training programmes. But there are at least 5 types of transfer:

1. *Lateral transfer*: Lateral transfer involves performance at the same level of complexity as the initial learning, but in a different context. In other words, they refer to the ability to complete new learnt tasks at work as well as in the training room.
2. *Sequential transfer*: Sequential transfer occurs when trainees build on a learning foundation. A skill learned today may have some relationship to a fact or idea learned tomorrow. For example, keyboard skills transfer to many tasks.
3. *Vertical transfer*: Vertical transfer occurs when learning at one level, such as comprehending statistical facts, facilitates the solution of problems. It amounts to transfer from the simpler components of a task to the more complex ones.
4. *Positive transfer*: When training or performance in one task can be transformed to another, positive transfer occurs. Positive transfer manifests itself in the following situations: learning Mandarin may aid the learning of Cantonese; and mastering the skill of word-processing results in the positive transfer of understanding spreadsheets.
5. *Negative transfer*: Negative transfer is said to occur when previous learning in a particular task hinders learning in another task. Errors may arise in a factory when an employee with experience of driving one particular model

of a fork-lift truck drives another model. The pedals for braking, reversing and accelerating can differ in position from one model to the next.

Transfer is important in evaluating the cost of training: the more transferable, the more cost-efficient. Related to the concept of transfer is the concept of generalizability. There are various types of generalizability – from the training room to the factory floor, from one highly specific skill to others, and over time. Most training programmes evaluate training immediately after it has ended, rather than, say, six months later. Of course, the extent to which information and skills have been retained depends on many factors apart from the course itself. The way an organization rewards skills acquisition and allows opportunity for practice is obviously important.

For researchers, the first problem is to identify the factors that maximize or minimize skill transfer and generalization; the second problem is to understand the processes by which this occurs; the third problem is to offer sound advice to maximize skill transfer and generalization.

Pitfalls of training

Lack of training is not the only reason for incompetence. If a manager's incompetence is the result of poor learning, then training is part of the answer. But there are also incompetent trainers and incompetent training methods. Researchers have listed a long series of potential problems of training:

- Inaccurate or incomplete training needs identification – that is, the need for training of a particular type was misdiagnosed in the first place.
- Failure to predetermine outcomes relevant to the business needs of the organization. Unless one sets a realistic and specific goal or outcome of training, it is very difficult to know whether it has succeeded or failed.
- Lack of objectives, or objectives expressed as 'will be able to' rather than 'will'. There is a difference between 'can do' and 'will do', often ignored by evaluators.
- Training seen by management and participants as having little or no relationship to real life. It is seen as a break and an alternative to work, rather than as a means to improve.
- Excessive dependence by trainers on theory and chalk-and-talk training sessions. This method is least effective for the training of specific skills.
- Trainers untrained or undertrained. It is far too easy to call yourself a trainer with little personal training in the skills required. Some courses have 'train-the-trainer' sessions, but these are all too rare.
- Training programmes too short to enable deep learning to take place or skills to be practised. The longer and more spaced out the programme, the more participants learn and the more it is retained.

- Use of inappropriate resources and training methods that have to be considered beforehand, particularly the fit between the trainer and the trainees' style.
- Trainer self-indulgence, leading to all sessions being fun sessions, rather than actual learning experiences.
- Failure to pre-position the participants in terms of the company's expectation(s) of them after training. This means having a realistic expectation, for each person, of what they should know, or should be able to do after the training.
- Failure to debrief participants effectively after training, particularly how best to practise and thus retain the skills they have acquired.
- Dependence on dated and invalid research to justify approaches. This is a very common problem.
- Excessive use of 'good intentions' and 'flavour of the month training', rather than those known to be effective.
- Training limited to lower levels of the organization, because it is cheaper and easier to deliver and evaluate.
- Inability of top management team to 'walk like they talk' – that is, managers do not model what trainers instruct.
- Use of training to meet social, ideological or political ends, either of trainers or senior management. That is, training is not really about skill acquisition but is rather about, for instance, a fight between various departments.
- Failure to relate to bottom-line performance. This means that training takes place without any consideration of its effect on productivity or profitability.
- Training design developed to accentuate enjoyable experiences and games rather than the transfer of learning to the workplace.

Training is the most favoured method of preventing or curing incompetence. It is also among the least effective, not because training per se does not work, but rather because it is an inappropriate response to the cause of the problem. It would be naïve to believe that a two-way negotiable skills course or a six-week-long statistics course would ever cure managerial incompetence. Indeed, attitudes to learning itself may predict managerial incompetence. For the incompetent manager training is often a nightmare because such courses often expose their inadequacies.

Training managers

In an important sense, all managers need training. A person with a lot of natural talent for management will still need a good bit of experience. An athletic analogy is appropriate – just because a person has a lot of hand–eye coordination does not mean that the person can hit a tennis ball. To be able to hit a tennis ball in a proficient way requires, in addition to natural talent, a lot of time on a court actually hitting tennis balls. Moreover, just as hand–eye coordination is normally distributed in a population – so that a few people have a lot of talent, most people don't have much talent and a few people have none whatsoever – so natural talent for management is normally distributed in a population. Consequently, every potential manager needs some training in order to do the job well.

The process of deciding what to train is relatively straightforward. It is necessary only to put the candidates for training through a well-designed assessment process and this will reveal what it is that needs to be trained. Again, an athletic model is apt. If you want to improve your tennis game, you will consult a tennis pro. The tennis pro will ask you to hit some balls, after which he or she will point out the shortcomings in your game – you are not getting sideways to the ball, you are not getting your raquet back soon enough, and so on. In the same way, a management assessment will reveal the critical shortcomings in your management performance. The trick, then, is to fix these shortcomings. And, once again, everyone will have some aspect of his or her performance that requires fixing.

This is the point at which the training process begins to get a bit sticky. The training problem turns into two general questions: what can be trained and who can be trained?

What can't be trained?

Personality is rooted in temperament, and temperament is rooted in genetics. Temperament is essentially fixed at birth. The bottom line is that temperament cannot be changed; it can only be understood and then accommodated and used when appropriate. But one needs first to understand what one's natural tendencies are, and this comes from assessment.

What can be trained?

What can be trained, however, are certain skills that are crucial for managerial effectiveness, and that are, in principle, learnable. Six skills seem particularly important for managers to learn. These include:

1. *Listening*: Listening is a skill that must be learned. And it is not enough simply to listen; the other person must receive the impression that he or she has been heard. Listening involves paying attention, making eye contact, not interrupting and rephrasing the other person's comments to indicate one's understanding.
2. *Writing*: Being able to write clearly, concisely and accurately is a crucial skill for managers – one that must be practised, and practised well.

3. *Speaking*: The ability to give clear, organized and persuasive presentations is an essential component of leadership, and one that must be learned.
4. *Providing feedback*: One of the most common complaints that subordinates have about their managers is that they do not receive enough feedback. The ability to give timely, useful, constructive feedback is an essential managerial skill.
5. *Assertiveness*: Being able to be appropriately assertive is another essential managerial skill. It involves being respectful but insistent, diplomatic but firm, demanding but fair.
6. *Conducting a meeting*: Being able to conduct a productive meeting is a crucial skill that is often overlooked. It involves judgement about when to have a meeting, who should be there, getting the right agenda, getting the agenda promulgated, sticking to the agenda, making sure that all voices are heard, leaving the group on a positive note, ending the meeting on time, and ending the meeting with the participants being clear about what is expected next.

Who can be trained?

There are substantial individual differences in trainability. People who are trainable can learn from their experience; people who are not trainable cannot learn from experience. Everyone who has examined the problem of managerial failure notes that a key cause of failure is an inability to learn, grow, adapt or profit from experience. There seem to be four components to the training process. First, the trainee must attend to the material – this requires having enough self-control to listen and pay attention. Second, the trainee must be smart enough to absorb and remember the training materials. Third, the trainee must have the relevant skills available to use the training materials. And finally, the trainee must believe that acquiring the new skills will make a difference to his or her performance. The first and fourth issues seem to be the most critical factors.

The empirical literature on individual differences in trainability leads to two reasonably well-replicated conclusions. First, people with very low self-esteem will listen carefully and eagerly to negative feedback regarding their performance because they are excessively self-critical and the feedback is a form of criticism. Paradoxically, it seems, these people will not listen to positive feedback regarding their performance; they discount positive feedback and dwell instead on the negative, which makes it difficult for them to improve their performance. They are so focused on what they are doing wrong that they are unable to build on what they are doing right. Their low self-esteem also makes it hard for them to experiment, to try doing things in new ways so that they can learn from positive experience.

The second, and equally paradoxical, finding concerns people with very high self-esteem. Such people will listen to positive feedback but will refuse to listen to negative feedback. They ignore it because they do not believe it. Because they will not listen, and because they do not think the feedback can improve their performance, people with very high self-esteem are very hard to train. There is an old joke that asks, 'How many psychologists does it take to change a light bulb?' The answer: 'One, but the bulb must really want to change.' And it is the same thing for people who are very self-confident.

In summary, every manager's performance can be improved with additional training. The really critical questions concern what can and cannot be trained, and who can and cannot be trained. Basic personality characteristics are fairly immutable and must be finessed rather than changed. Skills can be trained, changed and modified, but not everyone is trainable. People with low self-esteem ignore positive feedback, and those with high self-esteem ignore negative feedback; people who ignore feedback have trouble learning from experience.

8.5. Distraction and 'Other Lives'

The day is 24 hours long: people spend about a third asleep, a third at work and a third at home. That is a crude breakdown but near enough the truth. The time spent asleep is of little interest unless, of course, people cannot sleep, and then become overtired and, as a consequence, incompetent at work.

The important issue concerns the balance between work and home life. This is nearly always expressed in terms of the problems that women managers (and workers) have in balancing their work and family responsibilities. Anyone responsible for small children or aged relatives knows that family care is a full-time job that is as complex and as emotionally demanding as any management position.

It has long been recognized that there is considerable stress associated with the dual responsibilities of work and home. The dilemma of choosing between tending to a sick child and being at a senior management meeting discussing an aggressive merger is a real quandary. Family responsibilities can be very distracting. It is difficult to keep one's 'eye on the ball' when desperately worried about what is going on at home. But people often have problems and passions outside the workplace that clearly distract them. It is this distraction that means that manager's minds are elsewhere.

Distractions

Consider the following list of issues and how they can and do impact on a manager's competence.

Money-related addictions

Gambling: Serious gamblers are not very different from drug or alcohol addicts. They can easily become obsessed by one of the many forms of gambling and find it very difficult to give up. They become secretive about the addiction and when (inevitably) their losses mount up, they resort to dangerous and illegal behaviours to cover up their crisis. Stealing money from one's employer is a favourite ruse: most gamblers persuade themselves they will be able to 'pay it back' once they have won and it is, therefore, little more than a short-term loan.

Others make illegal payments and investments to pay for their habit. They may borrow legally excessive amounts from money lenders until they are given no more. They may fleece vulnerable and gullible relatives. They may secretly mortgage the house. And if they are senior managers, their actions could lead to the total collapse of a company. People who have been in this position often say that, retrospectively, they could spot there was something wrong but did nothing.

Speculation: Get-rich plans and schemes have always existed. But the ease of buying and selling shares has never been easier, or more strongly acceptable. A few easy wins early on can easily lead to a form of addiction. Many sorts of gambler's fallacies can 'kick in' and there are many cases of people getting up or staying up through the entire night to watch or trade shares. It can be very exciting and it can be easily hidden. The problem always starts when the early addicted money speculator runs out of spare money (discretionary cash) to invest further. Like traditional gamblers, they have an overpowering need to gamble and an ability to rationalize what they are doing.

For owner–managers the total company assets may easily become a chip in their gambling game. It is too easy for them to take their eye off the ball and for all the fallacies of the gambler to lead them to making terrible business decisions.

Drug-related addictions

Alcohol: The use of alcohol in the workplace is clearly changing. It is less acceptable, even illegal, to drink at work, and most organizations actively discourage the languid pub lunch or four-hour business luncheons. Senior managers who once may have had an executive liquor cabinet that was regularly 'refreshed' at company expense, are now discouraged even from having occasional cocktail parties on the premises.

But alcohol has traditionally been, and is still, used in some jobs for specific purposes. Alcoholism is associated with certain jobs such as the media, cooking and the armed services. Jobs with time deadlines, those with easy availability and those that involve training are often associated with heavy drinking. Alcohol is a physical depressant, but a social stimulant. It can 'bring you down' quickly and comfortably after meeting a difficult deadline. It can help people be braver or encourage them to admit fear, pain, anxiety and terror after witnessing terrible events. And it can 'cure boredom'.

For these and many other reasons people drift between the rather fuzzy stages along the path from social to heavy addicted drinkers. It takes a long time to occur and a long time to detect. Most adults can tell a story about an alcoholic manager who got away with it for years. Stories vary somewhat but are often about deadlines missed, erratic behaviour with staff and customers, long unexplained absences and illnesses, and an unkempt appearance. The longer the alcoholic manager stays, the more incompetence occurs.

Antidepressants: Some people become addicted to drugs through quite legal and legitimate medical prescriptions. Coping with emotional trauma may lead to prescriptions for a wide range of antidepressants, some of which have been shown to be addictive. The problem lies primarily in the fact that drugs are prescribed as a short-term emotionally stabilizing measure, but, if a person doesn't learn appropriate coping skills for the problem, the drugs may become the only crutch a person has.

Again, many adults can tell stories of the manager who was clearly dependent on antidepressant medication. There can be radical and frightening behaviour changes when, for any reason, the person cannot get his or her medication; in this case, anxiety attacks, inappropriate emotional outbursts or manic episodes may result.

Illness

It is difficult to imagine anything quite as distracting for any person as a seriously ill relative, particularly a child. Many people emerge from their own life-threatening illnesses visibly changed; they agree that they see things differently and that their priorities have changed. However, to have a seriously ill child, a terminally ill parent, or a chronically ill spouse/partner means that, for many, work becomes secondary. Nothing, many feel, is more important than one's family, and workplace problems and issues seem trivial compared with the potential enormity of life and death issues.

One reason for managerial incompetence may be illness. A particular problem here is that the manager, whose distraction may result in incompetence, may not disclose the nature of the problem. The illness may be socially embarrassing. Many mental illnesses are of this kind. A relative may have tried to take his or her own life while depressed. The relative may have recently been diagnosed with a hereditary illness and the manager may be worried about others finding out.

There are many reasons why managers attempt to hide issues around ill-ness. Yet attempting to deal with the illness can easily lead to considerable problems around issues of time keeping, tiredness and so on. The distracted manager is often not at work fully – they may be there in person but that is all.

Not only does the distracted manager not concentrate, but he or she may also be physically tired through volunteering personal nursing duties. Inevitably they themselves may become physically or mentally ill through the strain.

Relationships

Relationships such as marriage, and also close friendships, can be a tremen-dous source of pleasure and pain, support and frustration. There is a wealth of evidence that a good personal relationship can break the link between work stress and illness through the mechanism of social support. Equally, the relationship between work stress and illness can be exacerbated by a troublesome or crumbling relationship.

In many countries in the western world about one-third of marriages end in divorce, and a large percentage of these end acrimoniously in law courts. Ownership of property, custody of children and alimony settlements cause considerable emotional pain and soul searching. Most people have seen a friend or colleague go through a difficult divorce. There are many casualties of this experience and one casualty is often the workplace.

Subordinates of a manager rendered incompetent through divorce pro-ceedings tell a familiar story of moodiness, indecisiveness and absenteeism. This is of course all the more unusual if the cause is not known.

The cure for distraction

Distraction has many different sources – illness, addiction, relationships. Many senior managers who correctly understand that the cause of the per-ceived incompetence is distraction often do not know what to do. Most are understandably sympathetic and attempt to seek out professional help in the form of therapists, counsellors and the like.

Some big organizations have clear procedural guidelines when problems of alcohol or drug addiction are found. There are recommended counsel-lors, clinics and consultants. Incompetent addicts are given a specific period of sick-leave, are required to attend therapy and are given a formal warning. There are often set procedures in big organizations for these problems because they are well known and tend to reoccur. The problem is quite dif-ferent for relationships and illness. In most instances the incompetence that is the (partial) result of these situations drags on for a very long time before there is any serious intervention. And that is part of the problem.

The best solution involves three things. There is first the offer and even the provision of specialized help. There are various people who might be temporarily employed to help out – these may be counsellors, domestic help, babysitters and so on. The organization may feel that it is worthwhile sponsoring this. Second is a re-registration of contractual obligations over time keeping. Thus a person may be offered time off sick or (then) unpaid leave to sort out the matter. Or the person may go part-time or even leave the job (say to nurse the sick parent), but have a guaranteed option to return at a later date. The reason for their incompetence is, after all, that they are distracted and would rather be elsewhere most of the time. So the best solution is to allow them to be elsewhere for that time period. The third part of the solution involves discussing dates, not as threats but as points at which the issue should be revisited. These dates are marks in the sand where future decisions have to be made about the situation if at that time no solution has been found. This applies particularly to issues where self-control is involved, such as alcohol or drug dependency.

Clearly, getting the diagnosis wrong only makes the whole thing much worse. To send a distracted manager on a training course is nothing short of incompetence itself.

8.6. Historical Disaffection

The way many managers go about their job is often a history of their personal work experience. Thus management consultants will observe, if they work with senior managers who go from one organization to another, that they tend to adopt the same strategies and work in the same way. These recurring patterns are not the same as management style, which is a pattern of behaviour more related to personality factors. Rather, the recurring patterns seem to come from a belief in a particular way of doing things.

It is simple but important features of management that are learnt or copied; these include how much time should be proportionally spent on analysing business problems, planning a strategy of action, actually doing the work and reflecting on what they have learned. Some eschew analysis and planning and get into action as quickly as possible. Others like to spend considerable time getting advice, arranging committees and commissioning reports to understand the causes of the problem before doing anything.

Some job sectors are reactive – pharmaceuticals, banks, mining companies and hospitals; others are proactive – design companies, e-business and sales. The culture of the former is low risk, slow feedback and a ponderous pace where good ideas are given a proper chance to show success. Decisions are slow and consultation is top down. Senior managers have to cope with long-term ambiguity and demand because they are dependent on technical competence. Some believe they move with 'awesome slowness' (Deal and Kennedy, 1982).

The culture of the latter is the world of friendly, carousing, work-hard, play-hard extraverts. Success comes with persistence but quality is often sacrificed. Often these high-energy enthusiasts drift into scepticism and cynicism when quick-fix solutions fail or theories lose their shine or meaning.

More importantly, managers can learn to be disaffected. Organizational psychologists have talked about alienation from work or its opposite, work commitment/involvement. Karl Marx believed that work should be a voluntary, conscious activity that contributed to the development of one's mental and physical powers and that thus had its own intrinsic value. Marx spoke of alienation, in two senses: separation of workers from the product of their labour, when producers feel that they cannot influence what is produced and how it is made; and separation of workers from the means of production, when producers have no ownership or control of factories and equipment.

Seaman (1959) proposed five different types of separation. These may be summarized in terms of separation from control, prediction, moral values, other people and oneself, as follows:

Powerlessness: An inability to influence the course of events in one's lifespan
Meaninglessness: An inability to predict events and the outcomes of one's own and others' behaviour
Normlessness: A belief that morally undesirable means are often the only way to achieve desired ends
Isolation: A feeling that one is not a member of any important social network
Self-estrangement: A feeling that one's activities are undertaken for extrinsic reasons (for example, to provide the basis for mere survival) rather than for their intrinsic meaning and personal value.

Some psychologists have taken the above ideas and devised questionnaires to measure it. Thus Shephard (1972) developed a questionnaire with five sections. Examples of the questions in each category are set out below:

1. *Powerlessness*: To what extent can you vary the steps involved in doing your job? To what extent can you move from your immediate work area during working hours? To what extent can you control how much work you produce? To what extent can you help decide on the methods and procedures used in your job? To what extent do you have influence over what happens to you at work?

2. *Meaninglessness*: To what extent do you know how your job fits into the total work organization? To what extent do you know how your work contributes to company products? To what extent does management give workers enough information about what is going on in the company? To

what extent do you know how your job fits into the work of other departments? To what extent do you know how your work affects the jobs of others you work with?

3. *Normlessness*: To what extent do you feel that people who get ahead in the company deserve it? To what extent do you feel getting ahead in the company is based on ability?

4. *Instrumental Work Orientation*: Your job is something you have to do to earn a living – most of your real interests are centred outside the job. Money is the most rewarding reason for working. Working is a necessary evil to provide things your family and you want. You are living for the day when you can collect your retirement and do the things that are important to you.

5. *Self-evaluation Involvement*: You would like people to judge you for the most part by what you spend your money on, rather than by how you make your money. Success in the things you do away from the job is more important to your opinion of yourself than success in your work career. Your work is only a small part of who you are.

The opposite of alienation is involvement or commitment, about which a great deal has been written. But why do people become alienated? One constant factor associated with incompetent alienated managers is that they have *never* been given any significant, serious feedback on their performance – *ever*. If people are neither praised (stroked) for good work, nor punished for bad, then it is not surprising that they become alienated. They have been badly managed.

People who have worked in communist countries and people who have worked for state-owned bureaucracies often become incompetent because of alienation. Essentially there were few or even no serious consequences of your work. If you work hard, it did not matter, and it did not matter if you did not. Tasks had to be performed for no good reason and everyone opposed change. The job and promotion were guaranteed, based not on results but on length of service. Managers become particularly cross and alienated if their organization experiences considerable change – for example, from a length of service to a measured-performance model of work. They feel alienated from the organization which they believe has let them down and broken its side of the bargain.

Alienated incompetent managers are negative about every initiative and are jealous of people who are more successful and competent. They are 'work-to-rule' types, not in terms of union rules but in their personal style. They become 'quit-but-stay' workers who quit their enthusiasm, their commitment to the organization and their dedication, but who do not leave. They have torn up their emotional or psychological contracts but not their legal contract, and do the minimum required to stay employed.

Alienated workers seek each other out. They form the disgruntled cohort of workers whose memory is as long as their enthusiasm is short. They dwell over past 'injustices', resent young people and are deeply cynical about all initiatives made by companies. Many are happy to leave their brains with the car in the car park in the early morning, only bothering to refit it after knocking off exactly at the allotted time.

They are terrible managers. They resist change, care little about their staff and model the whole process extremely badly.

The cure for alienation

Furnham (1998) has suggested that there are, in essence, three cures for the problem:

1. *Buy them out*: It may seem costly in the short term but it may be the most cost-effective solution. Everyone has their price, and if the company is prepared to throw in some outplacement counselling and other services, even the most security-minded employee might be prepared to leap into the job pool of life. Most are frightened of what they perceive to be the icy-cold, shark-infested waters of the commercial world. The company environment, however much it has changed, still looks warm and protective. To sell the concept of a leaving package you need to reverse these perceptions, pointing out how cold and competitive the company must become and how warm and cosy the opportunities are out there in the real world.

2. *Raise the game*: Quit-but-stayers need to know that there are significant changes in the way things are done in the new organization. The talk of 'revenue up, cost down', 'lean-and-mean' organizations needs to be supported by tougher targets for individual workers. There are various ways to raise the game which includes changing equipment to the new technology which has to be mastered; removing or reducing support staff and functions; or, more simply, demanding more productivity. The thought of having perpetually to put in more effort frequently frightens off alienated individuals or they change into productive and committed workers.

3. *Introduce new blood*: This more risky strategy involves bringing in new (mostly young) people with no memory of the past. Forward-looking, enthusiastic and manageable new people show up the alienated workers. They prove that the new system can work and provide excellent models if carefully selected. As long as they outnumber and can outperform the alienated workers, the poisonous cynicism of the latter will not have a debilitating effect on the former. The 'passed-over-and-pissed-off' (POPOs) often appear more pathetic than wise and the ostracism from the young and upwardly mobile may succeed in either scaring them off or changing them.

8.7. Conclusion

This chapter has suggested that there are a few major causes of managerial incompetence: lack of ability, absence of training, distraction and alienation. There are, of course, others. One of the most obvious is a poor *fit* between the person and the job. This can occur because jobs change, rather more than people. The solution usually requires finding a job that fits better the abilities, needs and temperaments of the job holder, although one should admit that this may not be possible.

A second cause is more common and more intractable and it refers to psychological factors. As was noted in Chapter 5, the 'dark side' of personality can be a serious stumbling block for managerial success. Certain personality traits are closely associated with various sorts of dysfunctional behaviour. Thus some people are obsessional, some too impulsive. Extremes of obsessionality or impulsivity, along with a host of other issues, can lead to serious management failure. Lack of self-confidence, fear of failure and pathological risk aversion are also personality factors associated with management derailment.

The question is: What can be done about them? Can people be cured or changed? Can the obsessional be encouraged to 'lighten up' and stop checking? Can the habitual procrastinator be taught to deliver on time? The answer is sometimes yes, but often at great cost and determination. The quiet introvert can become a socialized extravert when the occasion requires it. He or she will still find socializing tiring and unnatural, but it can be done. Through patient commitment, delegation and retraining it is probably possible for many whose personality make-up is far from ideal to learn the skills of competence and leave behind the ghost of incompetent management practices.

References

Adams, K. (1997) Understanding and applying competencies: The views and experience of competencies' founding father, David McClelland. *Competency* 4: 18–23.

Adams, K. (1998) Three key methods of identifying competencies. *Competency* 5: 37–44.

Adorno, T., Frenkel-Brunswick, D., Levinson, D. and Sanford, N. (1948) *The Authoritarian Personality*. New York: Harper.

Albright, M. and Carr, C. (1997) *101 Biggest Mistakes Managers Make and How to Avoid Them*. New Brunswick, NJ: Prentice Hall.

American Psychiatric Association (1987) *Diagnostic and Statistical Manual of Mental Disorders* 3rd edn (DSM-III). Washington, DC: American Psychiatric Association.

American Psychiatric Association (1994) *Diagnostic and Statistical Manual of Mental Disorders* 4th edn (DSM-IV). Washington, DC: American Psychiatric Association.

Baldwin, T. and Ford, J. (1988). Transfer of training. *Personnel Psychology* 41: 63–105.

Barrick, M. and Mount, M. (1991) The big five personality dimensions and job performance: A meta-analysis. *Personnel Psychology* 44: 1–26.

Belbin, M. (1981) *Management Teams*. London: Heinemann.

Berman, J. (1997) Competency as a management practice in Europe and North America. *Competency* 4: 24–8.

Blum, M. and Naylor, J. (1968) *Industrial Psychology*. New York: Harper & Row.

Born, M. and Altink, W. (1996) The importance of behavioural and situational characteristics for entrepreneurial success. *International Journal of Selection and Assessment* 4: 71–7.

Boyatzis, R. (1982) *The Competent Manager: A model for effective performance*. New York: Wiley.

Boyatzis, R. (1999) Interview with Richard Boyatzis. *Competency* 4: 4–8.

Bramson, R. (1992) *Coping with Difficult Bosses*. London: Brealey.

Brinkman, R. (1994) *Dealing with People You Can't Stand*. New York: McGraw Hill.

Broucek, W.G. and Randall, G. (1996) An assessment of the construct validity of the Belbin Self-Report Inventory and Observer's Assessment from the perspective of the five-factor model. *Journal of Occupational and Organisational Psychology* 69: 389–405.

Broustein, M. (1993) *Handling the Difficult Employee*. Menlo Park, CA: Crisp.

Burn, D. and Dearlove, D. (1995). The competent organisation. *Competency* 2: 37–41.

Carlson, J. (1985). Recent assessment of the Myers-Briggs Type Indicator. *Journal of Personality Assessment* 49: 356–65.

Cattell, R. (1981) *Intelligence: Its Structure, Growth and Action*. Amsterdam: North Holland.

Cava, R. (1993) *Dealing with Difficult People*. London: Piatkus.

Cleckley, H. (1941) *The Mask of Sanity*. St Louis, MI: C.V. Mosby.

Conger, J. (1990) The dark side of leadership. *Organisational Dynamics* 19: 44–55.

Cook, M. (1998) *Personnel Selection and Productivity*. Chichester: Wiley.

Costa, P. (1996) Work and personality. *Applied Psychology* 45: 225–41.

Costa, P. and McCrae, R. (1989) *NEO PI-R Professional Manual*. Odessa, FL: Psychological Assessment Resources.

Costa, P, McCrae, R. and Kay, G. (1995) Persons, places and personality: Career assessment using the revised NEO personality inventory. *Journal of Career Assessment* 3: 123–29.

Courtis, J. (1986) *Managing by Mistake*. London: Institute of Chartered Accountants.

Deal, T. and Kennedy, A. (1982) *Corporate Culture*. Reading, MA: Addison-Wesley.

Deary, I. and Matthews, G. (1993) Personality traits are alive and well. *The Psychologist* 6: 299–311.

Devito, A. (1985) A review of the Myers-Briggs Type Indicator: In S. Mitchell (ed.) *Ninth Mental Measurement Yearbook*. Lincoln: University of Nebraska Press.

Dixon, N. (1981) *On the Psychology of Military Incompetence*. London: Jonathan Cape.

Drakeley, R. and White, A. (1999) Competencies: Foundation garments or emperor's clothes? *Selection and Development Review* 15: 7–13.

Dulewicz, V. (1989) Assessment centres as the route to competence. *Personnel Management* 11: 56–9.

Dulewicz, V. (1992) Assessment of management competencies by personality questionnaires. *Selection and Development Review* 8: 1–4.

Dulewicz, V. (1994) Personal competencies, personality and responsibility of middle managers. *Competency* 1: 20–9.

Dyce, J. (1999) The big five factors of personality and their relationship to personality disorders. *Journal of Clinical Psychology* 53: 589–93.

Dykeman, C. and Dykeman, J. (1996) Big five personality profile of executive search recruiters. *Journal of Employment Counselling* 33: 77–86.

Evers, F. and Rush, J. (1996) The basis of competence. *Management Learning* 27: 275–300.

Farson, R. (1996) *Management of the Absurd: Paradoxes in Leadership*. New York: Simon & Schuster.

Furnham, A. (1998) *The Psychology of Managerial Incompetence*. London: Whurr.

Furnham, A. (1999) *The Psychology of Behaviour at Work*. Hove: Psychology Press.

Furnham, A. (2000a) *The Hopeless, Hapless and Helpless Manager*. London: Whurr.

Furnham, A. (2000b) *Managerial Competency Frameworks*. London: Career Research Forum.

Garden, A.-M. (1991) Unresolved issues with the Myers-Briggs Type Indicator. *Journal of Psychological Types* 22: 3–13.

Gardner, H. (1999) *Intelligence Reframed*. New York: Basic Books.

Gerstein, M. and Reisman, H. (1983) Strategic selection: Matching executives to business conditions. *Sloan Management Review* 24: 118–39.

Goleman, D. (1998) *Emotional Intelligence*. New York: Bantam.

Hackman, J.R. (1989) Group influences on individuals in organizations. In M. Dunnette (ed.) *Handbook of Individual/Organizational Psychology*. Palo Alto, CA: Consulting Press, pp. 1455–525.

Haley, U. and Stumpf, J. (1989) Cognitive traits in strategic decision making. *Journal of Management Studies* 26: 477–91.

Herriot, P. and Pemberton, C. (1995) *Competitive Advantage Through Diversity*. London: Sage.

Herrnstein, R. and Murray, G. (1994) *The Bell Curve*. New York: Free Press.

Hicks, L. (1984) Conceptual and empirical analysis of some assumptions of an explicitly typological theory. *Journal of Personality and Social Psychology* 46: 1118–131.

Hirsh, S. and Kummerow, J. (1989) *Life Types*. New York: Warner.

Hogan, R. (1983) A socioanalytic theory of personality. In M.M. Page (ed.) *Nebraska Symposium on Motivation*. Lincoln, NE: University of Nebraska Press, pp. 336–55.

Hogan, R. (2000) Personality and effective team performance. Paper presented at the 8th Annual Symposium on Individual, Team and Organizational Effectiveness, University of North Texas.

Hogan, R. and Hogan, J. (1999) *Hogan Development Survey Manual*. Tulsa, OK: HAS.

Hogan, R. and Hogan, J. (2001) Assessing leadership: A view from the dark side. *International Journal of Selection and Assessment* 9: 40–51.

Honey, P. (1992) *Problem People: And How to Manage Them*. London: IPD.

Hough, L., Eaton, N., Dunnette, M., Kamp, J. and McCloy, R. (1990) Criterion-related validity of personality constructs and the effect of response distortion on these validities. *Journal of Applied Psychology* 75: 581–95.

Jacobs, R. (1989) Getting the measure of management competence. *Personnel Management* 6: 32–7.

Janis, I. (1972) *Victims of Group-Think*. Boston, MA: Houghton Mifflin.

Jones, A. and Cooper, C. (1980) *Combating Managerial Obsolescence*. London: Philip Allan.

Jones, T. (1999) *If It's Broken You Can Fix It: Overcoming Dysfunction in the Workplace*. New York: AMACOM.

Kets de Vries, M. (1994) The leadership mystique. *Academy of Management Executives* 8: 73–89.

Kets de Vries, M. (1999) Managing puzzling personalities. *European Management Journal* 17: 8–19.

Kets de Vries, M. and Miller, D. (1985) *The Neurotic Organisation*. San Fransisco, CA: Jossey-Bass.

Kofodimos, J. (1990) Why executives lose their balance. *Organisational Dynamics* 19: 58–73.

Kravitz, S. (1995) *Managing Negative People*. Menlo Park, CA: Crisp.

Lloyd, K. (1999) *Jerks at Work: How to Deal with Problems and Problem People*. Franklin Lake, NJ: Career Press.

Losey, M. (1999) Mastering the competencies of HR management. *Human Resource Management* 38: 95–102.

McCall, M. (1998) *High Flyers*. Cambridge, MA: Harvard Business School Press.

McClelland, D. (1973) Testing for competency rather than intelligence. *American Psychologist* 28: 1–14.

McCrae, R. and Costa, P. (1988) Reinterpreting the Myers-Briggs Type Indicator from the perspective of the five-factor model of personality. *Journal of Personality* 59: 19–40.

McKibbin, S. (1998) *A Cynic's Guide to Management*. London: Robert Hale.

Mansfield, R. (1999) What is 'competence' all about? *Competency* 6: 12–16.

Mars, G. (1984) *Cheats at Work*. London: Allen & Unwin.

Matthewman, J. (1997) Competencies in practice. *Competency* 9: 11–15.

Merry, U. and Brown, G. (1987) *The Neurotic Behaviour of Organisations*. London: Gardner Press.

Mick, D. (1996) Are studies of dark-side variables confounded by socially desirable responding? *Journal of Consumer Research* 23: 106–19.

Mischel, W. (1968) *Personality and Assessment.* New York: Wiley.

Moloney, K. (1997) Why competencies may not be enough. *Competency* 9: 33–7.

Moore, T. (1987) Personality tests are back. *Fortune* (30 March): 74–82.

Morgan, R. (1996) *Calming Upset Customers.* Menlo Park, CA: Crisp.

Mount, M. and Barrick, M. (1995) The Big Five personality dimensions: Implications for research and practice in human resources management. *Research in Personnel and Human Resources Management* 13: 153–200.

Oldham, J. and Morris, L. (1991) *Personality Self-Portrait.* New York: Bartam Books.

Peter, L. (1985) *Why Things Go Wrong.* London: Unwin.

Roberts, G. (1998) Competency management systems – the need for a practical framework. *Competency* 5: 8–10.

Roderick, C. (1997a) Team roles – The dark side. *Selection and Development Review* 13: 6–7.

Roderick, C. (1997b) Team roles – The dark side (Pt 2). *Selection and Development Review* 13: 18–19.

Roderick, C. (1998) Team roles – The dark side. *Selection and Development Review* 14: 18–19.

Salgado, J. (1997) The five factor model of personality and job performance in the European Community. *Journal of Applied Psychology* 82: 30–43.

Salovey, P. and Mayer, J. (1990) Emotional Intelligence. *Imagination, Cognition and Personality* 9: 185–211.

Schmidt, F. and Hunter, J. (1998) The validity and utility of selection methods in personnel psychology: Practical and theoretical implications of 85 years of research findings. *Psychological Bulletin* 124: 262–74.

Seaman, M. (1959) On the meaning of alienation. *American Sociological Review* 24: 783–91.

Shapiro, E. (1996) *Fad Surfing in the Boardroom: Reclaiming the Courage to Manage in the Age of Instant Managers.* London: Capstone.

Shephard, J. (1972) Alienation as a process: Work as a case in point. *Sociological Review* 13: 161–73.

Sternberg, R. (1990) *Metaphors of Mind: Conception of the Nature of Intelligence.* Cambridge: Cambridge University Press.

Sternberg, R. (1996) *Successful Intelligence.* New York: Plume.

Strebler, M., Robinson, D. and Heron, P. (1997) *Getting the Best Out of Your Competencies.* Brighton: Institute for Employment Studies.

Tett, R., Jackson, D. and Rothstein, M. (1991) Personality measures as predictors of job performance: A meta-analysis. *Personnel Psychology* 44: 703–35.

Thorndike R.L., et al. (1921) Intelligence and its measurement. *Journal of Educational Psychology* 12: 18–30.

Thurstone, L. (1938) *Primary Mental Abilities.* Chicago, IL: University of Chicago Press.

Turner, B. (1994) Causes of disaster: Sloppy management. *British Journal of Management* 5: 215–19.

Waibel, M. and Wicklund, R. (1994) Inferring competence from incompetence: An ironic process associated with person descriptors. *European Journal of Social Psychology* 24: 443–52.

Wareham, J. (1988) *Basic Business Types: The Characters You Need to Know about to Succeed in Business.* London: Thorsons.

Watson-Wyatt (1998) www.personalityresearch.org.pd.html (accessed 19 December 2002).

Widiger, T.A., Trull, T.J., Clarkin, J.F., Sanderson, C. and Costa, P.T. (2001) A description of the DSM-IV personality disorders with the five-factor model of personality. In P.T. Costa and T.A. Widiger (eds) *Personality Disorders and the Five-factor Model of Personality* 2nd edn. Washington, DC: American Psychological Association, pp. 89–99.

Woodruffe, C. (1993) *Assessment Centres: Identifying and Developing Competence*. London: IPM.

Zander, A. (1982) *Motives and Goals in Groups*. New York: Academic Press.

Ziyal, L. (1997) Definition of critical performance demands: A new approach to competency. *Competency* 4: 25–31.

Index

Kofodimos, J., 58–59
Kravitz, S., 31
Kumerow, J., 115–120

lateral transfer of learning, 238
leadership and competencies, 92–93
learning, 232–235
    competencies, 76–77
    curves, 235
    low-flyers, 30
    observational, 236–237
    and obsolescence, 22
    see also training and education
learning theorists, 194
leisurely personality style, 181–184
Levitation Principle, 28
lifeboat management, 38
listening, training in, 241
Lloyd, K., 35
locust management, 40
Losey, M., 85
low-flyers, 29–31
loyalty, brand, 17
luck, 11
lumpers, 224–225
lying, 62

McCall, M., 25, 67, 68, 232–233
McClelland, D., 73–74, 76
McCrae, R., 120, 123
McKibbin, S., 36–40, 42–43
madness, managerial, 49–55
management by walking about, 42
Manchester Airport, 82
manpower planning, 92
Mansfield, R., 74, 75
market driven managers, 25
Mars, G., 63
Marx, Karl, 248
massacre exacerbators, 204
mastery, striving for, 58, 59
mathematical intelligence, 226
matrix management, 25
Matthewman, J., 75–76
Matthews, G., 104
mavericks, 112–113
maybe person, 35
Mayer, J., 228
MBTI (Myers Briggs Type Indicator),
    115–121

meaninglessness, 248–249
measurement
    of competencies, 77
    of performance, 47
    of personality, 128
meddle management, 38
meetings
    second-chance, 216
    training in conducting, 242
    and under-employment, 41, 42
melancholic people, 121, 122
memory, 225
mental illness, 245
mentoring, 24–25
mercurial personality style, 163–167
Merry, U., 57–58
military incompetence, 4–9
Miller, D., 49–51
misbehaviour, organizational, 62–64
Mischel, W., 73
mischievous personality style, 159–163
mission statements, 16
mobility and obsolescence, 22
Moloney, K., 84
money-related addictions, 244
monitor evaluators, 200, 204
monitoring, and boredom, 41
moods, 105
Moore, T., 115
morale, 221
    absurd behaviour, 21
    teams, 207–208
Morgan, R., 31
Morris, L., 143, 146
    antisocial personality disorder, 160–161,
        162–163
    avoidant personality disorder, 176,
        177–178
    borderline personality disorder, 165,
        166–167
    dependent personality disorder,
        179–181
    histrionic personality disorder,
        169–170
    narcissistic personality disorder, 172,
        173–174
    obsessive–compulsive personality
        disorder, 186, 187–188
    paranoid personality disorder, 150,
        151–152

Made in the USA
San Bernardino, CA
07 July 2015